GMDH-Methodology and Implementation in MATLAB

GMDH-Methodology and Implementation in MATLAB

Editor

Godfrey Onwubolu

Sheridan Institute of Technology & Advanced Learning, Canada

Imperial College Press

ICP

Published by

Imperial College Press
57 Shelton Street
Covent Garden
London WC2H 9HE

Distributed by

World Scientific Publishing Co. Pte. Ltd.
5 Toh Tuck Link, Singapore 596224
USA office: 27 Warren Street, Suite 401-402, Hackensack, NJ 07601
UK office: 57 Shelton Street, Covent Garden, London WC2H 9HE

Library of Congress Cataloging-in-Publication Data
Names: Onwubolu, Godfrey C., editor.
Title: GMDH-methodology and implementation in MATLAB / [edited by] Godfrey Onwubolu
    (Sheridan Institute of Technology & Advanced Learning, Canada).
Description: London : Imperial College Press, [2016] | Includes bibliographical references.
Identifiers: LCCN 2015049361 | ISBN 9781783266128 (hc : alk. paper)
Subjects: LCSH: MATLAB. | GMDH algorithms. | System analysis--Data processing. |
    Quantitative research--Data processing.
Classification: LCC TA345.5.M42 G63 2016 | DDC 511/.8028553--dc23
LC record available at http://lccn.loc.gov/2015049361

British Library Cataloguing-in-Publication Data
A catalogue record for this book is available from the British Library.

Desk Editors: V. Vishnu Mohan/Mary Simpson

Typeset by Stallion Press
Email: enquiries@stallionpress.com

Printed in Singapore

PREFACE

The world around us is getting more complex, more interdependent, more connected, and global due to uncertainty, vagueness, and rapid developments that radically affect humanity. There are many cases in practice where it is impossible to create analytical models using classical theoretical systems analysis or common statistical methods since there is incomplete knowledge of the processes involved. In contrast, inductive models are derived from real physical data and represent the relationships that implicit within the system without or with only little knowledge of the physical processes or mechanisms involved. Many types of mathematical models require the modeler to know things about the system that are generally impossible to find. If modelers are forced to make wild guesses at the system's variables, they can hardly expect to produce a model with a great deal of reliability as to prediction. Inductive modeling is based on worldwide known Group Method of Data Handling (GMDH) initially originated by Prof. Ivakhnenko in 1968 and actively developing especially during last decade in many modified and generalized versions. This GMDH-based approach discourages modelers from putting their prejudices into models and encourages them to start building purely objective models: in other words, models that look only at the data and nothing else.

This book focuses on GMDH which is an inductive modeling method for prediction, modeling, and analysis of the behavior of complex systems. Since its inception is by Ivakhnenko, GMDH has been successfully applied to modeling real-world applications in the areas of:

- data and knowledge mining, relationships detection;
- knowledge discovery workflow automation, automated data pre-processing;
- time series analysis and prediction including stock market and exchange rate fluctuations;
- random fields including static images, random terrain (land-scapes), wind waves or composition variations of a heterogeneous material.

GMDH is very robust and offers modeling solutions to real-world applications, including solutions in agricultural-, aeronautical-, bio-engineering, chemical-, civil- environmental-, mechanical-engineering systems, ecological systems, socio-economic systems, solar activities, medical data, technology, bioinformatics and temporal and/or spatial modeling problems; signals such as speech, audio, and video.

Currently, there is no GMDH book (except *"GMDH: Methodology and Implementation in C"*) that makes this important technology **transparent** and **available** to users. If you Google "GMDH", what you will mostly read about is "GMDH SHELL" — virtually nothing else available! This new book fills the gap: that is our main objective.

Chapter Contributions: Experienced, internationally recognized researchers in GMDH have been invited to write MATLAB codes for GMDH, ranging from simple multilayer version to hybrid versions.

Chapter Format: *"GMDH: Methodology and Implementation in MATLAB"* chapters focus on authors explaining every procedure (subroutine) used for implementing their GMDH code. The remainder of each chapter describes every procedure (subroutine), with few examples, showing the data set(s) used, and steps that the end-user must follow to run the code successfully. The procedures (subroutines) are so clearly described such that users can understand them and modify them if they so wish. This is the main objective of *"GMDH: Methodology and Implementation in MATLAB"*.

Organization of the Chapters: In Chapter 1 an overview of the book in the context of the fundamentals of GMDH is presented. The book is divided into two sections: the first part presents the basic version of GMDH, while the second section presents hybrids of GMDH. Chapters 2 and 3 present the basic GMDH multilayered algorithm (well known as GMDH-MIA), which is the most common variant used in practice. Chapter 4 presents GMDH-based Polynomial Neural network (PNN) Algorithm. Chapter 5 presents designing GMDH Model using Modified Levenberg–Marquardt Technique. Chapter 6 presents GMDH using Differential Evolution (DE). The last three chapters present hybrid versions of GMDH which results in very efficient algorithms for solving very complex real-life engineering and economics problems encountered in practice.

In summary, this book presents mainly *hybrids* of GMDH and *focuses* on making available *workable* (*error-free*) codes in MATLAB for end-users who are ready to use these codes to solve real-life problems. It supplements an earlier version, *"GMDH: Methodology and Implementation in C"* edited by the same author and published by the same company. Consequently, end-users now have GMDH codes available in two programming languages, "C" and "MATLAB".

Audience: The book provides instructional material for senior undergraduate and entry-point graduate students in computer science, cybernetics, applied mathematics, statistics, engineering, bioinformatics, who are working in the areas of machine learning, artificial intelligence, complex system modeling and analysis, neural networks, and optimization. Researchers who want to know how to fundamentals of classical GMDH-based modeling approaches will find this book very useful as a starting point. Moreover, practitioners will find the book beneficial as it provides materials for those who want to apply methods that work on real-life problems to their challenging applications.

Appendix: Source codes in MATLAB language for Chapters 2–6 are hosted online on http://www.worldscientific.com/worldscibooks/10. 1142/p982. All codes were checked that they are in working condition before a decision was made for inclusion in the book.

Godfrey C. Onwubolu
Editor

Toronto, Canada
Summer 2015

ABOUT THE EDITOR

Dr. Godfrey Onwubolu currently teaches and researches in computer-aided design, additive manufacturing (3D printing) as well as inductive modeling and applies these techniques to industries in Canada. He holds a BEng in Mechanical Engineering, and both an MSc and PhD from Aston University, Birmingham, UK. He worked in a number of manufacturing companies in West Midland, UK, and he was a professor of manufacturing engineering having taught courses in design and manufacturing for several years. He is a Chartered Engineer (CEng) of UK, as well as a Professional Engineer in Canada. He is an active member of the American Society of Mechanical Engineers (ASME).

He has published several books with international publishing companies, such as Imperial College Press, Elsevier, and Springer-Verlag, and has published over 140 articles in international journals and conference proceedings.

LIST OF CONTRIBUTORS

Elaine Inácio Bueno

Instituto Federal de Educação, Ciência e Tecnologia — Campus Guarulhos
Av. Salgado Filho, 3501
07115-000 Guarulhos, SP, Brazil
ebueno@ifsp.edu.br

Donald Davendra

Department of Computer Science, Central Washington University, 400 East University Way, Ellensburg, WA 98926, USA
DonaldD@cwu.edu

Mohammed Abdalla Ayoub Mohammed

Universiti Teknologi Petronas-Perak-Malaysia, Malaysia
abdalla.ayoub@petronas.com.my

Godfrey C. Onwubolu

School of Mechanical and Electrical Engineering & Technology
Sheridan Institute of Technology and Advanced Learning
7899 McLaughlin Road, Brampton, ON, Canada, L6Y 5H9
godfrey.onwubolu@sheridancollege.ca

Iraci Martinez Pereira

Instituto de Pesquisas Energéticas e Nucleares, IPEN — CNEN/SP
Av. Professor Lineu Prestes 2242
05508-000 São Paulo, SP, Brazil
martinez@ipen.br

Maryam Pournasir Roudbaneh

Multimedia University
Malaysia mailing address: Maryam Pournasir,
No. 114, Shohada Street, Lahijan, Guilan 4419776593
Iran
pournasir_maryam@yahoo.com

Antonio Teixeira e Silva

Instituto de Pesquisas Energéticas e Nucleares, IPEN — CNEN/SP
Av. Professor Lineu Prestes 2242
05508-000 São Paulo, SP, Brazil
teixeira@ipen.br

Ivan Zelinka

Department of Computer Science, Faculty of Electrical Engineering
and Computer Science, VŠB-Technical University of Ostrava
17. listopadu 15, 708 33 Ostrava-Poruba, Czech Republic
ivan.zelinka@vsb.cz

CONTENTS

Preface   v

About the Editor   ix

List of Contributors   xi

Part A: Basic/Standard GMDH   1

Chapter 1:   Introduction   3
             Godfrey C. Onwubolu

1.   Group Method of Data Handling   7
       1.1.   Outline of GMDH and Its Applications . . .   7
       1.2.   Partial Model Construction   8
       1.3.   External Criteria of Accuracy   9
       1.4.   Sorting Out Procedure Description   10
       1.5.   GMDH Implementation and Algorithm . . .   11
               1.5.1.   Basic GMDH algorithm   11
               1.5.2.   External criteria   11
       1.6.   GMDH-Type Neural Networks   15
       1.7.   GMDH vs. Neural Network   16
       1.8.   Advantages of Basic GMDH Technique . . .   17
       1.9.   Limitations of GMDH Technique   20
       1.10.   Rationale for GMDH in MATLAB   21

1.11.   Recent Developments in GMDH-Type
Neural Networks   21

1.12.   Data Processing for Predictive Modeling
Using GMDH   22

 1.12.1.   Concept of preprocessing
 of data   22

 1.12.2.   Concept of data crossover   22

 1.12.3.   Predictive modeling using
 crossover data   23

1.13.   Conclusions   23

References   24

Chapter 2:   GMDH Multilayered Algorithm   27

Godfrey C. Onwubolu

2.   GMDH Multilayered Algorithms in MATLAB   27

 2.1.   Multilayered Algorithm Networks   27

  2.1.1.   GMDH layers   28

  2.1.2.   GMDH nodes   28

  2.1.3.   GMDH connections   30

  2.1.4.   GMDH network   31

  2.1.5.   Regularized model selection   31

  2.1.6.   GMDH algorithm   33

 2.2.   Computer Code for GMDH-MIA   34

  2.2.1.   Compute a tree of quadratic
  polynomials   34

  2.2.2.   Evaluate the Ivakhnenko
  polynomial using the tree
  of polynomials generated   41

  2.2.3.   Compute the coefficients
  in the Ivakhnenko polynomial
  using the same tree of polynomials
  generated   50

  2.2.4.   Main program   52

    2.3.   Case Studies 55
          2.3.1.   Case Study 1 55
          2.3.2.   Case Study 2 62
    2.4.   Summary 73
References 74

Chapter 3: GMDH Multilayered Algorithm in MATLAB   75

Mohammed Abdalla Ayoub Mohammed

Introduction 75
1.   Literature Review 78
    1.1.   Introduction 79
2.   Theory of Abductive Networks 80
    2.1.   Overview 80
    2.2.   History of GMDH 80
    2.3.   Fundamentals and Procedure
          of GMDH-Based Abductive Networks 81
    2.4.   Types of Abductive Networks 84
    2.5.   Polynomial Neural Network 85
          2.5.1.   Layer unit 85
          2.5.2.   Multilayer algorithm 85
          2.5.3.   Mathematical description
               of the system 86
3.   Research Methodology: Development and Testing
    of Universal Pressure Drop Models in Pipelines using
    Polynomial Group Method of Data Handling
    Technique 88
    3.1.   Overview 88
    3.2.   Network Performance Comparison 90
          3.2.1.   Trend analysis 91
          3.2.2.   Group error analysis 91
          3.2.3.   Statistical error analysis 92
    3.3.   Building AIM Model 92
    3.4.   Limitations 92

4.   Results and Discussion 93
      4.1. Development of AIM Model 93
            4.1.1. Summary of model's equation . . . 94
      4.2. Trend Analysis for the AIM Model 95
      4.3. Group Error Analysis for the AIM Model
            Against Other Investigated Models 96
      4.4. Statistical and Graphical Comparisons
            of the Polynomial GMDH Model 98
            4.4.1. Statistical error analysis 98
            4.4.2. Graphical error analysis of the
                    polynomial GMDH model 99
5.   Conclusion and Recommendations 105
      5.1. Conclusion 105
      5.2. Recommendation 106
References 106
Appendix A. Research Data 107
Appendix B. Pressure Drop Models in Pipelines
             using Polynomial Group Method of Data
             Handling Technique 109

Part B: HYBRID GMDH SYSTEM   125

Chapter 4: GMDH-Based Polynomial Neural Network
            Algorithm in MATLAB   127

Elaine Inácio Bueno, Iraci Martinez
Pereira and Antonio Teixeira e Silva

1.   Group Method of Data Handling and Neural
      Networks Applied in Temperature Sensors
      Monitoring of an Experimental Reactor 127
      1.1. Introduction 127
2.   Group Method of Data Handling — GMDH 129
      2.1. General Description of the GMDH
            Algorithm 135
3.   Artificial Neural Networks 136

4.   IPEN Research Reactor IEA-R1 137
       4.1.   IEA-R1 Data Acquisition System 138
5.   IEA-R1 Theoretical Model 138
6.   Monitoring and Fault Detection Model 142
7.   Results 146
       7.1.   Temperature Sensor Monitoring Using
               GMDH and Neural Networks
               MATLAB Code 146
       7.2.   Neural Networks Training 151
       7.3.   Sensors Monitoring Using Only Neural
               Network 154
8.   Conclusion and Future Work 159
References 160

Chapter 5: Designing GMDH Model Using Modified
            Levenberg Marquardt Technique in Matlab   163

            Maryam Pournasir Roudbaneh

1.   Introduction 165
2.   Reviewed Literature 167
       2.1.   Rationale for Hybrid Systems 167
       2.2.   Literature of Levenberg–Marquardt 169
3.   Group Method of Data Handling Model Using
       Modified Levenberg–Marquardt Technique
       for Inventory Systems 171
       3.1.   The Basic GMDH Algorithm 172
       3.2.   The Damped Least Squares
               (Levenberg–Marquardt) Method 175
               3.2.1.   Initial guess 176
               3.2.2.   Damping parameter 177
       3.3.   The Modified Levenberg–Marquardt–
               Fletcher Algorithm 178
4.   Experimental Results and Discussions 180
       4.1.   Experimental with Kanban System
               Data 182

4.2.   Experiment Results with Kanban System
Data 182
  4.2.1.   Comparison result for basic
  and GMDH-LM networks   185
4.3.   Experimental Result with (SVD, PI
and LM) Methods in Kanban System   186
  4.3.1.   Experimental result with two
  layers in kanban system 186
  4.3.2.   Experimental result with three
  layers in kanban system 186
  4.3.3.   Experimental result with four
  layers in kanban system 188
  4.3.4.   Analysis and description in kanban
  system 192
5.   Conclusions 206
References 208
Appendix 211

Chapter 6:   Group Method of Data Handing Using
Discrete Differential Evolution in Matlab   229

*Donald Davendra, Godfrey Onwubolu
and Ivan Zelinka*

1.   Group Method for Data Handling 229
  1.1.   Advantages of the Basic GMDH
  Technique 231
  1.2.   Limitations of GMDH Technique 231
2.   Differential Evolution Schema 233
3.   Discrete Differential Evolution   234
4.   Hybrid-GMDH Network 235
5.   GMDH-DDE in Matlab   237
  5.1.   Main Initialization Function 238
  5.2.   Data Read Function 238
  5.3.   Main Iteration Function 239
  5.4.   Propop Function 241
  5.5.   Repop Function   242

5.6. Lengha Function 244

5.7. DEIteration Function 245

5.8. DEForwardTransformation Function 246

5.9. DERoutine Function 246

5.10. DEBackwardTransformation Function 248

5.11. Muta Function 249

5.12. Fitn2 Function 249

5.13. Multip Function 255

6. Conclusion 259

Acknowledgment 259

References 260

Index   261

PART A
Basic/Standard GMDH

Chapter 1

INTRODUCTION

Godfrey C. Onwubolu

Group Method of Data Handling (GMDH)[1] is a family of algorithms for computer-based mathematical modeling and structural identification. Most of GMDH algorithms are characterized by inductive self-organizing procedure used for obtaining multi-parametric model. Specific behavior characteristics of GMDH enabled its successful use in such fields as data mining, knowledge discovery, forecasting, complex systems modeling, optimization and pattern recognition.

It is supposed that an object investigated with GMDH is represented by multiple inputs and at least one output. Also it is supposed that the object can be modeled by a certain subset of components of the *base function* (1.1):

$$Y(x_1, \ldots, x_n) = a_0 + \sum_{i=1}^{k} a_i f_i, \tag{1.1}$$

where x are inputs, Y is output, a are coefficients, f are elementary functions dependent on different sets of inputs, k is the number of base function components.

GMDH algorithm has to consider some *partial models* — component subsets of the base function (1.1) and choose an optimal model structure that is indicated by the minimum value of an *external criterion*. The main advantage derived from such a procedure is that the identified model has an optimal complexity adequate to the level of noise in the input data (noise resistant modeling).

3

The relationship between the inputs and the output of a multiple inputs single output self-organizing network can be represented by an infinite Volterra–Kolmogorov–Gabor (VKG) polynomial of the form [1]:

$$
y_n = a_0 + \sum_{i=1}^{M} a_i x_i + \sum_{i=1}^{M} \sum_{j=1}^{M} a_{ij} x_i x_j + \sum_{i=1}^{M} \sum_{j=1}^{M} \sum_{k=1}^{M} a_{ijk} x_i x_j x_k \ldots,
$$

$$(1.2)$$

where $X = (x_1, x_2, \ldots, x_M)$ is the vector of input variables and $A = (a_0, a_i, a_{ij}, a_{ijk}, \ldots)$ is the vector of coefficients or weights.

This is the discrete-time analogue of a continuous time Volterra series and can be used to approximate any stationary random sequence of physical measurements. Ivakhnenko showed that the VKG series can be expressed as a cascade of second-order polynomials using only pairs of variables [1, 2]. The corresponding network can be constructed from simple polynomial and delay elements. As the learning procedure evolves, branches that do not contribute significantly to the specific output can be pruned, thereby allowing only the dominant causal relationship to evolve. The multilayer GMDH network algorithm constructs hierarchical cascades of bivariate activation polynomials in the nodes, and variables in the leaves. The activation polynomial outcomes are fed forward to their parent nodes, where partial polynomial models are made. Thus, the algorithm produces high-order multivariate polynomials by composing simple and tractable activation polynomial allocated in the hidden nodes of the network.

In neural network idiom, the higher-order polynomial networks grown by the GMDH algorithm are essentially feed-forward, multilayered neural networks. The nodes are hidden units, the leaves are inputs, and the activation polynomial coefficients are weights. The weights arriving at a particular hidden node are estimated by ordinary least squares (OLS) fitting.

The very first consideration order used in GMDH and originally called multilayered inductive procedure is the most popular one. Multilayered procedure is equivalent to the Artificial Neural Network with polynomial activation function of neurons. Therefore the algorithm with such an approach is usually referred to as GMDH-type Neural Network or Polynomial Neural Network.

GMDH is a multilayered network with a certain structure determined through training. It has the feature that the nonlinear dynamics are expressed as a mathematical model as well as the polynomial can have higher order terms without instability problems [3]. Furthermore, GMDH is used to detect input–output relationships for various models. It aims to find relationships between one output and a frequently large set of possible inputs. The network decides which of the possible inputs are actually relevant to the system being identified. Therefore, the network is built up layer by layer during training. In each layer, there are neurons with only two inputs; the output of each neuron is a quadratic function of its both inputs. The parameters of the quadratic functions are obtained using linear regression analysis. Before adding a new layer, the previous layer is trained. During this training, for each unique combination of two inputs, a neuron is trained and on the basis of a certain selection criteria, only the best performing neurons are selected. Then, a new layer is added, and the whole procedure of training is performed again on this new layer. Adding new layers is done if some stopping criteria are achieved [4].

Based on this basic algorithm, many developed studies have been done to apply the GMDH approach in various applications such as data mining, forecasting, prediction and system identification, pattern recognition, and fault detection and isolation (FDI). For example, in the system identification filed, Kondo [5] applied GMDH algorithm to the medical image recognition problem. In his study, the shapes of the livers, obtained using stomach X-ray CT image, were recognized automatically and the interests regions were extracted using GMDH algorithm. The utilized image features were the statistics of the image density such as mean, standard deviation, variance, median, minimum, maximum and range. The final GMDH network had six layers with three neurons in each layer. The useful image features were found to be the mean, standard deviation and variance. Once the GMDH network was obtained, the regions of the livers were extracted by after processing of the resultant image. Finally, the output image of the GMDH network was compared with the original image. It was shown that GMDH algorithm had a good prediction accuracy for medical image recognition. Kondo [5] also applied GMDH algorithm to the nonlinear pattern identification problem. The input variables were the x, y and z coordinates while the output data was the pattern being identified. The inputs and output were trained using GMDH algorithm. The final network consisted of 10 layers with three neurons in each layer. The network was evaluated by comparing the actual values of the data with the predicted data from the GMDH network. The obtained results indicated that GMDH network was a very useful method for nonlinear pattern identification problem. Another study of the use of GMDH in system identification was proposed by Water *et al.* [4]. They applied GMDH on two synthetic examples in which the mathematical descriptions were known. The first example was a synthetic linear system while the second example was a synthetic switched randomized sine-wave system. It was shown that at least for these two examples, GMDH can be used in identification of dynamic systems. However, the authors stated that the excellent results obtained from synthetic examples do not guarantee such results for real systems.

Furthermore, Sakaguchi *et al.* [6] applied the GMDH approach to identify an atmospheric distillation process system. The set of inputs/output variables were obtained from real experimental setup. The inputs of the network were anti-forming chemical rate, feed rate, production rate of product A, production rate of product B, pre-fractionators reflux rate, pre-fractionators pressure and pre-fractionators feed temperature. The trained network consisted of four layers and eleven neurons: five neurons in the first layer, three neurons in the second layer, two neurons in the third layer and one neuron in the last layer. The network was then evaluated by comparing the predicted network output with the actual output. The obtained results indicated that GMDH can effectively identify an atmospheric distillation process system. In addition, Kondo [7] proposed a revised GMDH network and applied it to a nonlinear system whose mathematical description was known. The nonlinear system was identified using two approaches: revised GMDH and conventional radial basic function (RBF) neural network. In the first approach, the revised-GMDH network was trained using four inputs and one output. The revised-GMDH network had a feedback loop and the network parameter such as number of neurons, useful input variables and the number of feedback loop calculations were automatically determined so as to minimize the prediction sum of squares (PSS) criteria.

The constructed GMDH network consisted of only three input variables since the fourth variable was irrelevant to the system, four neurons in the hidden layer and three feedback loop calculations. On the other hand, in the second approach, the developed RBF neural network consisted of three layers, three inputs, one output and 20 hidden neurons.

The weights of the neural network were estimated using regression analysis. Finally, the results obtained from both revised GMDH network and conventional (RBF) neural network were compared. It was shown that both estimation and prediction errors of the revised GMDH algorithm were smaller than conventional (RBF) neural network.

Therefore, the revised GMDH algorithm provided an accurate identification method for the nonlinear system. The details of the neuron architectures, sorting out procedure, external criteria of accuracy and algorithm will be discussed in the following sections.

Figure 1.1 shows the architecture of GMDH network. A detailed description of GMDH, its application in system identification, external criteria and its algorithm, is provided in the subsequent section.

1. GROUP METHOD OF DATA HANDLING

In this section a detailed description of system identification using GMDH algorithm is provided, which includes the partial model construction, sorting out procedure description, external criteria of accuracy. This section also outlines the implementation and algorithm of GMDH network.

1.1. Outline of GMDH and Its Applications

GMDH is a modeling technique that provides an effective approach to the identification of higher order nonlinear systems. It was first introduced by Ivakhnenko [1]. Furthermore, GMDH is an inductive

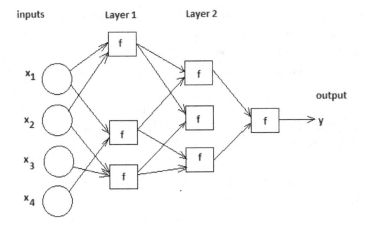

Fig. 1.1.   GMDH network architecture.

self-organizing algebraic model since it is not necessary to know the exact physical model in advance.

Instead, GMDH automatically learns the relations that dominate the system variables during the training process. In other words, the optimal neuron's structure is selected automatically in a way that minimizes the values of the prediction error criteria and unnecessary neurons are eliminated from the network. Therefore, the GMDH has good generalization ability and can fit the complexity of nonlinear systems [5].

1.2.   Partial Model Construction

GMDH network is a data-driven modeling technique. It uses mathematical functions to characterize the complex nonlinear relationships among the given inputs/output data sets. The GMDH network consists of a number of layers containing neurons. Each neuron has two inputs and one single output [8]. The output of each neuron is calculated using Ivakhnenko polynomial described in Eq. (1.1):

$$g(x_1, x_2) = w_0 + w_1 x_1 + w_2 x_2 + w_3 x_1 x_2 + w_4 x_1^2 + w_5 x_2^2. \quad (1.1)$$

The GMDH neuron architecture is shown in Fig. 1.2.

To construct a complete GMDH network, the combination of each two input variables in each layer is generated. Then, for each

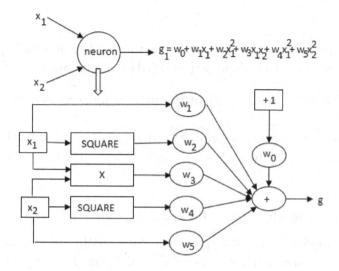

Fig. 1.2. GMDH neuron architecture.

combination and its associated output, the coefficients of the polynomials are estimated by least square fitting algorithm or regression
analysis that will be described later in Sec. 1.5. Once the polynomial coefficients are obtained, the output of the polynomials is then
evaluated and tested using external criteria of accuracy.

1.3. External Criteria of Accuracy

The external criterion, known as the regularity criteria, is used to
test the model adequacy. It evaluates and tests the output of each
neuron in the GMDH network by determining the mean square error
in the model between the actual and predicted output of each neuron.
The regularity criterion also indicates which of the input combination is more relevant to the network. Furthermore, the regularity
criterion tests the capability and fitness of the neuron polynomial to
the desired system output. The smaller the regularity criterion, the
better the fit of the neuron polynomial on the data. The regularity
criteria can be expressed by Eq. (1.2).

$$R^2 = \frac{\sum_{i=1}^{N}(y_i - g_i)^2}{\sum_{i=1}^{N}(y_i)^2},$$

(1.2)

where

R is the regularity criteria measure, N the number of samples, y the desired system output, and g the GMDH neuron output.

In GMDH network, the regularity criterion for each neuron output is evaluated.

Then, it is used to determine the surviving neurons to the next layer according to the sort out procedure described in the following section.

1.4. Sorting Out Procedure Description

GMDH modeling is self-organizing since neither the number of neurons nor the number of layer is predefined. The best performing neurons in each layer of the GMDH is selected based on the external criteria of accuracy described in the previous section. The neurons with regularity criteria that are less than a predefined threshold value will be selected while other neurons will be eliminated and discarded from the network. Figure 1.3 shows a GMDH network after

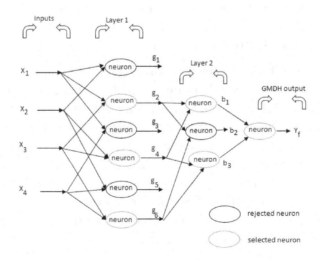

Fig. 1.3.   GMDH network with rejected neurons.

eliminating unnecessary neurons. Furthermore, the smallest regularity criterion in each layer is saved.

If the smallest regularity criterion in the next layer is larger than the smallest regularity criterion in the previous layer, adding new layers will stop. The final output of the GMDH network will be the output of the neuron with the smallest regularity criterion in the last layer [4].

1.5. GMDH Implementation and Algorithm

1.5.1. Basic GMDH algorithm

Basic GMDH algorithm makes the following steps:

1. Divides data sample onto parts A and B.
2. Generates structures for partial models.
3. Estimates coefficients of partial models using Least Squares Method and sample A.
4. Calculates value of *external criterion* for partial models using sample B.
5. Chooses the best model (set of models) indicated by minimal value of criterion.

1.5.2. External criteria

External criterion is one of the key features of GMDH (see Fig. 1.4). Criterion describes requirements to the model, for example minimization of list squares. It is always calculated with a separate part of data sample that have not been used for estimation of coefficients. There are several popular criteria:

- Criterion of Regularity (CR) — Least Squares of a model at the sample B.
- Criterion of Unbiasedness — Sum of CR value and special CR for which A is B and B is A. Ratio of sample lengths must be 1:1, i.e. size of A must be the same as size of B.

If a criterion does not define the number of observations for external data set, then the problem of data dividing ratio appears because

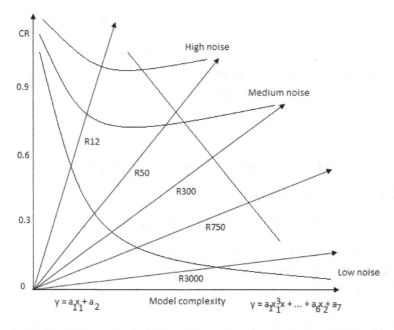

Fig. 1.4.   Optimal complexity of models evaluated with CR—criterion of regularity taken from [9].

the forecasting abilities of identified model are very dependent on the dividing ratio.

The main procedure for GMDH algorithm implementation is described in steps.

Step 1: The first step is the separation of the data into training and checking sets. The training data are used for the estimation of the weights of GMDH neurons while the checking data are used for organizing the network architectures. The division of data is conducted heuristically either by selecting random points for each set or based on the data variance. For example, the points with high variance are used in the checking set to ensure that the selected model is generalized and can extrapolate outside the data in the training set [10].

Step 2: The second step involves the generation of all possible combinations of two inputs among all the input variables. The number of combinations is given by $n = \frac{m(m-1)}{2}$ where m and n are the number of input variables and the number of combinations, respectively. Then, for each combination, expand the inputs to a quadratic polynomial Z.

$$Z = \begin{bmatrix} 1 & x_{11} & x_{21} & x_{11}x_{21} & x_{11}^2 & x_{21}^2 \\ 1 & x_{12} & x_{22} & x_{12}x_{22} & x_{12}^2 & x_{22}^2 \\ \vdots & \vdots & \vdots & \vdots & \vdots & \vdots \\ \vdots & \vdots & \vdots & \vdots & \vdots & \vdots \\ 1 & x_{1N} & x_{2N} & x_{1N}x_{2N} & x_{1N}^2 & x_{2N}^2 \end{bmatrix}_{N \times 6}.$$

Then, using the training data set, the coefficients of the polynomial (g), described previously in Eq. (1.1), are estimated for each combination in the training set. The weights of the polynomials are found by least square fitting algorithm and calculated by Eq. (1.3).

$$W = (Z^{\mathrm{T}}Z)^{-1}Z^{\mathrm{T}}y. \tag{1.3}$$

Step 3: The third step is to evaluate and test the output of each polynomial using the data points in the checking data. The output of each polynomial can be calculated using Eq. (1.4)

$$g = Z * W. \tag{1.4}$$

After calculating the output of each polynomial, the regularity criteria, for each neuron in the first layer, are calculated. Based on the regularity criteria calculations, the neurons with a regularity criterion that is less than a predefined is allowed to proceed to the next layer where the outputs of the selected neurons become the new input values. On the other hand, the remaining neurons are eliminated from the network.

Step 4: Finally, the whole procedure from the second step is repeated until the condition for terminating the GMDH network is satisfied. The GMDH network will stop when the lowest regularity criteria in the current layer is no longer smaller than that of the previous layer. To obtain the final GMDH model, the path of the neurons that corresponds to the lowest regularity criteria in each layer is tracked back. The flow chart that describes the GMDH algorithm is shown in Fig. 1.5.

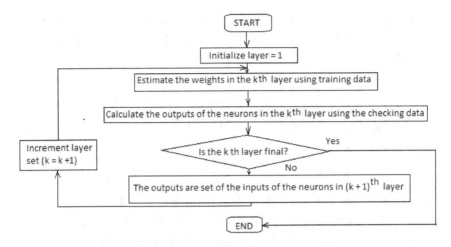

Fig. 1.5.   GMDH network flow chart.

The steps involved in the basic GMDH algorithm as shown in Algorithm 1.1.

Algorithm 1.1. Multilayer GMDH algorithm for growing higher order networks.

Initialization

Given a data series $\partial = \{(x_{ij}, y_i)\}$, $i = 1, 2, \ldots, n$; $j = 1, 2, \ldots, m$; where the number of training data is n_t and the number of testing data is n_c such that $n_t + n_t = n$.

Let the layer label be $l = 1$, the lowest error be $\varepsilon = MaxInt$ and the activation polynomials expressed as

$$p(x_i, x_k) = a_0 + a_1 x_i + a_2 x_k + a_3 x_i x_k + a_4 x_i^2 + a_5 x_k^2$$
$$\text{or} \quad p(x_i, x_k) = h(x_i, x_k)a \Rightarrow H[h_1, h_2, \ldots, h_N]^{\mathrm{T}}$$

Network construction and weight training

Step 1: Make all $c = \binom{m}{2}$ combinations of variables (x_i, x_k), $l \leq i, j \leq r$

Step 2: Make a polynomial $p_c^l(x_i, x_k)$ from each combination

2.1 Estimate its coefficients a_c by OLS fitting:

$$a_c = (H^T H)^{-1} H^T y$$

2.2 Evaluate the error or external criterion (EC) of the polynomial:

$$p_c^l(x_i, x_k) = h\, a_c$$

$$\mathrm{EC}_c = \left(\frac{1}{n_t}\right) \sum_{i=1}^{n_t} (y_i - p_c^l(x_i, x_k))^2$$

2.3 Compute the model selection criterion using the regularized average error (RAE):

$$\mathrm{RAE}_c = f(\mathrm{EC}_c)$$

Step 3: Order the polynomials with respect to their RAE_c, and choose r of these with lower criterion values

Step 4: Consider the lowest error from this layer: $\varepsilon^{l+1} = \min\{\mathrm{RAE}_c\}$

Step 5: If $\varepsilon^{l+1} > \varepsilon$ then terminate, else set $\varepsilon = \varepsilon^{l+1}$ and continue

Step 6: The polynomial outputs become current variables: $x_c \equiv p_c^l$

Step 7: Repeat the construction and training step with $l = l + 1$

Table 1.1 shows some data mining functions and more appropriate self-organizing (inductive) modeling algorithms and deductive algorithms for addressing these functions. As could be observed there are mainly three variants of GMDH needed to address most functions of data mining. Consequently, it is easier to design a unified system for variant data mining functions based on GMDH.

1.6. GMDH-Type Neural Networks

There are many different ways to choose an order for partial models consideration. The most common ways are:

- Multilayered Iterative Algorithm (MIA);
- Combinatorial (COMBI) Algorithm;
- Harmonic Algorithm;

Table 1.1.   Algorithms for self-organizing modeling.

Data mining functions	GMDH algorithms	Deductive algorithms
Classification	GMDH, AC	Decision trees (C4.5, etc.) Neural networks; k-NN Naïve Bayes; SVM
Clustering	AC†, OCA†	k-means spectral clustering; ISODATA
Modeling (prediction)	GMDH	CART (Classification and Regression Tree) Regression Bayesian Belief Networks (BBN) Bayesian Partition Model (BPM) Bayesian MARS Model Bayesian multivariate linear splines (MLS) Bayesian Radial Basis (RBF)
Time series forecasting	AC, GMDH	CART Regression Bayesian versions (as above)
Sequential patterns	AC	

†Known GMDH-nonparametric model selection methods are: Analog Complexing (AC) and Objective Cluster Analysis (OCA).

- Objective System Analysis (OSA);
- Objective Computer Clusterization (OCC);
- Pointing Finger (PF) clusterization algorithm;
- Analog Complexing (AC);
- Harmonical Rediscretization;
- Two-level (ARIMAD);
- Multiplicative-Additive (MAA);
- Algorithm on the base of Multilayered Theory of Statistical Decisions (MTSD);
- Group of Adaptive Models Evolution (GAME).

1.7.   GMDH vs. Neural Network

The GMDH algorithm can be viewed as a polynomial neural network, where the processing function of the node is a polynomial rather than a sigmoid function. Therefore, the optimization in the GMDH is based on a series of least-squares fitting rather than an iterative method of minimizing the errors like the back propagation neural networks. Training in the GMDH is a matter of performing linear algebra rather than a numerical method which requires a large amount of time for convergence. Another advantage of the GMDH is that it cannot overtrain.

Overtraining a neural network can be a problem when not enough points are given and too much iteration is used to train the network. Due to the training algorithm for the GMDH model, training stops when it reaches the best possible configurations [11].

Furthermore, the final model of GMDH is expressed mathematically in terms of high order polynomials. However, the final model extracted by neural networks is still hidden and distributed over the network. In addition, GMDH algorithm has systematically approach on the contrary of the neural network model which is based on a trial-and-error process [12]. In summary, the major differences between GMDH and neural networks are the ability of GMDH to objectively select the optimal model, avoid over-fitting problems, and select the most relevant input variables. Table 1.2 summarizes the differences between GMDH and neural network modeling [13].

1.8. Advantages of Basic GMDH Technique

The advantage of using pairs of input is that only six weights (coefficients) have to be computed for each neuron. The number of neurons in each layer increases approximately as the square of the number of inputs. During each training cycle, the synaptic weights of each neuron that minimize the error norm between predicted and measured values are computed and those branches that contribute least to the output of the neuron are discarded, the remaining branches being retained and their synaptic weights kept unchanged thereafter. A new layer is subsequently added and the procedure is repeated until the specified termination conditions are met.

There could be summarized that the GMDH-type polynomial networks influence the contemporary artificial neural network

Table 1.2.   Features of both GMDH and neural network modeling.

Features	GMDH	Neural network
Data analysis	Structure identifier	Universal approximator
Analytical model	Direct approximation	Indirect approximation
Architecture	Bounded network structure generated during the estimation process	• Pre-selected unbounded network structure • Selection of an adequate architecture requires time and experience
Network synthesis	Adaptive synthesized structure	Globally optimized fixed network structure
Threshold	Threshold objective functions	Threshold transfer function
Self-organization	Inductive: number of layers and nodes are estimated by minimum of external criterion	Deductive: require to specify number of layers and number of nodes
Parameter estimation	• Estimation in sets by means of maximum likelihood techniques using all the observational data • Extremely short samples	Recursive way that demands long samples
On/Offline	Data are usually stores and repeatedly accessible	Observation is available transiently in a real-time environment
Regularization	Estimation on training set, selection on testing set	Without: only internal information
Knowledge	Necessary knowledge about the task and the class of system (linear, nonlinear)	Requires knowledge about the theory of neural networks
Convergence	Existence of a model of optimal Complexity	Global convergence is difficult to guarantee

(Continued)

Table 1.2. (*Continued*)

Features	GMDH	Neural network
Optimizations	• Fast • Only include relevant terms • Irrelevant terms are eliminated	• Global search of a highly multimodal surface • Result depends on initial solutions • Slow and require the user to set various algorithmic parameters by trial and error • Time consuming
Computing	Efficient: for ordinary computers and for massively parallel computation	• Efficient: for implementation in hardware using massively parallel computation • Insufficient: for ordinary computers
A priori information knowledge	Used directly to select the reference functions and criteria	Not usable if they are not transformed in the world of neural networks
Feature	General-purpose, flexible linear or nonlinear, static or dynamic parametric models	General-purpose, flexible, Nonlinear (especially linear) static or dynamic nonparametric models

algorithms with several other advantages [14]:

(1) they offer adaptive network representations that can be tailored to the given task;

(2) they learn the weights rapidly in a single step by standard ordinary least square (OLS) fitting which eliminates the need to search for their values, and which guarantees finding locally good weights due to the reliability of the fitting technique;

(3) these polynomial networks feature sparse connectivity which means that the best discovered networks can be trained fast.

1.9. Limitations of GMDH Technique

Although standard GMDH provides for a systematic procedure of system modeling and prediction, it has also a number of shortcomings. Anastasakis and Mort [13] have carried out a comprehensive study of the shortcomings of GMDH:

Selection of Input Arguments: One of the main features of GMDH is its ability to objectively select the most appropriate input arguments amongst a set of candidates. However, the identification of these candidate input arguments is not straightforward and may affect its performance.

Inaccuracies in Parameter Estimation: The method of least square estimates is the most popular method to calculate the coefficients of partial descriptions. If the data matrix is well defined its estimates will be accurate however, in the majority of real world systems the data matrix is ill-defined and the least squares biased.

Multicollinearity: Another problem found exclusively in multilayer algorithm, which affects the stability of coefficients, is that of multicollinearity.

Reduction of Complexity: Another shortcoming found GMDH approach is a tendency to generate quite complex polynomial (since the complexity of the network increases with each training and selection cycle through addition of new layers) for relatively simple systems (data input); also, an inclination to producing overly complex network (model) when dealing with highly nonlinear systems owing to its limited generic structure (quadratic two-variable polynomial).

Formulas of Partial Descriptions: Despite the wide range of partial descriptions majority of researchers follow the argument that Volterra series are capable of identifying any nonlinear system and therefore have adopted polynomial partial descriptions similar to Ivakhnenko polynomial. However, due to the complexity of the model and the requirement of including the theory behind the object, many modifications have been designed in order to adapt to system's properties.

Over-fitting: A consequence of complexity is the over-fitting problem and poor generalization.

Partition of Data: The objectiveness of GMDH algorithm is based on the utilization of an external criterion to select the optimum model, which requires the partition of the data.

Low Accuracy in GMDH Method: In many cases and particularly in applications of long range prediction the GMDH has been observed to be inaccurate.

1.10. Rationale for GMDH in MATLAB

GMDH is robust, effective and efficient for modeling complex real-life system but there have been limited available functional codes available for end-users, until the recent book on GMDH in C [15]. The primary goal of this book is to further make available to the public, functional error-free GMDH codes in MATLAB programming language so that they could utilize these codes immediately to solve basic problems and be able to modify the codes for more challenging problems. With these books in the hands of end-users, the hitherto scarce public codes on GMDH are no longer a huddle.

1.11. Recent Developments in GMDH-Type Neural Networks

Due to the weaknesses of traditional GMDH, a number of computational intelligence methods [16, 17] have been used to hybridize GMDH, resulting in very efficient and robust hybrid modelers. The most common are (see [23] for details):

- GMDH-Genetic Programming [18],
- GMDH-Genetic Algorithm-based [19, 20],
- GMDH-Genetic Differential Evolution-based [21, 22],
- GMDH-Genetic Particle Swarm Optimization-based [23].

In this book, the native GMDH (MIA) is first presented then the GMDH-Genetic Algorithm-based, and GMDH-Genetic Differential Evolution-based modelers are presented in the second part. Each chapter briefly presents the background of the GMDH variant presented and then detail code is presented with the each step thoroughly explained so that readers can understand how GMDH works. This way is possible for end-users to re-use the codes for their own applications.

1.12.   Data Processing for Predictive Modeling Using GMDH

1.12.1.   Concept of preprocessing of data

Noisy data sets require some preprocessing. If original data sets are not processed the results obtained from GMDH may be significantly off tangent. End-users should be away of this problem, which may give the impression that the problem being solved cannot be handled using GMDH. Like any other modeling method, it is required that some raw data that are noisy need to be pre-processed.

1.12.2.   Concept of data crossover

This chapter present a new concept for data mining, herein referred to as the concept of data *crossover*. In the concept, a number of data sets for a family of products could be mixed in other to use the outcome to predict other members of the family of products which were not used for the simulation. For example, suppose we have three sizes of products belonging to a family. Then we can mix the data set by crossover of different lengths of the data sets, so that we have one new data set having the attributes of the different subcomponents (see Fig. 1.6). Let us consider an example.

Step 1: Design of Experiment (DOE) for input parameters/out
        Inputs: for three variants of a family of product
        Output: for three variants of a family of product
        Each data set has 33 data points (33 rows).
Step 2: Testing and recording of results of each variant.
Step 3: Crossover the original data sets (three of them) (see Fig. 1.6).

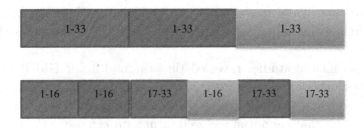

Fig. 1.6.   Crossover data set.

1.12.3.   Predictive modeling using crossover data

Step 1: Testing and recording of results of crossover data set.
Step 2: Use results of crossover data set results to generalize prediction for other variants "not seen" by the modeler.

The author has applied this concept to solve real-life problems of predicting a family of industrial products using few of the products for crossover, but having success in predicting the behavior of other members of the family of products which were not used in the simulation process. Results obtained are very satisfactory, and this type of modeling approach is very useful when studying the behavior of family products in an industrial setting. This way, it is possible for designers to anticipate how some other members of the family of a product might behave in practice even though there were not really tested, but depended on the tests of a small set of the products — this is data mining in action.

1.13.   Conclusions

GMDH-based algorithms and self-organization can be used to automate almost the whole knowledge discovery process, i.e. models have been created adaptively and data preparation will be self-organized in special missing values are estimated and dimensionality is reduced. Automated solutions are more or less based on techniques developed in a discipline named "machine learning" as an important part of artificial intelligence. These are various techniques by which computerized algorithms can learn which patterns actually do exist in data sets. They may not be as intelligent as humans but are error-free, consistent, formidable fast, and tireless compared to humans.

Experimental studies revealed that the multilayer GMDH often underperforms on nonparametric regression tasks; moreover, time series modeling GMDH exhibits a tendency to find very complex polynomials that cannot model well future, unseen oscillations of the series.

In order to alleviate the problems associated with standard GMDH approach, a number of researchers have attempted to hybridize GMDH with some evolutionary optimization techniques. This is the central theme of this book.

One main huddle with using GMDH is that codes that explain the process are very scarce, and where available, these are obsolete. Consequently effort has been made in the book to present codes in MATLAB so that end-users can understand the steps involved in implementing GMDH. This is main purpose of this book. It is hoped that researchers by sieving the contents of this book, will become active in investigating how standard GMDH could become more robust and flexible in solving complex, real-world problems which currently cannot be solved using standard GMDH approach.

REFERENCES

[1] Ivakhnenko, A. G. (1971) Polynomial theory of complex systems, *IEEE Trans. Syst. Man Cybernet.*, **SMC-1**, 364–378.

[2] Madala, H. R. & Ivakhnenko, A. G. (1994) *Inductive Learning Algorithms for Complex Systems Modelling*, CRC Press Inc., Boca Raton, Ann Arbor, London, Tokyo.

[3] Korbicz, J. & Mrugalski, M. (2008) Confidence estimation of GMDH neural networks and its application in fault detection systems, *Int. J. Syst. Sci.*, **39**, 783–800.

[4] Water, P. R., Kerckhoffs, J. H. & Welden, D. V. (2000) GMDH-based dependency modeling in the identification of dynamic systems, In: *European Simulation Multi-Conference (ESM)*, pp. 211–218.

[5] Kondo, T. (1998) The learning algorithms of the GMDH neural network and their application to the medical image recognition, In: *Proc. of the 37th SICE Annual Conf., International Session Paper*, pp. 1109–1114.

[6] Sakaguchi, A., Yamamoto, T., Fujii, K. & Monden, Y. (2004) Evolutionary GMDH-based identification for nonlinear systems, In: *2004 IEEE Int. Conf. on Systems, Man and Cybernetics*, Vol. 6, pp. 5812–5817.

[7] Kondo, T. (2004) Revised GMDH-type neural networks using PSS criterion, *The 2004 47th Midwest Symp. Circuits and Systems (MWSCAS '04)*, Vol. 3, pp. iii–81-4.

[8] Ehsan, N., Saeed, B. & Vesal, H. (2004) Evolutionary GMDH-based identification of building blocks for binary-coded systems, In: *2nd IEEE Int. Conf. Information & Communication Technologies (ICTTA'06)*, Damascus, Syria, pp. 1900–1904.

[9] http://www.gmdh.net — Articles, books and software.

[10] Onwubolu, G. C. (2007) Design of hybrid differential evolution and group method of data handling for inductive modeling, In: *Proc. Int. Workshop on Inductive Modeling*, Prague, Czech, pp. 87–95.

[11] Kondo, T., Ueno, J. and Kondo, K. (2005) Revised GMDH-type neural networks using AIC or PSS criterion and their application to medical image recognition, *J. Adv. Comput. Intell. Intell. Inform.*, **9**(3), 257–267.

[12] Müller, J. A. & Lemke, F. (1999) Self-organizing data mining based on GMDH principle, In: *ESIT '99, European Symp. Intelligent Techniques*, Greece.

[13] Anastasakis, L. (2001). The development of self-organization techniques, In: *Modeling: A Review of the Group Method of Data Handling (GMDH)*, ACSE Research Report No. 813, University of Sheffield, UK.

[14] Nikolaev, N. Y. & Iba, H. (2003) Polynomial harmonic GMDH learning networks for time series modeling, *Neural Netw.*, **16**, 1527–1540.

[15] Onwubolu, G. C. (ed.) (2015) *GMDH-Methodology and Implementation in C*, Imperial College Press, London.

[16] Turing, A. M. (1950) Computing Machinery and Intelligence, *Mind*, **59**, 433–460.

[17] Engelbrecht, A. P. (2001) *Computation Intelligence: An Introduction*, 2nd Edition, Wiley, Chichester.

[18] Iba, H., de Garis, H., & Sato, T. (1994) Genetic programming using a minimum description length priniciple, In: *Advances in Genetic Programming*, K. E. Kinnear, Jr. (ed.), MIT, Cambridge, pp. 265–284.

[19] Nariman-Zadeh, N., Darvizeh, A., Felezi, M. E. & Gharababaei, H. (2002) Polynomial modeling of explosive compaction process of metallic powders using GMDH-type neural networks and singular value decomposition, *Modeling Simul. Sci. Eng.* **10**, 727–744.

[20] Nariman-Zadeh, N., Darvizeh, A. & Ahmad-Zadeh, G. R. (2003) Hybrid genetic design of GMDH-type neural networks using singular value decomposition for modeling and predicting of the explosive cutting process, *Proc. Inst. Mech. Engrs.* **217**, Part B, 779–790.

[21] Onwubolu, G. C. (2007) Design of hybrid differential evolution and group method of data handling for inductive modeling, In: *Proc. Int. Workshop on Inductive Modeling*, Prague, Czech, pp. 87–95.

[22] Onwubolu, G. C. (2008) Design of hybrid differential evolution and group method of data handling networks for modeling and prediction, *J. Inform. Sci.*, **178**, No. 18, pp. 3616–3634.

[23] Onwubolu, G. C. (ed.) (2009) *Hybrid Self-Organizing Modeling Systems*, Springer-Verlag, Germany, Chapter 9.

Chapter 2

GMDH MULTILAYERED ALGORITHM

Godfrey C. Onwubolu

This chapter presents the basic GMDH multilayered iteration (MIA) network fundamentals which are well documented in the literature. The main steps for the computations of the GMDH algorithm are then presented. The functions are described as they appear in the zip file hosted on www.worldscientific.com containing the error-free computer code for this GMDH variant: this is the main goal of this chapter. Two examples are solved using the basic GMDH-MIA network: the first one which is easier to model is taken from Farlow's book [3], while the second one which is more difficult to model is taken from the author's laboratory experimental work on tool wear estimation. The results show that the basic GMDH-MIA network is useful for modeling; however, better results could be obtained by including some improvement strategies. Users can modify the code to meet their specific requirements and hence GMDH can become more useful to a wider range of the community involved in inductive modeling.

2. GMDH MULTILAYERED ALGORITHMS IN MATLAB

2.1. Multilayered Algorithm Networks

The Group Method of Data Handling (or GMDH) was introduced by Ivakhnenko (details are found in [1–6]) as a means of identifying nonlinear relations between input and output variables. The multi-layered iteration (MIA) network is one of the variants of GMDH. The MIA relationship between the inputs and the output of a multiple inputs single output self-organizing network can be represented by an infinite Volterra–Kolmogorov–Gabor (VKG) polynomial of the form [1]:

$$y_n = a_0 + \sum_{i=1}^{M} a_i x_i + \sum_{i=1}^{M} \sum_{j=1}^{M} a_{ij} x_i x_j$$

$$+ \sum_{i=1}^{M} \sum_{j=1}^{M} \sum_{k=1}^{M} a_{ijk} x_i x_j x_k \ldots, \tag{2.1}$$

where $X = (x_1, x_2, \ldots, x_M)$ is the vector of input variables and $A = (a_0, a_i, a_{ij}, a_{ijk}, \ldots)$ is the vector of coefficients or weights. The formulation of the GMDH framework here follows that of [6].

2.1.1.   GMDH layers

When constructing a GMDH network, all combinations of the inputs are generated and sent into the first layer of the network. The outputs from this layer are then classified and selected for input into the next layer with all combinations of the selected outputs being sent into layer 2. This process is continued as long as each subsequent layer$_{(n+1)}$ produces a better result than layer$_{(n)}$. When layer$_{(n+1)}$ is found to not be as good as the layer$_{(n)}$, the process is stopped.

2.1.2.   GMDH nodes

Self-organizing networks are constructed from elemental polynomial neurons each of which possesses only a *pair* of dissimilar inputs (x_i, x_j). Each layer consists of nodes generated to take a specific pair of the combination of inputs as its source. Each node produces a set of coefficients a_i where $i \in \{0, 1, 2, \ldots, m\}$ such that Eq. (2.2) is estimated using the set of *training* data. This equation is tested for fit by determining the mean square error of the predicted $\hat{y}$ and actual y values as shown in Eq. (2.3) using the set of *testing* data.

$$\hat{y}_n = a_0 + a_1 x_{i_n} + a_2 x_{j_n} + a_3 x_{i_n} x_{j_n} + a_4 x_{i_n}^2 + a_5 x_{j_n}^2, \quad (2.2)$$

$$e = \sum_{n=1}^{N} (\hat{y}_n - y_n)^2. \quad (2.3)$$

In determining the values of **a** that would produce the "best fit", the partial derivatives of Eq. (2.3) are taken with respect to each constant value a_i and set equal to zero:

$$\frac{\partial e}{\partial a_i} = 0. \quad (2.4)$$

Expanding Eq. (2.4) results in the following system of equations that are solved using the *training* data set.

$$\sum_{n=1}^{N} y = \sum_{n=1}^{N} a_0 + a_1 x_i + a_2 x_j + a_3 x_i x_j$$
$$+ a_4 x_i^2 + a_5 x_j^2, \quad (2.5)$$

$$\sum_{n=1}^{N} y x_i = \sum_{n=1}^{N} a_0 x_i + a_1 x_i^2 + a_2 x_i x_j + a_3 x_i^2 x_j$$
$$+ a_4 x_i^3 + a_5 x_i x_j^2, \quad (2.6)$$

$$\sum_{n=1}^{N} y x_j = \sum_{n=1}^{N} a_0 x_j + a_1 x_i x_j + a_2 x_j^2 + a_3 x_i x_j^2$$
$$+ a_4 x_i^2 x_j + a_5 x_j^3, \quad (2.7)$$

$$\sum_{n=1}^{N} y x_i x_j = \sum_{n=1}^{N} a_0 x_i x_j + a_1 x_i^2 x_j + a_2 x_i x_j^2 + a_3 x_i^2 x_j^2$$
$$+ a_4 x_i^3 x_j + a_5 x_i x_j^3, \quad (2.8)$$

$$\sum_{n=1}^{N} y x_i^2 = \sum_{n=1}^{N} a_0 x_i^2 + a_1 x_i^3 + a_2 x_i^2 x_j + a_3 x_i^3 x_j$$
$$+ a_4 x_i^4 + a_5 x_i^2 x_j^2, \quad (2.9)$$

$$\sum_{n=1}^{N} y x_j^2 = \sum_{n=1}^{N} a_0 x_j^2 + a_1 x_i x_j^2 + a_2 x_j^3 + a_3 x_i x_j^3$$

$$+ a_4 x_i^2 x_j^2 + a_5 x_j^4. \tag{2.10}$$

The equations can be simplified using matrix mathematics as follows:

$$Y = \begin{pmatrix} 1 & x_i & x_j & x_i x_j & x_i^2 & x_j^2 \end{pmatrix}, \tag{2.11}$$

$$X = Y^{\mathrm{T}} Y, \tag{2.12}$$

$$X = \begin{pmatrix} 1 & x_i & x_j & x_i x_j & x_i^2 & x_j^2 \\ x_i & x_i^2 & x_i x_j & x_i^2 x_j & x_i^3 & x_i x_j^2 \\ x_j & x_i x_j & x_j^2 & x_i x_j^2 & x_i^2 x_j & x_j^3 \\ x_i x_j & x_i^2 x_j & x_i x_j^2 & x_i^2 x_j^2 & x_i^3 x_j & x_i x_j^3 \\ x_i^2 & x_i^3 & x_i^2 x_j & x_i^3 x_j & x_i^4 & x_i^2 x_j^2 \\ x_j^2 & x_i x_j^2 & x_j^3 & x_i x_j^3 & x_i^2 x_j^2 & x_j^4 \end{pmatrix}, \tag{2.13}$$

$$a = \begin{pmatrix} a_0 & a_1 & a_2 & a_3 & a_4 & a_5 \end{pmatrix}, \tag{2.14}$$

$$b = (yY)^{\mathrm{T}}. \tag{2.15}$$

This system of equations then can be written as:

$$\sum_{n=1}^{N} aX = \sum_{n=1}^{N} b. \tag{2.16}$$

The node is now responsible for evaluating all inputs of x_{i_n}, x_{j_n}, y_n data values in **a** and **b** for the *training* set of data. Solving the system of equations results in **x** being the node's computed set of coefficients. Using these coefficients in Eq. (2.2), the node then computes its error by processing the set of *testing* data in Eqs. (2.2) and (2.3). The error is the measure of fit that this node achieved.

2.1.3.   GMDH connections

A GMDH layer sorts its nodes based on the error produced, saving the best **N** nodes. The generated y_n values (classifications) of each node become one set of inputs to be used by the next layer when it combines all outputs from the previous layer's nodes assigning them to the new layer's nodes (see Fig. 2.1). The layer must remember the nodes that were saved so that other data submitted to the network will follow the same generated path to the output.

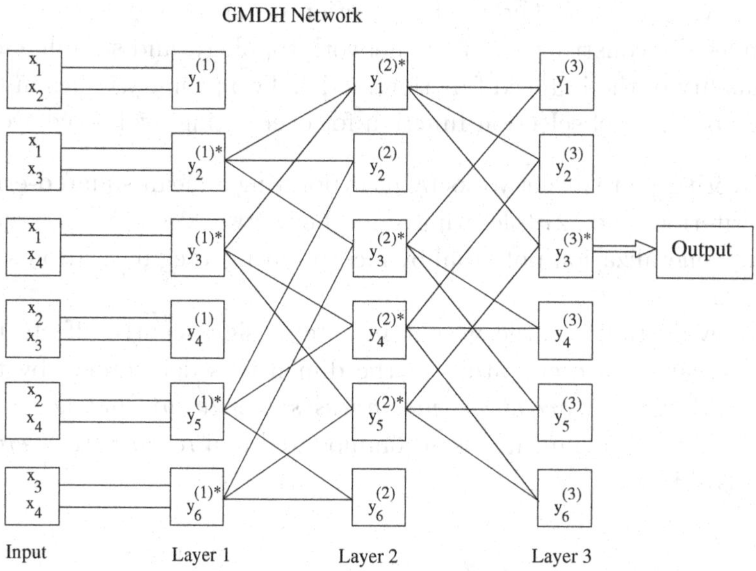

GMDH Network

Fig. 2.1.   GMDH forward feed functional network.

2.1.4.   GMDH network

When the GMDH network is completed, there is a set of original inputs that filtered through the layers to the optimal output node. This is the computational network that is to be used in computing predictions (in our application, classifications are implied). The best nodes in the input layer (starred nodes in Fig. 2.1) are retained and form the input to the next layer. The inputs for layer 1 are formed by taking all combinations of the surviving output approximations from the input layer nodes. It is seen that at each layer the order of the polynomial approximation is increased by two. The layer 2 best nodes for approximating the system output are retained and form the layer 3 inputs. This process is repeated until the current layer's best approximation is inferior to the previous layer's best approximation.

2.1.5.   Regularized model selection

A model selection criterion is necessary to achieve over-fitting avoidance; that is to pursue construction of not only accurate but also predictive networks. The model selection criterion is essential since it guides the construction of the network topology, and so influences the quality of the induced function model. Two primary issues in the design of a model selection function for over-fitting avoidance are:

(1) favoring more fit networks by incorporating a mean-squared-error sub-criterion; and (2) tolerating smoother network mappings having higher generalization potential by incorporating a regularization sub-criterion.

Knowing that a large weight in a term significantly affects the polynomial surface curvature in the dimensions determined by the term variables, a *correcting smoothness sub-criterion* that accounts for the weights' magnitude is accommodated in a *regularized average error* (RAE) as

$$RAE = (1/n_t) \left(\sum_{i=1}^{n_t} (y_i - F(x_i, x_k))^2 + \alpha \sum_{j=1}^{W} a_j^2 \right), \qquad (2.17)$$

where α is regularization parameter whose proper values are found using statistical techniques, a_j are the weights or coefficients, such that $1 \leq j \leq W$ and $F(x_i, x_k) = h(x_i, x_k)a$. This formula (2.17) is known as weight decay regularization and it requires the usage of regularized least square (RLS) fitting method for estimating the weights

$$a = (X^T X + \alpha I)^{-1} X^T y, \qquad (2.18)$$

where **a** is the coefficients vector. The regularized least square is also called the ridge regression. The $\alpha \geq 0$ is a parameter to control the amounts of shrinkage. Consequently, the advantage of regularization approach is that since the regression was used as a building block, the regularization techniques can be easily incorporated and provide more stable and meaningful solutions, especially when there exist a large amount of input variables.

2.1.6. GMDH algorithm

This section gives the steps involved in the basic GMDH algorithm as shown in Algorithm 2.1.

Algorithm 2.1. Multilayer GMDH algorithm for growing higher-order networks

---

Initialization

Given a data series $\partial = \{(x_{ij}, y_i)\}$, $i = 1, 2, \ldots, n$; $j = 1, 2, \ldots, m$; where the number of training data is n_t and the number of testing data is n_c such that $n_t + n_t = n$.

Let the layer label be $l = 1$, the lowest error be $\varepsilon = MaxInt$ and the activation polynomials expressed as

$$p(x_i, x_k) = a_0 + a_1 x_i + a_2 x_k + a_3 x_i x_k + a_4 x_i^2 + a_5 x_k^2$$

or

$$p(x_i, x_k) = h(x_i, x_k)a \Rightarrow H[h_1, h_2, \ldots, h_N]^{\mathrm{T}}.$$

Network construction and weight training

Step 1: Make all $c = \binom{m}{2}$ combinations of variables (x_i, x_k), $l \leq i$, $j \leq r$

Step 2: Make a polynomial $p_c^l(x_i, x_k)$ from each combination

2.1 Estimate its coefficients a_c by OLS fitting:

$$a_c = (H^{\mathrm{T}} H)^{-1} H^{\mathrm{T}} y$$

2.2 Evaluate the error or external criterion (EC) of the polynomial:

$$p_c^l(x_i, x_k) = h a_c$$

$$\mathrm{EC}_c = (1/n_t) \sum_{i=1}^{n_t} (y_i - p_c^l(x_i, x_k))^2$$

2.3 Compute the model selection criterion using the regularized average error (RAE):

$$\text{RAE}_c = f(\text{EC}_c)$$

Step 3: Order the polynomials with respect to their RAE_c, and choose r of these with lower criterion values

Step 4: Consider the lowest error from this layer: $\varepsilon^{l+1} = \min\{\text{RAE}_c\}$

Step 5: If $\varepsilon^{l+1} > \varepsilon$ then terminate, else set $\varepsilon = \varepsilon^{l+1}$ and continue

Step 6: The polynomial outputs become current variables: $x_c \equiv p_c^l$

Step 7: Repeat the construction and training step with $l = l + 1$

2.2.   Computer Code for GMDH-MIA

The computations of the GMDH algorithm are carried out by the following three main steps similar to those in [6]:

1. Compute a tree of quadratic polynomials (*function* gmdh).
2. Evaluate the Ivakhnenko polynomial using the tree of polynomials generated (*function* comp).
3. Compute the coefficients in the Ivakhnenko polynomial via regression analysis using the same tree of polynomials generated (*function* coeff).

These functions and the main function are in Chapter 2 folder of the zip file hosted on www.worldscientific.com.

2.2.1.   Compute a tree of quadratic polynomials

The function ***gmdh***() listed in Function 2.1 uses the input data array X and response data array Y together with the variables n, m, nt to compute a tree of quadratic polynomials. There are n data points, m independent variables, and nt number of observation in the training set in the array X. The number of observation in the training set is therefore $(n - nt)$. All the independent variables are taken two at a time and for each of these $\binom{m}{2}$ combinations we find the least squares polynomials of the form $y = A + Bu + Cv + Du^2 + Ev^2 + Fuv$ that best fits the y_i observations in the training set, where

$\binom{m}{2} = m(m-1)/2$. These coefficients are used to evaluate the polynomial at the n (all) data points. In other words, we have constructed new variables $z_1, z_2, \ldots, z_{\binom{m}{2}}$, where each of these new variables is a polynomial in the original variables $x_1, x_2, \ldots, x_m$ some of which will replace the original ones. The goal is to keep those new variables z_i that best estimate the output vector y and discard the others using the checking set. Function 2.1 gmdh describes this first step of the GMDH algorithm. There are seven stages in the function as shown in Function 2.1:

Stage: # 1: 1st & 2nd variables of $[m * (m-1)/2]$ pairs for training to define $xty[\,]$ and $xtx[\,][\,]$ for regression

Stage: # 2: Compute the coefficients $xyx[\,]$ via regression analysis using function coeff()

Stage: # 3: Constructed new variables $z_1, z_2, \ldots, z_{m(m-1)/2}$

Stage: # 4: Use checking data set to compute the goodness of fit statistics

Stage: # 5: Sort values of the statistics from low to high

Stage: # 6: Grow tree of Ivakhnenko polynomial

Stage: # 7: Determine minimum external criterion checking error and coefficient of correlation

One other function is called by $gmdh()$ function: this conv() for determining convergence. Unlike the functions in [6], the evaluation of coefficients is performed within the gmdh() function in method of this book.

Function 2.1 gmdh

```
    function [itree,tree,iter] = gmdh(n,m,nt,pii,niter,x,y,fout1)
%itree,tree,iter
    q = 0;
    rms = pii;
    ntp1 = nt+ 1;
    nc = n - nt;
    niter = niter + 1;
    mm = m; %save 'm' because it may change
    iter = 1; %layer
    dmin = 1.0E20; %minimum least square error, LSE
while (q == 0)
    l=1;
```

```
    mm1=m-1;
% begin loop to compute new m(m-1)/2 variables
for i=1:mm1 %number of variables
    ip1 = i + 1;
        for j=ip1:m % (i,j) are two consecutive variables for m(m-1)/2
combinations
    for ii=1:6
      xty(ii)=0.0;
        for jj=1:6
          xtx(ii,jj) = 0.0; %initialize 6x6 array, xtx
        end %end jj
    end %end ii
%STEP 1: use training set data to find the least square polynomial
        xtx(1,1) = nt; %number of data points in training set
      for k=1:nt %k = 1, nt
          xtx(1,2) = xtx(1,2) + x(k,i);
          xtx(1,3) = xtx(1,3) + x(k,j);
          xtx(1,4) = xtx(1,4) + power(x(k,i),2);
          xtx(1,5) = xtx(1,5) + power(x(k,j),2);
          xtx(1,6) = xtx(1,6) + x(k,i)*x(k,j);
          xtx(2,2) = xtx(2,2) + power(x(k,i),2);
          xtx(2,3) = xtx(2,3) + x(k,i)*x(k,j);
          xtx(2,4) = xtx(2,4) + power(x(k,i),3);
          xtx(2,5) = xtx(2,5) + x(k,i)*power(x(k,j),2);
          xtx(2,6) = xtx(2,6) + x(k,i)*x(k,i)*x(k,j);
          xtx(3,3) = xtx(3,3) + power(x(k,j),2);
          xtx(3,4) = xtx(3,4) + x(k,i)*x(k,i)*x(k,j);
          xtx(3,5) = xtx(3,5) + power(x(k,j),3);
          xtx(3,6) = xtx(3,6) + x(k,i)*power(x(k,j),2);
          xtx(4,4) = xtx(4,4) + power(x(k,i),4);
          xtx(4,5) = xtx(4,5) + power((x(k,i)*x(k,j)),2);
          xtx(4,6) = xtx(4,6) + x(k,j)*power(x(k,i),3);
          xtx(5,5) = xtx(5,5) + power(x(k,j),4);
          xtx(5,6) = xtx(5,6) + x(k,i)*power(x(k,j),3);
          xtx(6,6) = xtx(6,6) + power((x(k,i)*x(k,j)),2);
          xty(1) = xty(1) + y(k);
          xty(2) = xty(2) + x(k,i)*y(k);
          xty(3) = xty(3) + x(k,j)*y(k);
          xty(4) = xty(4) + x(k,i)*x(k,i)*y(k);
          xty(5) = xty(5) + x(k,j)*x(k,j)*y(k);
          xty(6) = xty(6) + x(k,i)*x(k,j)*y(k);
      end %end k=1,nt


    for ii=2:6 %ii = 2, 6
    im1 = ii-1;
        for jj=1:im1 %jj = 1, im1
        xtx(ii,jj) = xtx(jj,ii); %fill in lower-half of xtx(,)
        end % end jj
    end %end ii
%    solve regression equation for variables i and j
```

```
    zzz=xtx\xty'; %equivalence of subroutine sys(.) to find
coefficients/weights
    for iii=1:6
        poly(iii,1)=zzz(iii); %save weights (coefficients), zzz(.) in
poly(.)
    end
    for k=1:n %k = 1, n
        ww=0.0;
        ww = ww + poly(1,1) + poly(2,1)*x(k,i) + poly(3,1)*x(k,j)...
            + poly(4,1)*power(x(k,i),2) + poly(5,1)*power(x(k,j),2)...
            + poly(6,1)*x(k,i)*x(k,j);
        work(k,1) = ww; %columns of z for m(m-1)/2 new variables, z1, z2,...
        end %end k=1,n

        ind(1) = 100*(i+10) + (j+10);
        if (1 == nt)
            break; %goto: finish;
        end
        1 = 1+1; %increment counter until m(m-1)/2
    end     %end i=1,mm
end     % end j=ip1,m
                        %Note: (i,j) are two consecutive variables for
m(m-1)/2
                        %combinations
%           Construction of m*(m-1)/2 new variables is now completed
%///////////////////////////////////////////////////////////////
% STEP 2: Compute the LSE over checking observations, nc

    1 = 1-1; %decrement since this would have increased by 1
% finish: ;
    for i=1:nc
        ywork(i) = y(nt+i); % save y values over checking observations
    end
        for j=1:1 %consider all m(m-1)/2 data
            for i=1:nc
                xwork(i) = work(nt+i,j); % save x values over checking
observations
            end %end i=1,nc
%       compute the goodness of fit statistics
            st=stat(nc,ywork,xwork); %access subroutine 'stat'

            d(j) = st; %list of all fitness statistics
            index(j) = j;
        end %end j=1,1

%///////////////////////////////////////////////////////////////
% STEP 3: Replacement Strategy: ordering the columns of Z in increasing LSE
%           and choosing best columns of Z to replace some x columns
%sort the values of the statistics from low to high
    if (1 >0)
    [ir,d]=sorting(d,1,index); %sort all statistics from least to greatest
for
```

```
                              % all 1 or m(m-1)/2;
                              % d(1) is current minimum error
        for j=1:1
%           fprintf (fout1,'\n d[%d] = %8.3f',index(j), d(index(j)) );
            fprintf (fout1,'\n d[%d] = %8.3f',ir(j), d(index(j)) );

            WW1 = sprintf (' d[%d] = %8.3f',ir(j), d(index(j)) );
            disp (WW1)
            end
        end
        m=floor(m(1+rms)); %prescribed number of good statistics candidates
                           %Note: 'm' may change here

        if (m>1) m = 1;         end %limit upper bound of m(m-1)/2
%the largest number of var is set to 75
        if (m>75) m = 75;       end %limit to maximum of 75
        if (m<mm) m = mm;       end %limit lower bound of initial m
        for j=1:m
           itree(iter,j) = ind(ir(j));
            % fprintf (fout1,'\n itree[%d][%d] = %d',iter, j, ind(index(j)) );
            fprintf (fout1,'\n itree[%d][%d] = %d',iter, j, ind(ir(j)) );

            WW1 = sprintf (' itree[%d][%d] = %d',iter, j, ind(ir(j)) );
            disp (WW1)

            for k=1:6
               tree(iter,j,k) = poly(k,ir(j)); %return weights; poly is a 6xm
array
               fprintf (fout1,'\n tree[%d][%d][%d] = %g',iter, j, k,
tree(iter,j,k) );

            WW1 = sprintf (' tree[%d][%d][%d] = %g',iter, j, k,tree(iter,j,k));
            disp (WW1)

            end %end k=1,6
        end %end j=1,m

%/////test for convergence of gmdh algorithm/////
if (niter == 1)
    test = (d(1) - dmin+ 5E-4);
     if (test >0)
     conv(mm,iter,nt,x,y,fout1);
       return;
     end
else
     if (iter == niter)
     conv(mm,iter,nt,x,y,fout1);
       return;
     end
```

```
end
    dmin = d(1); %save minimum error
    fprintf (fout1,'\n Level number = %d',iter);
    fprintf (fout1,'\n No. variables saved = %d',m);
    fprintf (fout1,'\n rmin [minimum checking set error] value =
%8.3f',dmin);

    WW1 = sprintf ('\n Level number = %d',iter );
        disp (WW1)
    WW1 = sprintf ('\n No. variables saved = %d',m );
        disp (WW1)
    WW1 = sprintf ('\n rmin [minimum checking set error] value =
%8.3f',dmin );
        disp (WW1)

    ma(iter) = m; %save number of PDs
    iter = iter + 1; %increment layer
%   max number of iteration is 11
    for i=1:n
        for j=1:m %number of current polynomial variables
        x(i,j) = work(i,ir(j)); %replace original independent variable with
current polynomial outputs
        end
    end
    sum = 0.0;
    for i=1:nt
      sum = sum + y(i);
    end
    sum = sum/nt; %mean of y
    sum1 = 0.0;
    sum2 = 0.0;
    for i=1:nt
       sum1 = sum1 + power((sum - x(i,1)),2); %MSE for 1st dependent
variable (best so far)
       sum2 = sum2 + power((y(i) - sum),2); %MSE for y
    end
    sum = sum1/sum2; %MSE for y

    fprintf (fout1,'\n sum = %8.3f \n',sum);

    WW1 = sprintf ('\n sum = %8.3f \n',sum );
        disp (WW1)
end %while ////////////repeat 'construction' and 'training' step

% A=[ones(length(x),1)];
%    A=[A x x.*x];
%    for i=1:m-1
%      for j=i+1:m
%        A=[A x(:,i).*x(:,j)];
%      end
```

%   end

Let us illustrate with six input parameters (Example 2 in Sec. 2.3.2), so we have $p = 15$ pairs of inputs obtained from the relation $p = m(m-1)/2$ where $m = 6$. These pairs are as follows:

$$(x_{i,1}, x_{i,2}), \quad (x_{i,1}, x_{i,3}), \quad (x_{i,1}, x_{i,4}),$$
$$(x_{i,1}, x_{i,5}), \quad (x_{i,1}, x_{i,6}), \quad (x_{i,2}, x_{i,3}), \quad (x_{i,2}, x_{i,4}),$$
$$(x_{i,2}, x_{i,5}), \quad (x_{i,2}, x_{i,6}), \quad (x_{i,3}, x_{i,4}), \quad (x_{i,3}, x_{i,5}),$$
$$(x_{i,3}, x_{i,6}), \quad (x_{i,4}, x_{i,5}), \quad (x_{i,4}, x_{i,6}), \quad (x_{i,5}, x_{i,6})$$

and the indices $(1, 2)$, $(1, 3), \ldots, (5, 6)$ are used to compute the keys: $\text{ind}(1) = 100 * (i + 10) + (j + 10)$ such that

$$\text{ind} =$$

1112	1113	1114	1115	1116	1213
1214	1215	1216	1314	1315	1316
1415	1416	1516			

For each level (layer), let the first six best objective function (external criterion) values be arranged as:

d[10], d[6], d[13], d[7], d[8], d[12]
d[6], d[4], d[1], d[7], d[2], d[3]
d[1], d[8], d[5], d[2], d[4], d[3]

For example in level 1, we find the values of *ind* in positions 10, 6, 13, 7, 8, and 12 leading to 1314, 1213, 1415, 1214, 1215 and 1316 respectively; in level 2, we find the values of *ind* in positions 6, 4, 1, 7, 2, and 3 leading to 1213, 1115, 1112, 1214, 1113 and 1114 respectively; in level 3, we find the values of *ind* in positions 6, 4, 1, 7, 2, and 3 leading to 1112, 1215, 1116, 1113, 1115, and 1114 respectively. Using these two pieces of information, the keys for the tree are generated as follows:

$$\text{itree} =$$

1314	1213	1415	1214	1215	1316
1213	1115	1112	1214	1113	1114
1112	1215	1116	1113	1115	1114

The best m coefficients are stored in tree structure for each level such that:

$$tree[iter][j][k] = poly\,[k][index[j]]; \quad j = 1,\ldots,6; \quad k = 1,\ldots,m$$

2.2.2. Evaluate the Ivakhnenko polynomial using the tree of polynomials generated

This function **comp**() listed in Function 2.2 uses the tree of polynomials generated in **gmdh**() to evaluate the Ivakhnenko polynomial (Eq. (2.1)) for some value of the variables $x_1, x_2, \ldots, x_m$. We will continue with the six input parameters used in **gmdh**() for which,

itree =

1314	1213	1415	1214	1215	1316
1213	1115	1112	1214	1113	1114
1112	1215	1116	1113	1115	1114

There are basically two steps involved in this subroutine:

Step 1: Generate vector 'itr' from 'itree': **Comp6**():

At the time of accessing this subroutine, the value of layer or level is given by $iter = 3$.

There are some initializations such as $itr[1] = 1$; $i = 1$.

Loop 1: For $l = 0$, $nn = 2^{i-1} = 1$; $n1 = 2^i = 2$; $nz = 2^{i+1} - 1 = 3$; $j = n1 = 2$;

Loop 2:
$jj = itr[nn + l] = itr[1] = 1$;
$xx = itree[iter][jj] = itree[3][1] = 1112$
$itr[2] = itree[iter][jj]/100 - 10 = itree[3][1]/100 - 10 = (1112/100) - 10 = 1$
$iz = itree[iter][jj]/100 = itree[3][1]/100 = (1112/100) = 11$
$itr[3] = xx - 100 * iz - 10 = 1112 - 100 * 11 - 10 = 2$
$j = j + 2 = 4$
$itr[1, 2, 3] = [1\ 1\ 2]$

Loop 2 continues if j <nz, otherwise $l = l + 1$ and Loop 1 continues
$iter = iter - 1 := 2$

$i = i + 1 := 2$

$nn = 2^{i-1} = 2; \; n1 = 2^i = 4; \; nz = 2^{i+1} - 1 = 7; \; j = n1 = 4$

$jj = itr[nn + l] = itr[2] = 1;$

$xx = itree \; [iter][jj] = itree \; [2][1] = 1213$

$itr[4] = itree[iter][jj]/100 - 10 = itree[2][1]/100 - 10 = (1213/100) - 10 = 2$

$iz = itree[iter][jj]/100 = itree[2][1]/100 = (1213/100) = 12$

$itr[5] = xx - 100 * iz - 10 = 1213 - 100 * 12 - 10 = 3$

$j = j + 2 = 6$

$itr[1, 2, 3, 4, 5] = [1 \; 1 \; 2 \; 2 \; 3]$

Loop 2 continues if j <nz, otherwise $l = l + 1$ and Loop 1 continues (Note: j = 6; nz = 7 therefore we are still in Loop 2: iter = 2 and i = 2 and previous conditions hold)

$nn = 2^{i-1} = 2; \; n1 = 2^i = 4; \; nz = 2^{i+1} - 1 = 7; \; j = n1 = 4$

$jj = itr[nn + l] = itr[2 + 1] = itr[3] = 2;$

$xx = itree \; [iter][jj] = itree \; [2][2] = 1115$

$itr[4] = itree[iter][jj]/100 - 10 = itree[2][2]/100 - 10 = (1115/100) - 10 = 1$

$iz = itree[iter][jj]/100 = itree[2][2]/100 = (1115/100) = 11$

$itr[5] = xx - 100 * iz - 10 = 1115 - 100 * 11 - 10 = 5$

$j = j + 2 = 8$

$itr[1, 2, 3, 4, 5, 6, 7] = [1 \; 1 \; 2 \; 2 \; 3 \; 1 \; 5]$

Loop 2 continues if j <nz, otherwise $l = l + 1$ and Loop 1 continues (Note: j = 8; nz = 7 therefore control goes to Loop 1 after the following conditions)

$iter = iter - 1 := 1$

$i = i + 1 := 3$

$nn = 2^{i-1} = 4; \; n1 = 2^i = 8; \; nz = 2^{i+1} - 1 = 15; \; j = n1 = 8$

$jj = itr[nn + l] = itr[4] = 2;$

$xx = itree \; [iter][jj] = itree \; [1][2] = 1213$

$itr[8] = itree[iter][jj]/100 - 10 = itree[1][2]/100 - 10 = (1213/100) - 10 = 2$

$iz = itree[iter][jj]/100 = itree[1][2]/100 = (1213/100) = 12$

$itr[5] = xx - 100 * iz - 10 = 1213 - 100 * 12 - 10 = 3$

$j = j + 2 = 10$

$itr[1, 2, 3, 4, 5, 6, 7, 8, 9] = [1\ 1\ 2\ 2\ 3\ 1\ 5\ 2\ 3]$

Loop 2 continues if j <nz, otherwise $l = l + 1$ and Loop 1 continues (Note: j = 10; nz = 15 therefore we are still in Loop 2: iter = 1 and i = 3 and previous conditions hold and$l = l+1 = 1$)

$nn = 2^{i-1} = 4$; $n1 = 2^i = 8$; $nz = 2^{i+1} - 1 = 15$; $j = n1 = 8$

$jj = itr[nn + l] = itr[4 + 1] = itr[5] = 3$;

$xx = itree\ [iter][jj] = itree\ [1][3] = 1415$

$itr[10] = itree[iter][jj]/100 - 10 = itree[1][3]/100 - 10 = (1415/100) - 10 = 4$

$iz = itree[iter][jj]/100 = itree[1][2]/100 = (1415/100) = 14$

$itr[11] = xx - 100 * iz - 10 = 1415 - 100 * 14 - 10 = 5$

$j = j + 2 = 12$

$itr[1, 2, 3, 4, 5, 6, 7, 8, 9, 10, 11] = [1\ 1\ 2\ 2\ 3\ 1\ 5\ 2\ 3\ 4\ 5]$

(Note: j = 10; nz = 15 therefore we are still in Loop 2: iter = 1 and i = 3 and previous conditions hold and $l = l+1 = 2$)

$nn = 2^{i-1} = 4$; $n1 = 2^i = 8$; $nz = 2^{i+1} - 1 = 15$; $j = n1 = 8$

$jj = itr[nn + l] = itr[4 + 2] = itr[6] = 1$;

$xx = itree\ [iter][jj] = itree\ [1][1] = 1314$

$itr[12] = itree[iter][jj]/100 - 10 = itree[1][1]/100 - 10 = (1314/100) - 10 = 3$

$iz = itree[iter][jj]/100 = itree[1][1]/100 = (1314/100) = 13$

$itr[13] = xx - 100 * iz - 10 = 1314 - 100 * 13 - 10 = 4$

$j = j + 2 = 14$

$itr[1, 2, 3, 4, 5, 6, 7, 8, 9, 10, 11, 12, 13] = [1\ 1\ 2\ 2\ 3\ 1\ 5\ 2\ 3\ 4\ 5\ 3\ 4]$

(Note: j = 14; nz = 15 therefore we are still in Loop 2: iter = 1 and i = 3 and previous conditions hold and $l = l+1 = 3$)

$nn = 2^{i-1} = 4$; $n1 = 2^i = 8$; $nz = 2^{i+1} - 1 = 15$; $j = n1 = 8$

$jj = itr[nn + l] = itr[4 + 3] = itr[7] = 5$;

$xx = itree\ [iter][jj] = itree\ [1][5] = 1215$

$itr[14] = itree[iter][jj]/100 - 10 = itree[1][5]/100 - 10 = (1215/100) - 10 = 2$

$iz = itree[iter][jj]/100 = itree[1][1]/100 = (1215/100) = 12$

$itr[15] = xx - 100 * iz - 10 = 1215 - 100 * 12 - 10 = 5$

$j = j + 2 = 16$

$itr[1, 2, 3, 4, 5, 6, 7, 8, 9, 10, 11, 12, 13, 14, 15] = [1\ 1\ 2\ 2\ 3\ 1\ 5\ 2\ 3\ 4\ 5\ 3\ 4\ 2\ 5]$

We notice that the values of the array 'itr' are within the range of 1 and $m - 1$.

Step 2: Extract coefficients in 'itree' using information in 'itr'

At the time of accessing this subroutine, the value of layer or level is given by $iter = 3$.

There are some initializations such:

$$iter = 3, \quad nz = 2^{iter-1} = 4; \quad nzz = nz = 4; \quad n1 = 2^{iter} = 8.$$

Let us now first deal with the first level. Recall that the structure of $tree\,[iter][j][k]$ where $j = 1, \ldots, m$ and $k = 1, \ldots, 6$. We are now doing regression (see Eqs. (2.19) and (2.20)). From the tree structure the first term refers to the level (layer), the second refers to the best first m values and the last refers to six coefficients needed for regression, which means that we are extracting the best coefficients for regression. The index for the extraction of coefficients is 'jj1' while the indices for x_i and x_j are 'jj2' and 'jj3' respectively. For example $jj1 = itr[nz] = itr[4] = 2; \ jj2 = itr[n1] = itr[8] = 2; \ jj3 = itr[n1+1] = itr[9] = 3;$ which means that we need to use the following pieces of information:

tree[1][2][1] $= -0.842936$
tree[1][2][2] $= -10.5842$
tree[1][2][3] $= 17.7297$
tree[1][2][4] $= 1.97805$
tree[1][2][5] $= -1.0362$
tree[1][2][6] $= -2.34478$

as well as the second and third columns of x values (see Table 2.2 where we use for example the values of 2 and 1.5 for the first row) so that we now have the estimated value of:

$$work[1] = -0.842936 - 10.5842 * 2 + 17.7297 * 1.5 + 1.97805 * 2 * 2$$
$$-1.0362 * 1.5 * 1.5 - 2.34478 * 2 * 1.5 = 3.1296.$$

The values of nz and n1 are updated as $nz = nz + 1$ and $n1 = n1 + 2$ so that after the first iteration $nz = 5$ and $n1 = 10$ leading to the use of the following flags (last three columns):

nz	n1	n1 + 1	jj1	jj2	jj3
4	8	9	2	2	3
5	10	11	3	4	5
6	12	13	1	3	4
7	14	15	5	2	5

$jj1 = itr[nz] = itr[5] = 3$; $jj2 = itr[n1] = itr[10] = 4$; $jj3 = itr[n1 + 1] = itr[11] = 5$; which means that we need to use the following pieces of information:

tree[1][3][1] = 1211.82
tree[1][3][2] = −20.4177
tree[1][3][3] = −3.52863
tree[1][3][4] = 0.084853
tree[1][3][5] = 0.00730125
tree[1][3][6] = 0.0285809

as well as the fourth and fifth columns of x values (sec Table 2.2 where we use for example the values of 131 and 34.48 for the first row) so that we now have the estimated value of:

$$\text{work}[2] = 1211.82 - 20.4177 * 131 - 3.52863 * 34.48$$
$$+ 0.084853 * 131^2 + 0.00730125 * 34.48^2$$
$$+ 0.0285809 * 131 * 34.48 = 9.3732.$$

In the next iteration (level), jj1 = 1, jj2 = 3 and jj3 = 4 which means that we need to use the following pieces of information:

tree[1][1][1] = −0.551931
tree[1][1][2] = −14.9265
tree[1][1][3] = 0.13005
tree[1][1][4] = −0.904898
tree[1][1][5] = −0.00157262
tree[1][1][6] = 0.202222

as well as the third and fourth columns of x values (see Table 2.2 where we use for example the values of 1.5 and 131 for the first row) so that we now have the estimated value of:

$$\text{work}[3] = -0.551931 - 14.9265 * 1.5 + 0.13005 * 131$$
$$- 0.904898 * 1.5^\wedge 2 - 0.00157262 * 131^\wedge 2$$
$$+ 0.202222 * 1.5 * 131 = 4.8077.$$

In the next iteration (level), jj1 = 5, jj2 = 2 and jj3 = 5 which means that we need to use the following pieces of information:

tree[1][5][1] = −21.5588
tree[1][5][2] = −6.5823
tree[1][5][3] = 1.59529
tree[1][5][4] = 4.3734
tree[1][5][5] = 0.00797934
tree[1][5][6] = −0.591555

as well as the second and fifth columns of x values (see Table 2.2 where we use for example the values of 2 and 34.48 for the first row) so that we now have the estimated value of:

$$\text{work}[4] = -21.5588 - 6.5823 * 2 + 1.59529 * 34.48 + 4.3734 * 2^\wedge 2$$
$$+ 0.00797934 * 34.48^\wedge 2 - 0.591555 * 2 * 34.48 = 6.4686$$

work[i] = [3.1296 9.3732 4.8077 6.4686], which are the outputs of the neurons in the first level (or layer). We then move to the second layer and increment i by 1 so that $i = 2$.

At this point, the value of iter is decremented by 1, so that iter = 2.

$$iter = 2, \quad nz = 2^{iter-1} = 2; \quad n1 = 2^{iter} = 4;$$
$$nzz = nz = 2; \quad n11 = n1 = 4.$$

We now enter a loop for j from 2 to nzz, here it is done only once because nzz = 2. Let us compute the flag values of jj and jj1 as follows:

j	nz	n1	n1+1	jj	jj1
1	2	4	5	1	1
2	3	6	7	3	2

We are calculating a new set of estimated output using indices jj and jj1 in the tree structure using the following information:

tree[1][1][1] = -0.551931
tree[1][1][2] = -14.9265
tree[1][1][3] = 0.13005
tree[1][1][4] = -0.904898
tree[1][1][5] = -0.00157262
tree[1][1][6] = 0.202222

as well as the first and second calculated values of **work[i]** so that we now have the new estimated value of work[n11+1] = work[4+1] = work[5]:

$$\text{work}[5] = -0.551931 - 14.9265 * 3.1296 + 0.13005 * 9.3732$$
$$- 0.904898 * 3.1296^2 - 0.00157262 * 9.3732^2$$
$$+ 0.202222 * 3.1296 * 9.3732 = -49.1160$$

$nz = nz + 1 = 3$; $n1 = n1 + 2 = 6$.
Therefore we use the following information:

tree[1][2][1] = -0.842936
tree[1][2][2] = -10.5842
tree[1][2][3] = 17.7297
tree[1][2][4] = 1.97805
tree[1][2][5] = -1.0362
tree[1][2][6] = -2.34478

as well as the third and fourth calculated values of **work[i]** so that we now have the new estimated value of work[n11 + 2] = work[4 + 2]

$= \text{work}[6]$:

$$\begin{aligned} \text{work}[6] = {} & -0.842936 - 10.5842 * 4.8077 + 17.7297 * 6.4686 \\ & + 1.97805 *^{\wedge} 4.80772 - 1.0362 * 6.4686^{\wedge}2 \\ & - 2.34478 * 4.8077 * 6.4686 = -7.5993 \end{aligned}$$

We further decrement iter by 1 so that iter $= 1$.

$$iter = 1, \quad nz = 2^{iter-1} = 1; \quad n1 = 2^{iter} = 2;$$
$$nzz = nz = 1; \quad n11 = n1 = 2.$$

$$\begin{aligned} \text{work}[5] = {} & -0.551931 - 14.9265 * -49.1160 + 0.13005 * (-7.5993) \\ & - 0.904898 * (-49.1160)^{\wedge}2 - 0.00157262 * (-7.5993)^{\wedge}2 \\ & + 0.202222 * (-49.1160)(-7.5993) \end{aligned}$$

When iter $= 0$ the estimated value is returned as $y = \text{work}[3]$, otherwise updated is needed as follows:

$$\text{work}[j] = \text{work}[n11 + j], \quad \text{where } j = 1, \dots, nzz$$

So far, we have only considered one row of the data set. This process is carried out for the number of testing data set.

Function 2.2 comp

```
function [yy,itr]=comp(zz,itree,tree,iter)
    it = iter; %layer
    itr(1) = 1; %initialize
    i = 1;
q=0; r=0;

%Step 1: Generate vector 'itr' from 'itree'
while (r ==0 ) %not equal to        [I]
    l = 0; %layer
    nn = power(2,double(i-1));
    n1 = power(2,double(i));
    nz = power(2,double(i+1))-1;
    j = n1;

while (q == 0) %not equal to        [II]
    jj = floor(itr(nn+1));
```

```
    xx = floor(itree(iter,jj));
    itr(j) = floor(itree(iter,jj)/100-10);        %reconstruction
    iz = floor(itree(iter,jj)/100);
    itr(j+1) = floor(xx -100*iz - 10);             %reconstruction
    j = j + 2;
    if (j>nz) break;
    else
    l = l + 1;
    end
end      %while q==0                   [II]


    if (iter==1) break; end
    iter = iter - 1;
    i = i + 1;
    end      %while r==0                [I]
%=====


%Step 2: Extract coefficients in 'itree' using information in 'itr'
    iter = it;
    nz = (power(2,double(iter-1)));
    nzz = nz;
    n1 = (power(2,double(iter)));
    for j=1:nzz
        wk=0.0; % initialize
        jj1 = itr(nz);
        jj2 = itr(n1);
        jj3 = itr(n1+1);
        wk = wk+tree(1,jj1,1) + tree(1,jj1,2)*zz(jj2) +
tree(1,jj1,3)*zz(jj3)...
              + tree(1,jj1,4)*power(zz(jj2),2) +
tree(1,jj1,5)*power(zz(jj3),2)...
              + tree(1,jj1,6)*zz(jj2)*zz(jj3);
        work(j) = wk;
        nz = nz + 1;
        n1 = n1 + 2;
    end
    iter = iter -1;


    if (iter ==0)
    yy = work(1);
    iter = it;
    end


    i = 2;


    q=0;
```

```
while (q == 0) %not equal to
    nz = (power(2,double(iter-1)));
    n1 = (power(2,double(iter)));
    nzz = nz;
    n11= n1; %%%


    for j=1:nzz
        wk=0.0; % initialize
        jj = 2*j-1;
        jj1 = itr(nz);
%       jj2 = itr(n1); %GCO
%       jj3 = itr(n1+1); %GCO
        wk = wk+tree(i,jj1,1) + tree(i,jj1,2)*work(jj) +
tree(i,jj1,3)*work(jj+1)...
                + tree(i,jj1,4)*power(work(jj),2) +
tree(i,jj1,5)*power(work(jj+1),2)...
                + tree(i,jj1,6)*work(jj)*work(jj+1);
        work(n11+j) = wk;
      nz = nz + 1;
        n1 = n1 + 2;
        end %end for j=1:nzz


    iter = iter - 1;
    %work


    if (iter==0)


%               yy = work(3); %GCO -- this is the original syntax
            yy = max(work);
          iter = it;
        break;
    end
    for j=1:nzz
    work(j) = work(n11+j); %UP-DATING is taking place here!
    end
    i = i + 1;
end %while iter ~=0
```

2.2.3. Compute the coefficients in the Ivakhnenko polynomial using the same tree of polynomials generated

This subroutine uses the same tree of polynomials generated in **gmdh**() to compute the coefficients $a_0, a_i, a_{ij}, a_{ijk}, \ldots$ in the

Ivakhnenko polynomial (Eq. (2.1)) using only training data set. The equations used are as follows:

$$X = \begin{pmatrix} 1 & \sum x_{ki} & \sum x_{kj} & \sum x_{ki}x_{kj} & \sum x_{ki}^2 & \sum x_{kj}^2 \\ \sum x_{ki} & \sum x_{ki}^2 & \sum x_{ki}x_{kj} & \sum x_{ki}^2 x_{kj} & \sum x_{ki}^3 & \sum x_{ki}x_{kj}^2 \\ \sum x_{kj} & \sum x_{ki}x_{kj} & \sum x_{kj}^2 & \sum x_{ki}x_{kj}^2 & \sum x_{ki}^2 x_{kj} & \sum x_{kj}^3 \\ \sum x_{ki}x_{kj} & \sum x_{ki}^2 x_{kj} & \sum x_{ki}x_{kj}^2 & \sum x_{ki}^2 x_{kj}^2 & \sum x_{ki}^3 x_{kj} & \sum x_{ki}x_{kj}^3 \\ \sum x_{ki}^2 & \sum x_{ki}^3 & \sum x_{ki}^2 x_{kj} & \sum x_{ki}^3 x_{kj} & \sum x_{ki}^4 & \sum x_{ki}^2 x_{kj}^2 \\ \sum x_{kj}^2 & \sum x_{ki}x_{kj}^2 & \sum x_{kj}^3 & \sum x_{ki}x_{kj}^3 & \sum x_{ki}^2 x_{kj}^2 & \sum x_{kj}^4 \end{pmatrix}, \quad (2.19)$$

$$Y = \left[\sum y_k \quad \sum x_{ki}y_k \quad \sum x_{kj}y_k \quad \sum x_{ki}^2 y_k \right.$$
$$\left. \sum x_{kj}^2 y_k \quad \sum x_{kij}y_k \right]. \quad (2.20)$$

The regularized least square (RLS) fitting method for estimating the weights is given as

$$a = (X^T X + \alpha I)^{-1} X^T Y, \quad (2.21)$$

where **a** is the coefficients vector. There are numerous methods available such as Gauss method, etc and any of these could be used.

2.2.4.   Main program

The main program is listed in Function 2.3 main. The main functions called are:

function [itree,tree,iter] = gmdh(n,m,nt,pii,niter,x,y, fout1) //main function for computing the tree of quadratic polynomials
function [yy,itr]=comp(zz,itree,tree,iter) // for evaluating the Ivakhenko polynomials and coefficients

The auxiliary functions called are:

function conv(mm,iter,nt,x,y,fout1) //for checking convergence
function st = stat(nc,ywork,xwork) // for statistics
function [ir,d] = sorting(d,1,index) // for sorting statistics
function Measured_Predicted(Y,Ym,string)// for plotting
function Model_results(Y,Ym,string) //plots results for series y and y_model

Function 2.3 main

```
% Onwubolu, G. C.
% GROUP METHOD FOR DATA HANDLING (GMDH): Analysis Applying MATLAB %

% GROUP METHOD FOR DATA HANDLING (GMDH): Analysis Applying MATLAB Toolbox
Version 1.0
%
% MATLAB's power applied to GMDH
% Commenced: July 24, 2006
% Fully debugged: December 13, 2008


clear all;
close all;


'GMDH'                 % Display label.
% Group Method for Data Handling


global iter;

percent=75; %percentage of total for training, nt: 75% is good
niter=0;
nprnt=1;
pii=0.0;
```

```
%data: last column is Y (the response) remaining columns are covariates, X
file_name='input.txt';
aa = load (file_name);
[len wid]=size(aa);
n=len; % # of data points
m=wid-1; % # of columns for X
nt = floor((percent/100)*len);
% Pre-processor
x(:,1:wid-1)=aa(:,1:wid-1); %copy from 1st to last but one columns of
original data into X
y(:,1)=aa(:,wid); %copy from last column of original data into Y
%
%make a copy of array x(i,j) to ev(i,j), vector y(i) to ysave(i)
for i=1:n
    ysave(i)=y(i); %save y
    for j=1:m
        ev(i,j)=x(i,j); %save x
    end
end

%open files
fout1 =fopen('gmdh.txt','w+');
fout2 =fopen('observed.txt','w+');
fout3 =fopen('estimate.txt','w+');

%compute a tree of quadratic polynomials
[itree,tree,iter]=gmdh(n,m,nt,pii,niter,x,y,fout1); %itree,tree,iter

        fprintf (fout1,'\n\n # Observed Estimate    Diff    PercDiffError\n');
        fprintf (fout1,'\n============================== \n');

% for i=1:nt %==============////
  for i=nt+1:n %==============////
    for j=1:m
      zz(j) = ev(i,j); %read each row of X for processing
    end
    %call subroutine to evaluate the Ivakhnenko polynomial
[yy,itr]=comp(zz,itree,tree,iter);
    er = abs(ysave(i) - yy); %yy is from comp(zz) and is global

    if (ysave(i) ~= 0 && i >nt)
    perer = abs(100.0*er/ysave(i)); %save only testing data
    error(i,1)= power(er,2); error(i,2)= perer; %errors
    %save output in files
    out(i)=yy; % save in array
    diff(i)=er; %save in array
    percent_diff(i)=perer; %save in array

        fprintf (fout1,'\n %d %8.3f %8.3f %8.3f %8.3f', i, ysave(i), yy, er,
perer);
```

```
     fprintf (fout2,'\n %8.3f', ysave(i));
     fprintf (fout3,'\n %8.3f', yy);


   end %if
   end % for i%=============////
fprintf (fout1,'\n\n Testing MSE error =%8.3f \n', mean(error(:,1)));
fprintf (fout1,'\n Testing PDiff error =%8.3f \n', mean(error(:,2)));

% The Ivakhnenko polynomial is printed only if it is a simple quadratic
%if (iter==1)
     fprintf (fout1,'\n\n Ivakhnenko polynomial\n');
     fprintf (fout1,'\n ===================== \n');
     fprintf (fout1,' \n y = a + b*u + c*v + d*u*u + e*v*v + f*u*v \n');
     fprintf (fout1,'a = %f, b = %f, c = %f, d = %f, e = %f, f =
%f',tree(1,1,1),tree(1,1,2),tree(1,1,3),tree(1,1,4),tree(1,1,5),
tree(1,1,6));
     fprintf (fout1,'\n u = x[%d], v = x[%d]',itr(2),itr(3));
%end


%close files
fclose(fout1);
fclose(fout2);
fclose(fout3);


%print on screen
 disp (' # Observed Estimate          Diff           PercDiffError');
 disp (' ======================================');


for i=nt+1:n
 XX = sprintf (' %d %8.3f %8.3f %8.3f %8.3f', i, ysave(i), out(i), diff(i),
percent_diff(i));
 disp (XX)
end


YY1=sprintf('\n Testing MSE error =%8.3f \n', mean(error(:,1)));
YY2=sprintf('\n Testing PDiff error =%8.3f \n', mean(error(:,2)));
disp (YY1)
disp (YY2)
% The Ivakhnenko polynomial is printed only if it is a simple quadratic
   disp (' Ivakhnenko polynomial');
   disp (' =====================');
   disp (' y = a + b*u + c*v + d*u*u + e*v*v + f*u*v ');
   WW1 = sprintf (' a = %f, b = %f, c = %f, d = %f, e = %f, f =
%f',tree(1,1,1),tree(1,1,2),tree(1,1,3),tree(1,1,4),tree(1,1,5),
tree(1,1,6));
   WW2 = sprintf ('\n u = x[%d], v = x[%d]',itr(2),itr(3));

disp (WW1)
disp (WW2)
```

```
% plot graphs of observed and estimated
Plot_Observed_Estimated_Values;

%end of program
```

2.3. Case Studies

2.3.1. Case Study 1

This problem is taken from Farlow's book: "A SAS Program for Simplified GMDH Models": Michael H. Prager, pp. 291–315. There are 26 data points consisting of five input variables (not described) and one output variable as shown in Table 2.1.

Input:

Number of independent variables = 5
Number of data points = 26
Number of levels GMDH performs before stopping = 1
Fractional increase in the number of variables at each iteration = 0.2

Output:

Since there are five inputs, $\binom{m}{2} = m(m-1)/2 = 5(5-1)/2 = 10$ pairs of two variables taken at a time. Consequently, there are 10 objective functions (external criterion values) arranged in a non-decreasing order in the array d. It is important to understand how to interpret the outputs of the GMDH algorithm, listed as *GMDH output information*. In this example, we have used 70% of the total data set for training.

Starting from the first iteration (level), there are five input parameters, so we have p = 10 pairs of inputs obtained from the relation $p = m(m-1)/2$ where $m = 5$. We can list these pairs as follows: $(x_{i,1}, x_{i,2})$, $(x_{i,1}, x_{i,3})$, $(x_{i,1}, x_{i,4})$, $(x_{i,1}, x_{i,5})$, $(x_{i,2}, x_{i,3})$, $(x_{i,2}, x_{i,4})$, $(x_{i,2}, x_{i,5})$, $(x_{i,3}, x_{i,4})$, $(x_{i,3}, x_{i,5})$, and $(x_{i,4}, x_{i,5})$, where $i \in [n_t + 1, n]$ representing the checking data set. The minimum value of the checking error is given by, $EPI = 0.006$, while the next value is 0.007. These values correspond to neurons 2 and 8 respectively in the first layer of the GMDH network. This shows that neuron 2 is the best

Table 2.1.   Five-input, one-output problem (from Farlow's book).

#	x_1	x_2	x_3	x_4	x_5	y
1	1.4324	21.482	1.3957	1.4309	23.5353	22.185
2	0.3434	21.6878	−0.0306	−4.7577	22.1819	15.2626
3	0.2527	22.2133	1.8564	−4.0028	24.1853	15.1236
4	−1.0725	22.8959	−0.9865	−1.006	23.6404	16.1317
5	−0.6404	23.0648	−1.9811	−0.535	21.2181	15.0551
6	−1.0965	23.3373	0.8944	2.819	23.4471	18.493
7	1.0645	24.8361	−1.4909	3.495	22.1102	15.4711
8	0.6644	26.582	−1.0806	0.7533	25.8578	15.4483
9	−0.6407	26.9486	−0.6113	−7.0433	25.5455	15.0973
10	0.648	27.2197	0.4729	−0.511	28.3249	16.2165
11	−0.8836	27.7938	−1.0194	2.3419	25.581	15.656
12	0.7592	28.8897	1.83	−4.83	31.906	17.2672
13	1.2589	29.3235	0.6369	−4.5846	27.9323	19.076
14	−0.2705	30.1815	0.1823	−1.4904	29.8858	15.1402
15	−1.0699	30.4115	−1.3615	0.1228	29.6108	15.7351
16	−0.6103	30.9182	−0.279	−5.1598	31.744	15.6332
17	−0.054	31.2739	1.4213	−1.8428	33.0698	15.0727
18	−0.0472	31.7831	−0.3899	0.0973	30.9779	14.9354
19	0.2489	23.8578	−1.4783	0.0080	22.4089	15.0456
20	0.0113	24.4009	−0.8482	1.0198	23.7643	15.1338
21	−1.2599	25.3547	1.9878	1.4693	26.5690	21.4214
22	−0.9801	25.8602	1.4438	1.2403	25.5077	18.1862
23	0.8444	26.0204	1.0789	2.3604	27.3899	17.2739
24	0.9876	28.3329	1.3969	−2.4026	30.8196	18.4304
25	−1.1676	28.9977	0.5527	−4.3260	30.2351	18.6360
26	−0.6454	32.2099	−0.2656	−2.0461	31.0517	15.7772

because it has the least *EPI* value of 0.006 followed by neuron 8. This means that neuron 2 is connected to $(x_{i,1}, x_{i,2})$, while neuron 8 is connected to $(x_{i,3}, x_{i,4})$ respectively at the first layer. The six coefficients of neuron 2 are given in $tree[1][1][i]$ while those of neuron 8 are given in $tree[1][2][i]$ corresponding to the six coefficients used for the Ivakhnenko polynomial, where $i = 1, \ldots, 6$. We accept 50% of the best solutions corresponding to neurons 2, 8, 3, 9, and 4 to proceed to the next level or iteration.

At the second iteration (level) of the GMDH network, the minimum value of the checking error, *EPI* = 0.002. This value corresponds to neuron 1 or 8. This shows that neuron 1 or 8 is the best. The best neurons are in the order of 1, 8, 5, 10, and 3, with the overall best neuron being 1 or 8 since there is a tally. This overall best neuron must be connected to neurons 2 and 3 of the first (previous) level. The six coefficients are given in $tree[2][1][i]$ corresponding to the six coefficients used for the Ivakhnenko polynomial. Therefore, it is seen that using the information encoded in $d[k]$; $k = 1, \ldots, p = m(m-1)/2$, $tree[l][j][i]$; $l = 1, \ldots, level$; $j = 1, \ldots, m$; $i = 1, \ldots, 6$ it is possible to grow the GMDH network with all node connections from level (layer) to level and also obtain the model relating the optimal output neuron to intermediate neuron connections and input variables. The network information can be summarized as:

$$(x_{i,1}, x_{i,3}) \leftarrow 2 \; (u_{i,2}, u_{i,8}) \leftarrow 1$$
$$(x_{i,3}, x_{i,4}) \leftarrow 8 \; (u_{i,2}, u_{i,3}) \leftarrow 8$$
$$(x_{i,1}, x_{i,4}) \leftarrow 3 \; (u_{i,2}, u_{i,9}) \leftarrow 5$$
$$(x_{i,3}, x_{i,5}) \leftarrow 9 \; (u_{i,2}, u_{i,4}) \leftarrow 10$$
$$(x_{i,1}, x_{i,5}) \leftarrow 4 \; (u_{i,8}, u_{i,3}) \leftarrow 3$$

Therefore, the equations that define the models for checking data set are given as follows:

$$u = 14.8015 + 0.270268x_1 + 0.647376x_2 + 2.45283x_1^2 - 0.172079x_2^2$$
$$+ 0.258625x_1x_2,$$
$$v = 16.2919 + 1.16017x_3 + 0.345908x_4 + 0.245674x_3^2 + 0.037816x_4^2$$
$$+ 0.240052x_3x_4,$$
$$y = 59.2604 - 1.45536 - 4.55512u + 0.0707519u^2 + 0.144948v^2$$
$$- 0.0103056uv.$$

We can check that this model is correct (values agreeing with those in Table 2.2), using the script:

a1 = 59.2604; b1 = −1.45536; c1 = −4.55512; d1 = 0.0707519; e1 = 0.144948; f1 = −0.0103056;
a2 = 14.801535; b2 = 0.270268; c2 = 0.647376; d2 = 2.452825; e2 = −0.172079; f2 = 0.258625;
a3 = 16.2969; b3 = 1.16017; c3 = 0.345908; d3 = 0.245674; e3 = 0.0378316; f3 = 0.240052; c = 0;

Table 2.2.   Observed, estimated, and error values for the checking points.

#	Observed	Estimated	Difference	% Diff Error
19	15.046	14.832	0.213	1.417
20	15.134	14.571	0.563	3.717
21	21.421	20.404	1.017	4.748
22	18.186	17.868	0.318	1.751
23	17.274	17.524	0.251	1.450
24	18.430	17.871	0.559	3.033
25	18.636	17.154	1.482	7.952
26	15.777	15.399	0.378	2.396

```
for i=nt+1:n
   c=c+1;
   u=a2 + b2*x(i,1) + c2*x(i,3) + d2*x(i,1)*x(i,1) + e2*x(i,3)*x
(i,3) + f2*x(i,1)*x(i,3);
   v=a3 + b2*x(i,3) + c3*x(i,4) + d3*x(i,3)*x(i,3) + e3*x(i,4)*x
(i,4) + f3*x(i,3)*x(i,4);
   yc(c)=a1 + b1*u + c1*v + d1*u*u + e1*v*v + f1*u*v;
end
```

After the first iteration, the checking error decreases while the coefficient of determination increases; the final values are 0.002 and 0.975 respectively. The GMDH algorithm converged after 2 generations. Table 2.2 shows the observed, estimated, and error values. Figure 2.2 shows the absolute difference between the measured and estimated test data while Fig. 2.3 shows the percentage difference between the measured and estimated test data.

GMDH output information:

$d[2] = 0.006$
$d[8] = 0.007$
$d[3] = 0.008$
$d[9] = 0.008$
$d[4] = 0.008$
$d[5] = 0.009$

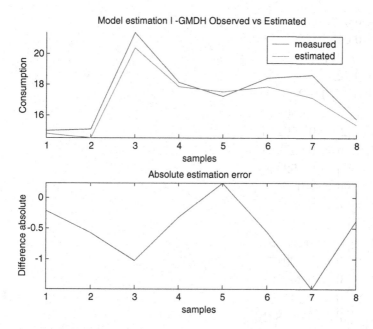

Fig. 2.2.   Absolute difference between the measured and estimated test data (Farlow's book).

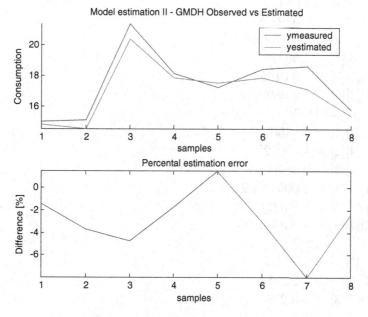

Fig. 2.3.   Percentage difference between the measured and estimated test data (Farlow's book).

d[1] = 0.011
d[7] = 0.015
d[10] = 0.017
d[6] = 0.021
itree[1][1] = 1112
tree[1][1][1] = 14.8015
tree[1][1][2] = 0.270268
tree[1][1][3] = 0.647376
tree[1][1][4] = 2.45283
tree[1][1][5] = −0.172079
tree[1][1][6] = 0.258625
itree[1][2] = 1113
tree[1][2][1] = 16.2969
tree[1][2][2] = 1.16017
tree[1][2][3] = 0.345908
tree[1][2][4] = 0.245674
tree[1][2][5] = 0.0378316
tree[1][2][6] = 0.240052
itree[1][3] = 1114
tree[1][3][1] = 14.5459
tree[1][3][2] = 0.529278
tree[1][3][3] = −0.118524
tree[1][3][4] = 2.60376
tree[1][3][5] = −0.015543
tree[1][3][6] = −0.0899773
itree[1][4] = 1115
tree[1][4][1] = 5.34507
tree[1][4][2] = 1.89072
tree[1][4][3] = 0.989005
tree[1][4][4] = 0.00540389
tree[1][4][5] = −0.0211966
tree[1][4][6] = −0.0384795
itree[1][5] = 1213
tree[1][5][1] = 17.3266
tree[1][5][2] = −2.23833
tree[1][5][3] = −0.279194

tree[1][5][4] = 2.6447
tree[1][5][5] = 0.0064092
tree[1][5][6] = 0.109679
Level number = 1
No. variables saved = 5
rmin [minimum checking set error] value = 0.006
sum = 0.912

d[1] = 0.002
d[8] = 0.002
d[5] = 0.003
d[10] = 0.003
d[3] = 0.003
d[7] = 0.004
d[4] = 0.005
d[2] = 0.006
d[6] = 0.011
d[9] = 0.013
itree[2][1] = 1112
tree[2][1][1] = 59.2604
tree[2][1][2] = −1.45536
tree[2][1][3] = −4.55512
tree[2][1][4] = 0.0707519
tree[2][1][5] = 0.144948
tree[2][1][6] = −0.0103056
itree[2][2] = 1113
tree[2][2][1] = 92.697
tree[2][2][2] = −3.94332
tree[2][2][3] = −6.75897
tree[2][2][4] = −0.12214
tree[2][2][5] = −0.038118
tree[2][2][6] = 0.52933
itree[2][3] = 1114
tree[2][3][1] = 38.5469
tree[2][3][2] = −1.48666
tree[2][3][3] = −2.42114

tree[2][3][4] = 0.0116821
tree[2][3][5] = 0.0476717
tree[2][3][6] = 0.0958784
itree[2][4] = 1115
tree[2][4][1] = 98.336
tree[2][4][2] = −7.42368
tree[2][4][3] = −3.96332
tree[2][4][4] = 0.0452571
tree[2][4][5] = −0.0631488
tree[2][4][6] = 0.407283
itree[2][5] = 1213
tree[2][5][1] = 68.3656
tree[2][5][2] = −3.79777
tree[2][5][3] = −3.67638
tree[2][5][4] = −0.103583
tree[2][5][5] = −0.121068
tree[2][5][6] = 0.486902
Level number = 2
No. variables saved = 5
rmin [minimum checking set error] value = 0.002
sum = 0.977
GMDH converged after 2 generations
Multiple correlation (summed over training set) = 0.977

2.3.2.   Case Study 2

This problem is taken from the author's work on tool wear. There are 50 data points consisting of six input variables and one output variable as shown in Table 2.3. The descriptions of the input variables are given as follows: x_1 = speed (m/min); x_2 = # of tool teeth (Z); x_3 = depth of cut, DOC (mm); x_4 = material hardness, BHN; x_5 = tool/work-piece interface temp (C); x_6 = chip thick (mm); y = tool wear (μm). In this example, we have used 75% of the total data set for training.

Table 2.3. Six-input, one-output tool wear problem (laboratory results).

#	x_1	x_2	x_3	x_4	x_5	x_6	y
1	10	2	1.5	131	34.48	0.324	3.2
2	10	2	2	131	40.12	0.38	5.4
3	10	2	2.5	131	37.08	0.57	9.2
4	10	2	3	131	37.04	0.586	17.6
5	10	2	3.5	131	39.24	0.796	18.6
6	10	2	1.5	100	40.08	0.001104	1.4
7	10	2	2	100	38.68	0.001198	2.6
8	10	4	2.5	100	39.88	0.000544	0.6
9	10	4	3	100	48.08	0.000762	2.2
10	10	4	3.5	100	49.4	0.001156	3.8
11	13	2	1.5	131	37.21	0.258	4.4
12	13	2	2	131	44.2	0.268	14.2
13	13	2	2.5	131	35.8	0.282	14.4
14	13	2	3	131	39.04	0.372	14.6
15	13	2	3.5	131	35.88	0.41	15
16	13	2	1.5	100	36.6	0.000926	2.8
17	13	2	2	100	35.64	0.00083	3.4
18	13	4	2.5	100	48.84	0.000328	3.8
19	13	4	3	100	43.92	0.000518	4.4
20	13	4	3.5	100	37.84	0.000758	5.2
21	19	2	1.5	131	35.02	0.214	4.6
22	19	2	2	131	37.84	0.25	11.4
23	19	2	2.5	131	40.96	0.256	14.8
24	19	2	3	131	42.88	0.33	18
25	19	2	3.5	131	35.52	0.304	18.8
26	19	2	1.5	100	34.4	0.00076	3.6
27	19	2	2	100	35.68	0.000634	4
28	19	4	2.5	100	62.96	0.000284	4.4
29	19	4	3	100	56.28	0.000428	5.6
30	19	4	3.5	100	36.12	0.000634	6.2
31	27	2	1.5	131	37.36	0.142	5
32	27	2	2	131	38.68	0.162	6.4
33	27	2	2.5	131	38.28	0.194	12.4
34	27	2	3	131	37.8	0.232	18.4
35	27	2	3.5	131	42.16	0.24	19.6
36	27	2	1.5	100	34.88	0.000638	4.2
37	27	2	2	100	35.36	0.000428	6
38	27	4	2.5	100	38	0.00017	5
39	27	4	3	100	73.32	0.000334	6.4
40	27	4	3.5	100	69.58	0.000518	7.4

(*Continued*)

Table 2.3.   (*Continued*)

#	x_1	x_2	x_3	x_4	x_5	x_6	y
41	36	2	1.5	131	39.8	0.022	12
42	36	2	2	131	38	0.076	17.2
43	36	2	2.5	131	37.6	0.116	19.2
44	36	2	3	131	42.32	0.146	20.8
45	36	2	3.5	131	37.92	0.172	25.2
46	36	2	1.5	100	32.16	0.00025	7.8
47	36	2	2	100	39.12	0.000238	12
48	36	4	2.5	100	38.08	0.00006	5.8
49	36	4	3	100	42.44	0.000148	8.4
50	36	4	3.5	100	43.56	0.005514	9.2

Output:

Since there are six inputs, $\binom{m}{2} = m(m-1)/2 = 6(6-1)/2 = 15$ pairs of two variables taken at a time. Consequently, there are 15 objective functions (external criterion values) arranged in a non-decreasing order in the vector d. In this example, we have used 75% of the total data set for training. It is important to understand how to interpret the outputs of the GMDH algorithm, listed as *GMDH output information*.

Starting from the first iteration (level), there are six input parameters, so we have $p = 15$ pairs of inputs obtained from the relation $p = m(m-1)/2$ where $m = 6$. We can list these pairs as follows: $(x_{i,1}, x_{i,2})$, $(x_{i,1}, x_{i,3})$, $(x_{i,1}, x_{i,4})$, $(x_{i,1}, x_{i,5})$, $(x_{i,1}, x_{i,6})$, $(x_{i,2}, x_{i,3})$, $(x_{i,2}, x_{i,4})$, $(x_{i,2}, x_{i,5})$, $(x_{i,2}, x_{i,6})$, $(x_{i,3}, x_{i,4})$, $(x_{i,3}, x_{i,5})$, $(x_{i,3}, x_{i,6})$, $(x_{i,4}, x_{i,5})$, $(x_{i,4}, x_{i,6})$, and $(x_{i,5}, x_{i,6})$ where $i \in [n_t + 1, n]$ representing the checking data set. The minimum value of the checking error is given by, $EPI = 0.157$, while the next value is 0.160. These values correspond to neurons 10 and 6 respectively in the first layer of the GMDH network. This shows that neuron 10 is the best because it has the least *EPI* value of 0.157 followed by neuron 6. This means that neuron 10 is connected to $(x_{i,3}, x_{i,4})$, while neuron 6 is connected to $(x_{i,2}, x_{i,3})$ respectively at the first layer. The six coefficients of neuron 10 are given in $tree[1][1][i]$ while those of neuron 6 are given in $tree[1][2][i]$ corresponding to the six coefficients used for the Ivakhnenko polynomial, where $i = 1, \ldots, 6$. We accept 50% of the best solutions corresponding to neurons 10, 6, 13, 7, 8, and 12 to proceed to the next level or iteration.

At the second iteration (level) of the GMDH network, the minimum value of the checking error, $EPI = 0.151$. This value corresponds to neuron 6. This shows that neuron 6 is the best. The best neurons are in the order of 6, 4, 1, 7, 2, and 3, with the overall best neuron being 6. This overall best neuron must be connected to neurons 10 and 6 of the first (previous) level. The six coefficients are given in $tree[2][1][i]$ corresponding to the six coefficients used for the Ivakhnenko polynomial. Therefore, it is seen that using the information encoded in $d[k]$; $k = 1, \ldots, p = m(m-1)/2$, $tree[l][j][i]$; $l = 1, \ldots, level$; $j = 1, \ldots, m$; $i = 1, \ldots, 6$, it is possible to grow the GMDH network with all node connections from level (layer) to level and also obtain the model relating the optimal output neuron to intermediate neuron connections and input variables. The network information can be summarized as:

$$(x_{i,3}, x_{i,4}) \leftarrow 10 \ (u_{i,10}, u_{i,6}) \leftarrow 6$$
$$(x_{i,2}, x_{i,3}) \leftarrow 6 \ (u_{i,10}, u_{i,13}) \leftarrow 4$$
$$(x_{i,4}, x_{i,5}) \leftarrow 13 \ (u_{i,10}, u_{i,7}) \leftarrow 1$$
$$(x_{i,2}, x_{i,4}) \leftarrow 7 \ (u_{i,10}, u_{i,8}) \leftarrow 7$$
$$(x_{i,2}, x_{i,5}) \leftarrow 8 \ (u_{i,10}, u_{i,12}) \leftarrow 2$$
$$(x_{i,3}, x_{i,6}) \leftarrow 12 \ (u_{i,6}, u_{i,12}) \leftarrow 3$$

Therefore, the equations that define the models for checking data set are given as follows:

$$u = -0.551931 - 14.9265x_3 + 0.13005x_4 - 904898x_3^2$$
$$- 0.00157262x_4^2 + 0.202222x_3x_4,$$
$$v = -0.842936 - 10.5842x_2 + 17.7297x_3 + 1.97805x_2^2 - 1.03626x_3^2$$
$$- 2.34478x_2x_3,$$
$$y = 1.09213 + 0.315835u + 0.106076u + 0.00475923u^2$$
$$+ 0.00281245v^2 + 0.035183uv.$$

We can check that this model is correct (values agreeing with those in Table 2.2), using the script:

a1 = −0.551931; b1 = −14.9265; c1 = 0.13005; d1 = −0.904898; e1 = −0.00157262; f1 = 0.202222;
a2 = −0.842936; b2 = −10.5842; c2 = 17.7297; d2 = 1.97805; e2 = −1.0362; f2 = −2.34478;
a3 = 1.09213; b3 = 0.315835; c3 = 0.106076; d3 = 0.00475923; e3 = 0.00281245; f3 = 0.035183;
c=0;
for i = nt+1:n
    c=c+1;
    u=a1 + b1*x(i,3) + c1*x(i,4) + d1*x(i,3)*x(i,3) + e1*x(i,4)*x
(i,4) + f1*x(i,3)*x(i,4);
    v=a2 + b2*x(i,2) + c2*x(i,3) + d2*x(i,2)*x(i,2) + e2*x(i,3)*x
(i,3) + f2*x(i,2)*x(i,3);
    yc(c)=a3 + b3*u + c3*v + d3*u*u + e3*v*v + f3*u*v;
end

After the first iteration, the checking error decreases while the coefficient of determination increases; the final values are 0.151 and 0.903 respectively. The GMDH algorithm converged after two generations. Table 2.2 shows the observed, estimated, and error values. Figure 2.2 shows the absolute difference between the measured and estimated test data while Fig. 2.3 shows the percentage difference between the measured and estimated test data (see also Figs. 2.4 and 2.5, Table 2.4).

d[10] = 0.157
d[6] = 0.160
d[13] = 0.187
d[7] = 0.196
d[8] = 0.206
d[12] = 0.265
d[2] = 0.330
d[15] = 0.351
d[9] = 0.377
d[14] = 0.392
d[11] = 0.393
d[3] = 0.443

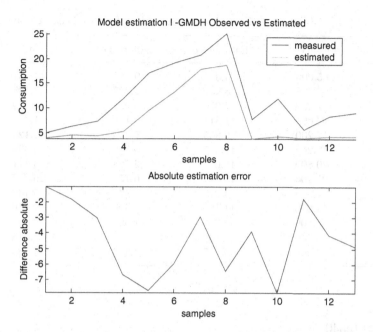

Fig. 2.4. Absolute difference between the measured and estimated test data (author's work).

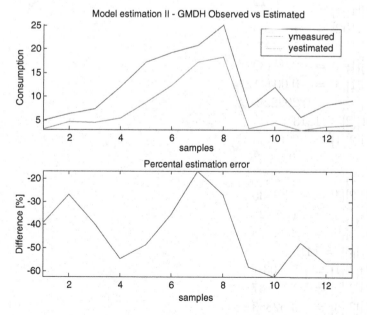

Fig. 2.5. Percentage difference between the measured and estimated test data (author's work).

Table 2.4.   Observed, estimated, and error values for the checking points.

#	Observed	Estimate d	Difference	% Diff Error
38	5.000	4.313	0.687	13.737
39	6.400	8.457	2.057	32.143
40	7.400	7.076	0.324	4.379
41	12.000	11.814	0.186	1.546
42	17.200	9.955	7.245	42.121
43	19.200	12.415	6.785	35.336
44	20.800	18.072	2.728	13.117
45	25.200	18.424	6.776	26.887
46	7.800	4.279	3.521	45.146
47	12.000	11.106	0.894	7.450
48	5.800	4.300	1.500	25.862
49	8.400	4.434	3.966	47.218
50	9.200	4.187	5.013	54.485

$d[1] = 0.448$

$d[4] = 0.540$

$d[5] = 1.063$

$itree[1][1] = 1314$

$tree[1][1][1] = -37.7575$

$tree[1][1][2] = -14.9265$

$tree[1][1][3] = 0.786117$

$tree[1][1][4] = -0.904898$

$tree[1][1][5] = -0.00441274$

$tree[1][1][6] = 0.202222$

$itree[1][2] = 1213$

$tree[1][2][1] = -216.135$

$tree[1][2][2] = 150.885$

$tree[1][2][3] = 17.7297$

$tree[1][2][4] = -24.9335$

$tree[1][2][5] = -1.0362$

$tree[1][2][6] = -2.34478$

$itree[1][3] = 1415$

$tree[1][3][1] = 1042.03$

$tree[1][3][2] = -17.4237$

$tree[1][3][3] = -3.52863$

tree[1][3][4] = 0.0718921
tree[1][3][5] = 0.00730125
tree[1][3][6] = 0.0285809
itree[1][4] = 1214
tree[1][4][1] = −5.59357
tree[1][4][2] = −3.05544
tree[1][4][3] = 0.00798075
tree[1][4][4] = 0.462909
tree[1][4][5] = 0.00114766
tree[1][4][6] = 0.00539094
itree[1][5] = 1215
tree[1][5][1] = −76.155
tree[1][5][2] = 34.3648
tree[1][5][3] = 1.59529
tree[1][5][4] = −2.45112
tree[1][5][5] = 0.00797934
tree[1][5][6] = −0.591555
itree[1][6] = 1316
tree[1][6][1] = −5.76757
tree[1][6][2] = 7.56775
tree[1][6][3] = −4.87076
tree[1][6][4] = −1.35347
tree[1][6][5] = −67.1268
tree[1][6][6] = 21.3114

Level number = 1

No. variables saved = 6

rmin [minimum checking set error] value = 0.157

sum = 0.892

d[6] = 0.151
d[4] = 0.156
d[1] = 0.156
d[7] = 0.156
d[2] = 0.158
d[3] = 0.159

d[8] = 0.159
d[10] = 0.184
d[13] = 0.188
d[11] = 0.191
d[9] = 0.205
d[15] = 0.248
d[12] = 0.261
d[14] = 0.264
d[5] = 0.557
itree[2][1] = 1213
tree[2][1][1] = 1.09213
tree[2][1][2] = 0.315835
tree[2][1][3] = 0.106076
tree[2][1][4] = 0.00475923
tree[2][1][5] = 0.00281245
tree[2][1][6] = 0.035183
itree[2][2] = 1115
tree[2][2][1] = 1.62794
tree[2][2][2] = 0.85725
tree[2][2][3] = −0.428741
tree[2][2][4] = −0.00122192
tree[2][2][5] = 0.0273732
tree[2][2][6] = 0.0131112
itree[2][3] = 1112
tree[2][3][1] = −0.314391
tree[2][3][2] = −0.0329745
tree[2][3][3] = 1.17614
tree[2][3][4] = 0.00220945
tree[2][3][5] = −0.137765
tree[2][3][6] = 0.127179
itree[2][4] = 1214
tree[2][4][1] = −5.94933
tree[2][4][2] = 0.17928
tree[2][4][3] = 2.739
tree[2][4][4] = −0.0183785
tree[2][4][5] = −0.18153

tree[2][4][6] = 0.0916022
itree[2][5] = 1113
tree[2][5][1] = 2.23792
tree[2][5][2] = 0.844499
tree[2][5][3] = −0.638497
tree[2][5][4] = 0.00155366
tree[2][5][5] = 0.0411527
tree[2][5][6] = 0.00591047
itree[2][6] = 1114
tree[2][6][1] = 4.94246
tree[2][6][2] = 0.615199
tree[2][6][3] = −1.34742
tree[2][6][4] = −0.0220728
tree[2][6][5] = 0.0595322
tree[2][6][6] = 0.0743392

Level number = 2

No. variables saved = 6

rmin [minimum checking set error] value = 0.151

sum = 0.903

d[1] = 0.154
d[8] = 0.154
d[5] = 0.154
d[2] = 0.155
d[4] = 0.155
d[3] = 0.155
d[11] = 0.156
d[10] = 0.156
d[14] = 0.156
d[12] = 0.156
d[13] = 0.159
d[15] = 0.162
d[6] = 0.163
d[7] = 0.165
d[9] = 0.166

itree[3][1] = 1112
tree[3][1][1] = 0.44997
tree[3][1][2] = 1.15671
tree[3][1][3] = −0.251346
tree[3][1][4] = −0.247173
tree[3][1][5] = −0.11188
tree[3][1][6] = 0.363565
itree[3][2] = 1215
tree[3][2][1] = −0.696556
tree[3][2][2] = −7.24703
tree[3][2][3] = 8.3373
tree[3][2][4] = 18.613
tree[3][2][5] = 17.7302
tree[3][2][6] = −36.3466
itree[3][3] = 1116
tree[3][3][1] = −0.34888
tree[3][3][2] = 0.605213
tree[3][3][3] = 0.458668
tree[3][3][4] = 0.140037
tree[3][3][5] = 0.144779
tree[3][3][6] = −0.288377
itree[3][4] = 1113
tree[3][4][1] = −0.451223
tree[3][4][2] = 0.448326
tree[3][4][3] = 0.619906
tree[3][4][4] = 0.268383
tree[3][4][5] = 0.269631
tree[3][4][6] = −0.54262
itree[3][5] = 1115
tree[3][5][1] = 0.464853
tree[3][5][2] = 1.03245
tree[3][5][3] = −0.116239
tree[3][5][4] = −0.300181
tree[3][5][5] = −0.18936
tree[3][5][6] = 0.493379
itree[3][6] = 1114

tree[3][6][1] = −0.237742
tree[3][6][2] = 0.463103
tree[3][6][3] = 0.566683
tree[3][6][4] = 0.262184
tree[3][6][5] = 0.265796
tree[3][6][6] = −0.530991

Testing MSE error = 4.260

Testing PDiff error = 6.989

Ivakhnenko polynomial ===================
y = a + b*u + c*v + d*u*u + e*v*v + f*u*v
a = −37.757461, b = −14.926539, c = 0.786117, d = −0.904898,
e = −0.004413, f = 0.202222
u = x[1], v = x[2]

2.4. Summary

This main focus of this chapter is to describe in a very clear manner the functions of the basic GMDH multilayered iteration (MIA) network so that end-users could easily understand how it works. The computer code is then presented and described as they appear in the error-free code in Chapter 2 folder of the zip file hosted on www.worldscientific.com. Two examples are solved using the basic GMDH-MIA network: the first one which is easier to model is taken from Farlow's book [3], while the second one which is more difficult to model is taken from the author's laboratory experimental work on tool wear estimation. The results show that the basic GMDH-MIA network is useful for modeling; however, better results could be obtained by including some improvement strategies. Users can modify the code to meet their specific requirements and hence GMDH can become more useful to a wider range of the community involved in inductive modeling.

However, it should be noted that basic GMDH multilayered iteration (MIA) network has high level of error, requiring major enhancement though hybridization of GHDH with other optimization techniques such as genetic algorithm, differential evolution, to mention a few. These are applied in this book.

REFERENCES

[1] Ivakhnenko, A. G. (1971) Polynomial theory of complex systems, *IEEE Trans. Syst. Man Cybernetics*, **SMC-1**, 364–378.

[2] Madala, H. R. & Ivakhnenko, A. G. (1994) *Inductive Learning Algorithms for Complex Systems Modelling*, CRC Press Inc., Boca Raton, Ann Arbor, London, Tokyo.

[3] Farlow S. J. (ed.) (1984) *Self-Organizing Methods in Modeling GMDH-Type Algorithms*, Marcel Decker, New York.

[4] Mueller J.-A., Lemke F. & Ivakhnenko A. G. (1997) GMDH algorithm for complex systems modeling, *Math. Model. Syst.* **4**, 275–316.

[5] Mueller J.-A. & Lemke F. (1999) Self-Organizing Data Mining, www.knowledgeminer.net.

[6] Onwubolu, G. C. (ed.) (2015) *GMDH-Methodology and Implementation in C (With CD-ROM)*, Imperial College Press.

Chapter 3

GMDH MULTILAYERED ALGORITHM IN MATLAB

Mohammed Abdalla Ayoub Mohammed

INTRODUCTION

Two phase flow phenomenon; namely liquid and gas, or what is synonymously called Multiphase flow (MPF), occurs in almost all upstream oil production, as well as in many surface downstream facilities. It can be defined terminologically as a concurrent flow of a *stream* containing a liquid hydrocarbon phase (crude oil or condensate), a gaseous phase (natural gas, and nonhydrocarbon gases), a produced water phase, and solids phase (wax, asphaltene sand, or even hydrates). Usually the amount of solid phase can be neglected because of its low contribution in the stream line. This process has raised considerable attention from nuclear and chemical engineering disciplines as well as petroleum engineering. The phenomenon is governed mainly by bubble point pressure; whenever the pressure drops below bubble point at any point inside the production conduit, gas will evolve from liquid, and from that point to the surface, multiphase gas–liquid flow will occur. Additional governing factor is the gas–liquid components and their changing physical characteristics along the pipe length and configuration with the change of temperature. Furthermore, certain flow patterns will develop while the pressure decreases gradually below the bubble point. The flow patterns depend mainly on the relative velocities of gas and liquid, and gas/liquid ratio. Needless to mention that sharp distinction between these regimes is quite intricate [1]. However, multiphase flow mixture can be transported horizontally, vertically, or at any angle of inclination. Furthermore, defining the pressure profile as a general case for all these configurations has quite limitations in relation with changing liquid hold-up and flow patterns, slippage criterion, and friction factor determination. In addition to that, velocity profile of each phase is hard to be determined inside the pipe.

The pressure drop (ΔP) mainly occurs between wellhead and separator facility. It needs to be estimated with a high degree of precision in order to execute certain design considerations. Such considerations include tubing size and operating wellhead pressure in a flowing well; direct input for surface flow line and equipment design calculations [2]. There is a pressing need for estimating the pressure drop in pipeline systems using a simple procedure that would eliminate the tedious and yet the inaccurate and cumbersome methods. Numerous attempts have been tried since the early fifties to come up with precise procedures to estimate pressure drop in multiphase flow pipes using conventional ways. The latter, were managed through the application of empirical correlations and mechanistic models [3]. Previous attempts fail to provide satisfactory accuracy for estimation of pressure drop in multiphase flow pipe systems. Most of these correlations were derived for two phase flow and none of them had accounted for the water phase, which may add to the difficulty and accuracy of modeling. These correlations and mechanistic models had been used by the industry despite of their low accuracies because there is no alternative. The conventional approach proved to be unsuitable for dealing with highly complex problem.

There are two reasons to justify conducting this study; firstly, empirical correlations used in the derivation of some of mechanistic models were acquired by small-scale facilities which will not be reliable for industrial applications [1]. Secondly, most of these mechanistic models were developed under limited laboratory conditions such as small test section, small pipe diameters, and low outlet pressure (not exceeding 120 psi) [1]. Thus, there is a pressing need for accurate modeling of pressure drop in pipeline systems under multiphase flow conditions using real field data. This should be done by using the most relevant data and the right technique. This can be achieved through the application of the latest statistical and computing technique which will be able to discover the highly nonlinear relationship between relevant input parameters and the output.

Approach: The approach that will be followed to model the pressure drop for pipeline system with a wide range of inclination angles is through the Abductory Induction Mechanism (AIM). In order to overcome limitations encountered in previous empirical and mechanistic models, a new approach has been developed by a Ukraine scientist named Alexy G. Ivakhnenko, which has gained wide acceptance in the past few years called Group Method of Data Handling (GMDH) or Abductory Induction Mechanism (AIM) will be utilized [12].

Aims of the Research: The overall objective of this study is to minimize the uncertainty in the multiphase pipeline design by developing a representative model for pressure drop determination in downstream facilities (gathering lines) with the use of the most relevant input variables and with a wide range of inclination angles.

To help achieve the overall objectives; the Abductory Induction Mechanism, (AIM) techniques will be utilized. Data from selected different fields will be used in this study. Specific objectives are:

1. To construct a model for predicting pressure drop in pipeline systems under multiphase flow conditions for a wide range of angles of inclination using AIM techniques.
2. To test the constructed models against real field data collected from Middle Eastern fields.
3. To assess the model's validity by conducting thorough trend analysis and comprehensive comparative study with the models adopted by the oil and gas industry.

Benefits of the Research: The benefits of the current research to the oil and gas industry can be summarized as follows:

1. Modeling of pressure drop in pipeline system can aid in offering sound design considerations for the pipeline engineer and designer

in terms of choosing the best pumping components of the system that are consistent with the physical properties.

2. Determining the most relevant and influential input parameters involved in estimating pressure drop can improve the modeling procedure. This can be done through the automated framework to exploit information inherent in modeled data sets in order to estimate the pressure drop by GMDH approach. This helps reduce the curse of dimensionality, which is greatly affecting modelling running time, overfitting, suspected collinearity and numerical instability [16].

3. Investigating the potential of using AIM technique in this new area, while no past research had been conducted to model such a feature (generic model).

4. Exploring the suitability of the best current empirical correlations and mechanistic models in estimating pressure drop in pipeline systems with a wide range of angle of inclinations and under field conditions.

5. GMDH model will serve as an easy and applicable mathematical correlation with the most relevant input parameters to the pressure drop target.

1.   LITERATURE REVIEW

This part of the research deals with the revision of the most commonly used correlations and mechanistic models and their drawbacks in estimating pipeline pressure drop in multiphase flow. It is worthy to mention that no single study in the literature could be found presenting pressure drop estimation in pipelines under multiphase conditions using Abductive networks and taking into consideration wide range of angles of inclination. In this chapter, only publications from literature that have pronounced major contribution to this study will be reviewed. Special emphasis will be given to Beggs and Brill correlation, because it has been designed originally to be applied for all angles of pipe inclination [3]. Additional prominence will be devoted to some mechanistic models, which show reliable performance in estimating pressure drop by industry.

1.1. Introduction

Multiphase flow panacea is quite complex since the problem has no analytical solution. Numerous factors are contributing to the nature of this problem such as slippage of the gas past the oil, change of the flow patterns with decreasing pressure to the surface, and mass transfer change between coexisting phases. Two schemes had been proposed in literature to solve this problem, namely empirical correlations and mechanistic models.

The first approach had been conceived in 1940s [9]. It was based on experimental observations and limited laboratory data. The main target of this approach had to meet certain individual design considerations. The second (semi-empirical) approach called mechanistic modeling had appeared in the early 1980s [6] which had been based on combining the resulting steady state equations and experimental data of multiphase fluids. This approach received wide acceptance from the oil industry since it was adopting the physical phenomenon and conservation of mass and energy principles.

There are many correlations and mechanistic models used for estimating pressure drop in pipelines. However, only a few of them are designed to estimate the pressure drop at all angles of inclination. Researchers had noticed that most of these correlations were developed under laboratory conditions and are, consequently, inaccurate when scaled-up to oil field conditions [15].

Empirical correlations fail to address the true and complex behavior of multiphase flow since adding more data to the latest empirical models resulted in no improvement in accuracy of pressure drop estimation and design of multiphase systems. Application of empirical correlations to a broad range of data usually results in errors in the range of ± 20% in pressure drop prediction [4].

The mechanistic method is a semi-empirical approach that deals with addressing physical phenomena of multiphase flow. The mechanisms of multiphase flow are established using mathematical modeling approach. Each flow pattern and its transition phase are comprehensively studied using fluid dynamics. Such flow patterns are presented in horizontal, deviated, and vertical flow [4]. The technique of mechanistic modeling has coupled the laboratory, field measurements and the most important factors affecting the multiphase mechanism. The prediction capability of these models is greatly enhanced when compared to the empirical correlations [13].

2. THEORY OF ABDUCTIVE NETWORKS

2.1. Overview

This part deals with addressing the concept of AIM. It consists of fundamentals and procedure of GMDH-Based Abductive Networks, and types of Abductive networks. Comprehensive mathematical representation however will be presented along with most commonly used algorithm types.

2.2. History of GMDH

The GMDH-based abductive networks algorithm was built up by Professor Alexey G. Ivakhnenko in the year 1968 at the Institute of Cybernetics in Kyiv (Ukraine). The major purpose of its introduction was the recognition of relationships in large complex nonlinear multidimensional systems, their approximation, and prediction. To reach its current status, the GMDH-based abductive network algorithm has passed several rejuvenations and modifications by several researchers. However, Japanese and Polish scientists had contributed significantly to the update of the algorithm [14]. They concluded that "GMDH is the best method for solving the AI problems-identification, short-term and long-term forecast of random processes and pattern recognition in complex systems". Mathematical GMDH theory showed that regression analysis can be described as the particular case of GMDH [7]. Most of the updated GMDH theory has been reported in Ukrainian journal "Automatica"). It is clearly shown that the journal subdivided the progress in GMDH theory into five sub eras. Major contributions will be reported as follows:

Period 1968–1971: This period is distinguished by application of one regularity criterion for solving of the problems of clustering, pattern detection and short-term forecasting. As reference functions polynomials, logical nets and Bayes probability formulas were used. However, noise-immunity was not investigated in this period.

Period 1972–1975: This period is featured by solving the problem of modeling of noised data and with incomplete information basis. Multi-criteria selection and utilization of additional priory information for noise-immunity increasing were proposed.

Period 1976–1979: This period is marked by the investigation of the convergence of multilayered GMDH algorithms. It was shown that some multilayered algorithms have "multilayerness error". The solution of objective systems analysis problems by multilayered GMDH algorithms was proposed.

Period 1980–1988: Many important theoretical results were received. It became evident that full physical models are not suitable to be used for long-term forecasting. It was confirmed, that nonphysical models of GMDH are more accurate for approximation and forecast than physical models of regression analysis.

Period 1989–to present time: This period is characterized by the development of new algorithms for nonparametric modeling of fuzzy objects and Simplified Learning Programming algorithm for expert systems. The current progress is devoted to development of twice-multilayered neuronets and parallel combinatorial algorithms for multiprocessor computers.

2.3. Fundamentals and Procedure of GMDH-Based Abductive Networks

The proposed algorithm is based on a multilayer structure using the general form, which is referred to as the Kolmogorov–Gabor polynomial (Volterra functional series)

$$y = a_0 + \sum_{i=1}^{m} a_i x_i + \sum_{i=1}^{m} \sum_{j=1}^{m} a_{ij} x_i x_j$$
$$+ \sum_{i=1}^{m} \sum_{j=1}^{m} \sum_{k=1}^{m} a_{ij} x_i x_j x_k \ldots, \tag{2.1}$$

where the external input vector is represented by $X = (x_1, x_2, \ldots)$, y is the corresponding output value, and a is the vector of weights and coefficients. The polynomial equation represents a full mathematical description. The whole system of equations can be represented using a matrix form as shown below in (2.2).

$$X = \begin{bmatrix} x_{11} & x_{12} & \cdots & \cdots & x_{1M} \\ x_{21} & x_{22} & \cdots & \cdots & x_{2M} \\ \cdots & \cdots & \cdots & x_{ij} & x_{iM} \\ \vdots & \vdots & \vdots & \vdots & \vdots \\ x_{N1} & x_{N2} & \cdots & \cdots & x_{NM} \end{bmatrix}, \quad y = \begin{bmatrix} y_1 \\ y_2 \\ \vdots \\ y_{N1} \end{bmatrix}. \quad (2.2)$$

Equation (2.1) can be replaced by a system of partial polynomial for the sake of simplicity as shown by (2.3)

$$y = a_0 + a_1 x_i + a_2 x_j + a_3 x_i x_j + a_4 x_i^2 + a_5 x_j^2, \quad (2.3)$$

where $i, j = 1, 2, \ldots, M; i \neq j$.

The inductive algorithm follows several systematic steps to finally model the inherent relationship between input parameters and output target [10]. Data sample of N observations and M independent variables (as presented by (2.2)) corresponding to the system under study is required; the data will be split into training set A and checking set $B(N = N_A + N_B)$.

Firstly, all the independent variables (matrix of X represented by (2.2)) are taken as pair of two at a time for possible combinations to generate a new regression polynomial similar to the one presented by (2.3) where p and q are the columns of the X matrix.

$$y_i = a_{pq} + b_{pq} x_{ip} + c_{pq} x_{iq} + d_{pq} x_{iq}^2 + e_{pq} x_{iq}^2 + f_{pq} x_{ip} x_{iq},$$

$$\begin{cases} p = 1, 2, \ldots, M, & p \neq q, \\ q = 1, 2, \ldots, M, & p \prec q, \\ i = 1, 2, \ldots, N. \end{cases} \quad (2.4)$$

A set of coefficients of the regression will be computed for all partial functions by a parameter estimation technique using the training data set A and (2.4).

The new regression coefficients will be stored into a new matrix C:

$$C_i = a_{pq} + b_{pq} + c_{pq} + d_{pq} + e_{pq} + f_{pq}, \quad \begin{cases} p = 1, 2, \ldots, M, & p \neq q, \\ q = 1, 2, \ldots, M, & p \succ q, \\ i = 1, 2, \ldots, N. \end{cases}$$

(2.5)

According to the mathematical law, the number of combinations of input pairs is determined by

$$\text{Number of combinations} = \frac{M(M-1)}{2}.$$

(2.6)

The polynomial at every N data points will be evaluated to calculate a new estimate called z_{pq} as follows:

$$z_{i,pq} = a_{pq} + b_{pq}x_{ip} + c_{pq}x_{iq} + d_{pq}x_{ip}^2 + e_{pq}x_{iq}^2 + f_{pq}x_{ip}x_{iq}. \quad (2.7)$$

The process will be repeated in an iterative manner until all pairs are evaluated to generate a new regression pairs that will be stored in a new matrix called Z matrix. This new generation of regression pairs can be interpreted as new improved variables that have a better predictability than the original set of data X (presented by (2.9)):

$$Z = \{z_{ij}\}, \quad \begin{cases} i = 1, 2, \ldots, N, \\ j = 1, 2, \ldots, \dfrac{M(M-1)}{2}, \end{cases}$$

(2.8)

$$Z = \begin{bmatrix} z_{11} & z_{12} & \cdots & \cdots & z_{1,\frac{M(M-1)}{2}} \\ z_{21} & z_{22} & \cdots & \cdots & \cdots \\ \cdots & \cdots & \cdots & z_{ij} & \cdots & \cdots \\ \vdots & \vdots & \vdots & \vdots & \vdots & \vdots \\ z_{N1} & z_{N2} & \cdots & \cdots & z_{N,\frac{M(M-1)}{2}} \end{bmatrix}.$$

(2.9)

Quality measures of these functions will be computed according to the objective rule chosen using the testing data set B. This can be done through comparing each column of the new generated matrix Z with the dependent variable y. The external criterion may somewhere be called regularity criterion (root mean squared values) and defined as follows:

$$r_j^2 = \sum_{i=1}^{nt} \frac{(y_i - z_{ij})^2}{(y_i^2)}, \quad j = 1, 2, \ldots, \frac{M(M-1)}{2}. \quad (2.10)$$

The whole procedure is repeated until the regularity criterion is no longer smaller than that of the previous layer. The model of the data can be computed by tracing back the path of the polynomials that corresponds to the lowest mean squared error in each layer.

The best measured function will be chosen as an optimal model. If the final result is not satisfied, then F the number of partial functions will be chosen which are better than all (this is called "freedom-of-choice") and do further analysis. The schematic diagram of self-organizing GMDH algorithm is depicted in Fig. 2.1.

2.4. Types of Abductive Networks

A variety of algorithms differ in how they go through partial functions. They are grouped into two types: single-layer and multilayer

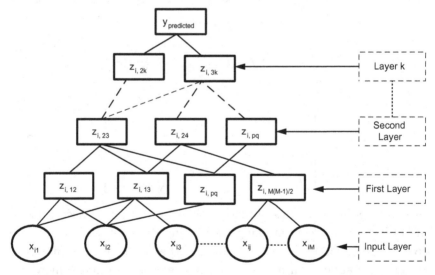

Fig. 2.1. Schematic diagram of self-organizing algorithm with M inputs and K layers.

algorithms. Combinatorial is the main single-layer algorithm. Multilayer algorithm is the layered feed-forward algorithm. Harmonic algorithm uses harmonics with nonmultiple frequencies and at each level the output errors are fed forward to the next level. Other algorithms like multilevel algorithm are comprised of objective system analysis and two-level, multiplicative-additive, and multilayer algorithms with error propagations [10].

A short description of the multilayered algorithm will be provided in this section. It is synonymously known as polynomial neural network.

2.5. Polynomial Neural Network

2.5.1. Layer unit

As presented in the section of fundamentals and procedure of AIM, the system consists of a sequence of layers and each layer has a group of units connected to the adjacent layer. Each unit has a weight value that is estimated through the application of regularity criterion, or simply minimizing the error by generally applying an external criterion. This measurement will serve two missions. First, it makes the unit "on" or "off" in comparison with the checking data N_B which is another part of the total data set N. Secondly, it is reflected to attain the optimum output response. The "on" unit, which is judged to connect to the unit in the next layer, will become a new input for it. The process continues layer after layer in an iterative manner.

2.5.2. Multilayer algorithm

Multilayer network is a parallel bounded structure that is built up based on the type of connection approach given in the basic iterative algorithm with linearized input variables and information in the network flows forward only. Each layer has a number of simulated units depending upon the number of input variables. Two input variables are passed on through each unit. If there are M input variables, the first layer generates $M_1(= c_M^2)$ functions. Now $F_1(\leq M_1)$ units as per the threshold values are made "on" to the next layer. Outputs of these functions become inputs to the second layer and the same procedure is repeated in the second layer. It is further repeated in successive layers until a global minimum on the error criterion is achieved [10].

2.5.3.   Mathematical description of the system

The system can be described as a system of nonlinear function in its arguments, which may include higher order terms and delayed inputs

$$y = f(x_1, x_2, \ldots, x_1^2, x_2^2, \ldots, x_1 x_2, x_1 x_3, \ldots, x_{1(-1)}, \ldots, x_{2(-1)}, \ldots),$$
(2.11)

where $f()$ is a function of higher degree and y is its estimated output. However, all arguments of x can be calculated as follows:

$$y = f(u_1, u_2, \ldots, u_M) = a_0 + a_1 u_1 + a_2 u_2 + \cdots + a_M u_M, \quad (2.12)$$

where u_i, $i = 1, 2, \ldots, M$, are the reconstructed terms of x, a_k, $k = 0, 1, \ldots, M$, are the coefficients and M is total number of arguments. These M input variables become inputs to the first layer (as illustrated previously). The partial functions generated at this layer can be rewritten as follows:

$$\begin{bmatrix} y_1 = v_{01}^{(1)} + v_{11}^{(1)} u_1 + v_{21}^{(1)} u_2 \\ y_2 = v_{01}^{(2)} + v_{11}^{(2)} u_1 + v_{21}^{(2)} u_3 \\ y_3 = v_{01}^{(3)} + v_{11}^{(3)} u_1 + v_{21}^{(3)} u_4 \\ \vdots \\ y_{m1} = v_{01}^{(M1)} + v_{11}^{(M1)} u_{(M-1)} + v_{21}^{(M1)} u_M \end{bmatrix}, \quad (2.13)$$

where $M_1 (= c_M^2)$ is the number of partial functions generated at the first layer, y_j and $v_{i1}^{(j)}, j = 1, 2, \ldots, M_1$, $i = 0, 1, 2$, are the estimated outputs and corresponding coefficients of the functions. Let us assume that F_1 functions are selected for the second layer and that there are $M_2(= c_{F_1}^2)$ partial functions generated at the second layer. The generated partial function can be formalized as follows:

$$
\begin{bmatrix}
z_1 = v_{02}^{(1)} + v_{12}^{(1)} y_1 + v_{22}^{(1)} y_2 \\
z_2 = v_{02}^{(2)} + v_{12}^{(2)} y_1 + v_{22}^{(2)} y_3 \\
\vdots \\
y_{m2} = v_{02}^{(M2)} + v_{12}^{(M2)} y_{(M-1)} + v_{22}^{(M2)} y_M
\end{bmatrix},
\tag{2.14}
$$

where z_j and $v_{i2}^{(j)}$, $j = 1, 2, \ldots, M_2$, $i = 0, 1, 2$, are the estimated outputs and corresponding coefficients of the functions. Following the same trend, assume that F_2 functions are passed on to the third layer; this means that there are $M_3(= c_{F_2}^2)$ partial functions generated in this layer. The generated partial function can mathematically be expressed as follows:

$$
\begin{bmatrix}
v_1 = v_{03}^{(1)} + v_{13}^{(1)} z_1 + v_{23}^{(1)} z_2 \\
v_2 = v_{03}^{(2)} + v_{13}^{(2)} z_1 + v_{23}^{(2)} z_3 \\
\vdots \\
v_{m3} = v_{02}^{(M3)} + v_{13}^{(M3)} z_{(M-1)} + v_{23}^{(M3)} z_M
\end{bmatrix},
\tag{2.15}
$$

where v_j and $v_{i3}^{(j)}$, $j = 1, 2, \ldots, M_3$, $i = 0, 1, 2$, are the estimated outputs and corresponding weights of the functions. The process is repeated by imposing threshold levels of $M \geq F_1 \geq F_2 \geq F_3 \geq \cdots \geq F_1$ so that finally a distinctive function is selected at one of the layers. The multilayer network structure with five input arguments and five selected nodes is depicted in Fig. 2.2.

Finally, to get the optimal function in terms of the input arguments, the final model can be traced back as follows:

$$
\begin{aligned}
v_2 &= f(z_1, z_3) \\
&\equiv f(f(y_1, y_2), f(y_1, y_4)) \\
&\equiv f(u_1, u_2, u_3, u_5) = f(X).
\end{aligned}
\tag{2.16}
$$

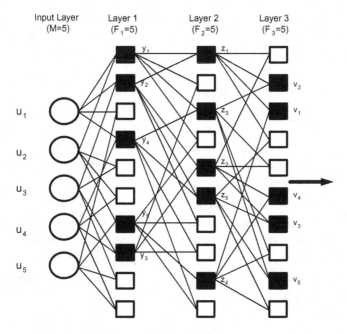

Fig. 2.2.   Multilayer network structure with five input arguments and selected nodes, redrawn from [10].

3. RESEARCH METHODOLOGY: DEVELOPMENT AND TESTING OF UNIVERSAL PRESSURE DROP MODELS IN PIPELINES USING POLYNOMIAL GROUP METHOD OF DATA HANDLING TECHNIQUE

3.1. Overview

The research methodology involves filling the gap exists in the literature by assessing and evaluating the best MPF (multiphase flow) empirical correlations and mechanistic models. The assessment will be dealing with their performance in estimating pressure drop whilst using available statistical and graphical techniques. The performance of the developed models will be compared against the best available correlations used by the industry. The following schematic diagram (Fig. 3.1) illustrates the sequence of research events.

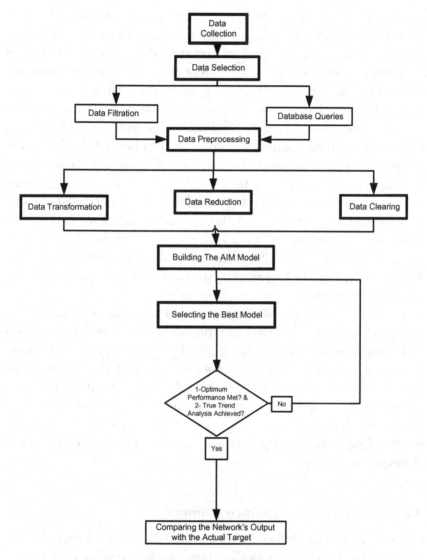

Fig. 3.1. Methodology chart for models generation.

It is clearly evident that data collection is the first step in generating a successful modeling study. However, data collection means gathering the relevant information pertinent to the course of study. The attributes should be well known to be contributing to the desired output. Irrelevant information can mislead the desired target. In addition to that the collected data must answer a simple question. Are the quality and quantity of collected data able to provide an improvement for the solution of current problem? Without collecting useful data nobody can tell if the generated model will simply succeed in providing an answer for the questions posed. In the problem of estimating pressure drop in pipelines with a wide range of angles of inclination, so many parameters are known to be contributing in the estimation of pressure drop. However, not all these parameters might be significantly contributed to the final output. Interestingly, some of these parameters cannot be available in the collected data due to some technical problems. Although this insufficiency in the data can reduce the information fed to the model, on the other hand, it might not significantly affect the precision of modeling procedure. Additionally, some of these input parameters were removed from the final data selection due to their low ranges.

A total number of 335 data sets had been utilized during the course of this study for modeling purposes (range of collected data had been presented in Appendix A). Relevant input variables were selected based on the most commonly used empirical correlations and mechanistic models used by the industry. Eight attributes were thought to have a strong impact on the pressure drop estimation, which are: oil rate, water rate, gas rate, diameter of the pipe, length of pipe, wellhead pressure, wellhead temperature, and angle of deviation.

3.2.   Network Performance Comparison

Pressure drop calculation for Beggs and Brill correlation, Gomez *et al.* model, Xiao *et al.* model had been conducted using the freeware *DPDLSystem* (*Delta Pressure Drop-Length System*). The stand-alone system involves an iterative approach to predict the length of the pipe's increment corresponding to the values of pressure drop. The software allows great flexibility in selecting PVT (Pressure–Volume–Temperature) methods, type of pressure drop correlation (vertical, inclined, and horizontal), operating conditions, and flow-rate type data. Only test data had been chosen for comparison for each selected model against the proposed AIM models. The network performance comparison had been conducted using the most critical statistical and analytical techniques. Trend analysis, group error analysis, and graphical and statistical analysis are among these techniques.

3.2.1. Trend analysis

A trend analysis was performed for each generated model to check whether it was physically correct or not. Interchangeably, this analysis is the synonyms of sensitivity analysis. However, it serves as a major ingredient in assessing model building and quality assurance. For this purpose, synthetic sets were prepared where in each set only one input parameter was varied between the minimum and maximum values while other parameters were kept constant at their mean (base) values. This means that each input parameter was changed Once-At-a-Time (OAT) to check its effect at the final output. This helped increase the comparability of the results (all "effects" are computed with reference to the same central point in space).

3.2.2. Group error analysis

To demonstrate the robustness of the developed model, another statistical analysis was conducted, which was group error analysis. The purpose of this analysis was to quantify the error produced by each input when grouped to a number of classes based on the average absolute relative error as an indicator. The reason for selecting average absolute relative error is that it is a good indicator of the accuracy of all empirical correlations, mechanistic model; as well as for the new developed AIM model. This effective comparison of all investigated correlations and mechanistic models provides a good means of evaluating models performance. Average absolute relative error was utilized in this analysis by grouping input parameter and hence plotting the corresponding values of average absolute relative error for each set.

3.2.3.   Statistical error analysis

This error analysis had been utilized to check the accuracy of the models. The statistical parameters used in the present work were: average percent relative error, average absolute percent relative error, minimum and maximum absolute percent error, root mean square error, standard deviation of error, and the correlation coefficient. Those statistical parameters are well known for their capabilities to analyze models' performance, and have been utilized by several authors (see Ayoub [2], Osman *et al.* [11] and El-Sebakhy *et al.* [5]).

Crossplots. In this graphical-based technique, all estimated values had been plotted against the measured values and thus a crossplot was formed. A 45° straight line between the estimated vs. actual data points was drawn on the crossplot, which denoted as a perfect correlation line. The tighter the cluster about the unity slope line, the better the agreement between the actual and the predicted values. This may give a good sign of model coherence.

3.3.   Building AIM Model

The process of generating AIM model started by selecting the most input parameters used to generate the previous empirical and mechanistic models. Free software was being used for this purpose [8]. This source code was tested with MATLAB version 7.1 (R14SP3). Despite the software allows great flexibility in selecting the model parameters, it also provides ample interference.

3.4.   Limitations

The results of the proposed AIM model may be limited in its nature due to data attributes range. The obtained results may suffer degradation due to the type of data used in generating the model. However, the accuracy obtained by the AIM model depends on the range of each input variable and the availability of that input parameter (parameters). Although the main purpose was to explore the potential of using GMDH technique, optimum performance can be obtained using this limited data range in attributes and variables.

Care must be taken when obtained results applied for data type and range beyond that used in generating the AIM model.

4. RESULTS AND DISCUSSION

4.1. Development of AIM Model

AIM (Polynomial Group Method of Data Handling technique) is a smart type of regression, which utilizes three steps to reach the final output (representation, selection, and stopping). The technique is capable of producing high degree polynomial in effective predictor. In addition, the process starts with initially simple regression relationship to derive more accurate representation in the next iteration. Polynomial GMDH technique is offering a sound representation of input regime to output through the application of regularity criterion. Usually this one can be average absolute percentage error. It is implemented to reduce the error between the actual and estimated target in each layer. A threshold level is applied before each layer is added since addition of a new layer and neurons depends on this threshold level.

As described initially in Sec. 3.3, software was utilized for building the final AIM model. The constructed model consists of two layers. A total number of 28 neurons were tried initially in the first layer before starting the optimization. At the end of optimization process only two hidden neurons were included, which have been texted z_1 and z_2. These two hidden neurons have no units rather they statistically responsible for mapping the relationship between input and output layer. The default selection is only one neuron for the second layer, which was the pressure drop target. The generation of hidden layer which contains these hidden units has been obtained after optimizing the model performance. However three input parameters had shown pronounced effect on the final pressure drop estimate, which were: wellhead pressure, length of the pipe, and angle of inclination. The selection of these three inputs had been conducted automatically without any interference from the user. They were selected based on their mapping influence inside the data set on the pressure drop values.

This topology was achieved after a series of optimization processes by monitoring the performance of the network until the best network

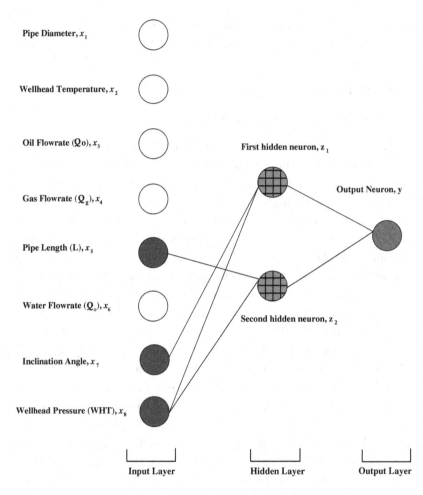

Fig. 4.1.   Schematic diagram of the proposed AIM topology.

structure was accomplished. Figure 4.1 shows the schematic diagram of the proposed AIM topology. Trend analysis has been checked for each model's run to make sure the modeling procedure was sound.

4.1.1.   Summary of model's equation

As described in the previous section the model consists of two layers as follows:

Total Number of layers: 2

Layer #1

Number of neurons: two (neurons z_1 and z_2)

$$z_1 = \alpha_0 + \alpha_1 x_8 + \alpha_2 x_7 + \alpha_3 x_7 x_8 + \alpha_4(x_8)^2 + \alpha_5(x_7)^2$$
$$z_2 = \alpha_6 + \alpha_7 x_8 + \alpha_8 x_5 + \alpha_9 x_5 x_8 + \alpha_{10}(x_8)^2 + \alpha_{11}(x_5)^2$$

where

$\alpha_0 = -428.13059484218$ $\qquad$ $\alpha_1 = 3.32804279841806$

$\alpha_2 = -0.395894375895042$ $\qquad$ $\alpha_3 = 0.00219488561608562$

$\alpha_4 = -0.00470613525745107$ $\qquad$ $\alpha_5 = -0.000813801551583036$

$\alpha_6 = -404.104040068822$ $\qquad$ $\alpha_7 = 3.28280927457335$

$\alpha_8 = -0.00560599702533417$ $\qquad$ $\alpha_9 = 1.7395894539217e - 005$

$\alpha_{10} = -0.00474009259349089$ $\qquad$ $\alpha_{11} = 3.53811231021166e - 008$

Layer #2

Number of neurons: one

$$y = \sigma_0 + \sigma_1 z_2 + \sigma_2 z_1 + \sigma_3 z_1 z_2 + \sigma_4(z_2)^2 + \sigma_5(z_1)^2$$

where

$\sigma_0 = 38.6163548411764$ $\qquad$ $\sigma_1 = -0.357238550745703$

$\sigma_2 = 0.349279607055502$ $\qquad$ $\sigma_3 = 0.0477387718410476$

$\sigma_4 = -0.0185457588736114$ $\qquad$ $\sigma_5 = -0.0242018021448686$

where x_5 is length of the pipe, ft; x_7 is the angle of inclination, degrees; x_8 is the wellhead pressure, psia; and y is the simulated pressure drop by AIM model.

4.2.   Trend Analysis for the AIM Model

A trend analysis was conducted for every model run to check the physical accuracy of the developed model. Depending on the final parameters involved in estimating pressure drop that obtained automatically by the model; three input variables were found strongly affecting the final output compared to at least eight input parameters needed for other empirical correlations or mechanistic models. Those are angle of deviation, length of the pipe, and wellhead pressure. Only the effect of the first two input parameters will be investigated that should be compatible with the physical phenomenon of

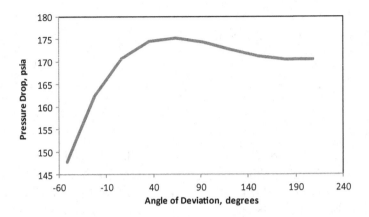

Fig. 4.2.   Effect of angle of inclination on pressure drop.

the general energy equation. Figure 4.2 shows the effect of angle of inclination on the pressure drop. The effect of angle of inclination was investigated where all range of angles of inclination was plotted against pressure drop. The model was able to generate the sound track where pressure drop is known to be an increasing function up to 90° and beyond that angle it is known to be a decreasing function. Additionally, the relationship between the pressure drop and length of the pipe was examined by trend analysis where the length of the pipe was plotted against the simulated pressure drop at four different angles of inclination as shown in Fig. 4.3.

Again, and as expected the AIM model was able to predict the correct phenomenon where the pressure drop is known to be an increasing function with respect to pipe length. Also it is clear that with increasing angle of inclination from downhill to uphill the pressure drop is an increasing function. Again the AIM model was able to produce the right physical trend with respect to angle variation.

4.3.   Group Error Analysis for the AIM Model Against Other Investigated Models

To demonstrate the robustness of the developed model, group error analysis was performed. Average absolute relative error is utilized

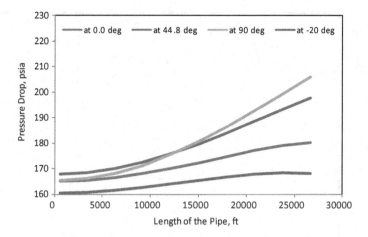

Fig. 4.3.   Effect of pipe length on pressure drop at four different angles of inclination.

as a powerful tool for evaluating the accuracy of all empirical correlations, mechanistic model, as well as the polynomial GMDH model. This effective comparison of all investigated correlations and mechanistic models provides a good means of evaluating models performance since it is used as a main criterion for models evaluation. Average absolute relative error was utilized in this analysis by grouping input parameter and hence plotting the corresponding values of average absolute relative error for each set. Figures 4.4 and 4.5 present the statistical accuracy of pressure drop correlations and models under different groups. Figure 4.4 shows the statistical accuracy of pressure drop grouped by length of the pipe. Length of the pipe had been partitioned into five groups and plotted against the respective average absolute percent relative error for each group. Polynomial GMDH model was found superior in obtaining the lowest average absolute percent relative error for range of two pipe length groups ($11901 < L < 16000$ and $16001 < L < 25000$).

Furthermore, the statistical accuracy of pressure drop estimation for the polynomial GMDH model against other investigated models grouped by the angle of inclination is plotted in Fig. 4.5. Data were partitioned into four categories to include all possible inclination (downhill, horizontal, uphill, and vertical).

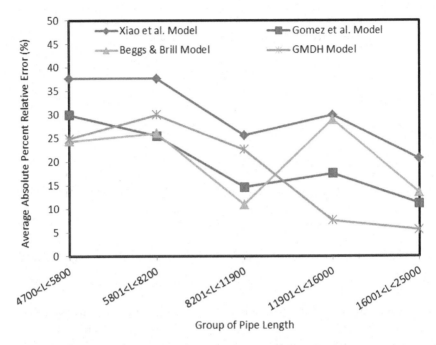

Fig. 4.4.   Statistical accuracy of pressure drop for the polynomial GMDH model and other investigated models grouped by pipe length (with corresponding data points).

As shown in the respective figure, the GMDH model's performance was superior especially for horizontal pipes (0°) and achieved the lowest average absolute percent relative error for the range of angle of inclination between $-7° < \theta < -52°$ (downhill angles) and $90° < \theta < 208°$ (uphill angles).

4.4.   Statistical and Graphical Comparisons of the Polynomial GMDH Model

4.4.1.   Statistical error analysis

Statistical error analysis was conducted for all sets. Summary of statistical comparisons between all sets (training, validation, and testing) of the polynomial GMDH Model is presented in Table 4.1.

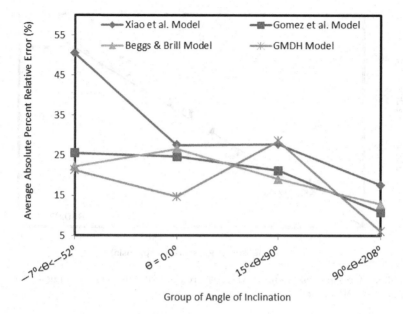

Fig. 4.5. Statistical accuracy of pressure drop for the polynomial GMDH model and other investigated models grouped by angle of inclination (with corresponding data points).

Table 4.1. Statistical analysis results of the polynomial GMDH model.

Statistical Parameters	Training	Validation	Testing
E_a (Average Absolute Percent Relative Error)	18.5282	31.6448	19.5921
E_r (Average Percent Relative Error)	−6.6299	−21.1243	−0.9040
E_{Max} (Maximum Absolute Percent Relative Error)	286.9142	583.0868	130.6760
E_{Min} (Minimum Absolute Percent Relative Error)	0.0862	0.2303	0.0904
RMSE (Root Mean Square Error)	38.2075	90.9291	33.5273
R "fraction" (The Correlation Coefficient)	0.9771	0.9544	0.9750
STD (Standard Deviation)	12.0291	14.0404	14.3347

4.4.2. Graphical error analysis of the polynomial GMDH model

Three graphical analysis techniques were employed to visualize the performance of the polynomial GMDH model and other investigated

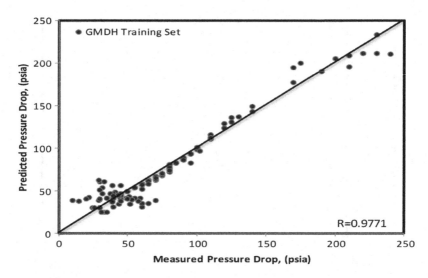

Fig. 4.6.   Crossplot of predicted vs. measured pressure drop for training set (polynomial GMDH model).

models. Those include crossplots, error distribution, and residual analysis.

Crossplots of the polynomial GMDH model: Figures 4.6–4.8 present crossplots of predicted pressure drop vs. the actual one for polynomial GMDH model (training, validation, and testing sets). Figure 4.5 shows a crossplot between predicted and actual pressure drop values for the training set where a correlation coefficient of 0.9771 was obtained by the GMDH model.

The GMDH model showed good agreement between actual and estimated values especially at the middle range (from 70 to 150 psia). However, this measure (correlation coefficient) was not taken as a main criterion for evaluating models performance since it may not give clear insight into the actual error trend while points under the 45° may be recovered by others under the same line. Figure 4.6 shows another crossplot created by the validation set where predicted pressure drop was plotted against the actual values. Now 0.9544 is obtained by this model for this data set. Validation set was introduced during training of GMDH model to avoid overtraining.

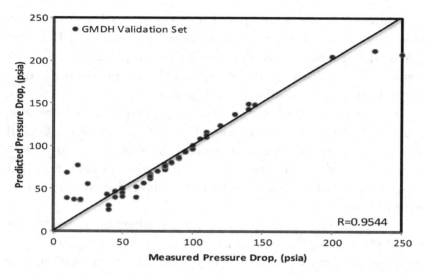

Fig. 4.7. Crossplot of predicted vs. measured pressure drop for validation set (polynomial GMDH model).

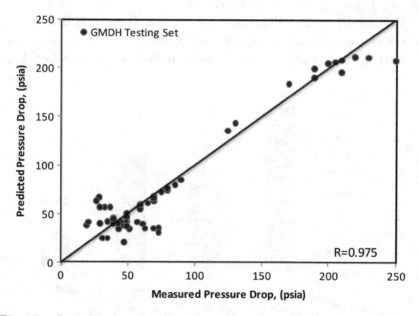

Fig. 4.8. Crossplot of predicted vs. measured pressure drop for testing set (polynomial GMDH model).

Figure 4.7 shows a crossplot between estimated and measured pressure drop values for the test set created by the GMDH model. The model achieved reasonable correlation coefficient between estimated and actual values where a value of 0.975 was obtained. Bear in mind that this correlation coefficient was achieved with only three input parameters, which are angle of inclination, wellhead pressure, and length of the pipe. In addition, the performance of the GMDH may be improved further if more data sets have been introduced with a wide range of tested variables. This may give an indication that most of the input variables used for other investigated models may serve as noise data.

The main purpose of utilizing this technique is to explore the potential of using GMDH as a tool, for the first time, to predict the pressure drop under wide range of angles of inclination. The exploration includes finding the most influential input parameters in estimating the pressure drop under this wide range of angles of inclination. Figure 4.8 shows a comparison of correlation coefficients for GMDH model against all investigated models. Beggs and Brill model achieved the highest correlation coefficient as shown by Fig. 4.9. GMDH model ranked the last if this criterion has been selected as

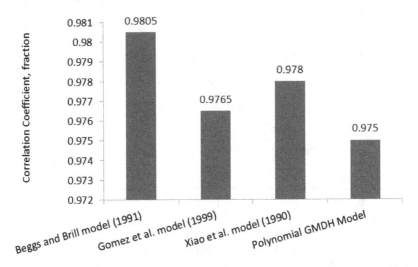

Fig. 4.9.   Comparison of correlation coefficients for the polynomial GMDH model against all investigated models.

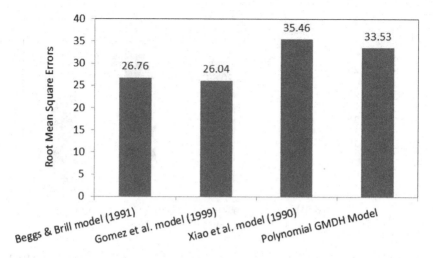

Fig. 4.10. Comparison of average absolute percent relative errors for the polynomial GMDH model against all investigated models.

a main performance indicator. However, the main criterion for evaluating model's performance, which is the Average Absolute Percent Relative Error, revealed that the GMDH test set outperformed all investigated models in AAPE with a value of approximately 19.6%, followed by Beggs and Brill model as shown in Fig. 4.10. The comparison of root mean square errors for the polynomial GMDH model against all investigated models was shown in Fig. 4.11. This time, the lowest RMSE is achieved by Gomez *et al.* model (26.04%) while the GMDH model ranked third before the worse model (Xiao *et al.* model) with a value of 33.53%. Additional criteria for evaluating model's performance are Standard Deviation, Root Mean Square Error (RMSE), Minimum Absolute Percent Relative Error, and Maximum Absolute Percent Relative Error. The GMDH model failed to provide low maximum absolute percent relative error where a value of 130.6% is obtained. If this criterion was selected to evaluate models performance, the GMDH model will be considered as the worst among the rest of investigated models. On contrary, if the minimum absolute percent relative error is considered as the only parameter for evaluating models performance, the GMDH will be ranked first among all investigated models with a value of 0.0904. Moreover,

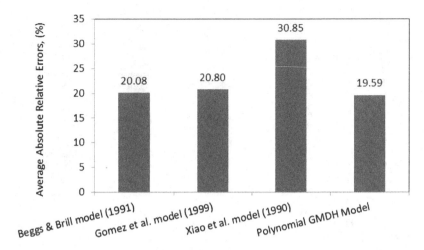

Fig. 4.11.   Comparison of root mean square errors for the polynomial GMDH model against all investigated models.

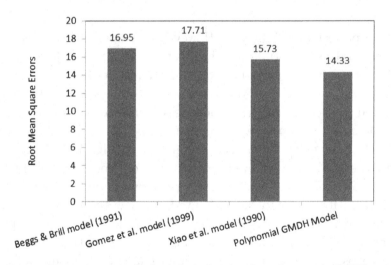

Fig. 4.12.   Comparison of standard deviation for the polynomial GMDH model against all investigated models

Fig. 4.9 shows a comparison of correlation coefficient for the polynomial GMDH model against all investigated models.

Root Mean Square Error (RMSE) is used to measure the data dispersion. A lower value of standard deviation indicates a smaller degree of scatter. As shown in Fig. 4.12, GMDH model achieves the

Table 4.2. Statistical analysis results of empirical correlations, mechanistic models, against the proposed AIM models.

Model Name	E_a	E_r	E_{Max}	E_{Min}	RMSE	R	STD
Beggs and Brill model	20.076	−10.987	79.00	0.3333	26.7578	0.9805	16.9538
Gomez et al. model	20.802	−2.046	72.65	0.525	26.0388	0.9765	17.7097
Xiao et al. model	30.845	29.818	71.4286	0.0625	35.4582	0.9780	15.7278
Polynomial GMDH model	19.592	−0.904	130.68	0.0904	33.5273	0.9750	14.3347

lowest STD with a value of 14.33%, followed by Xiao *et al.* model (15.73%).

Table 4.2 summarizes the performance comparison indicators for all investigated models as well as for the polynomial GMDH model.

5.   CONCLUSION AND RECOMMENDATIONS

5.1.   Conclusion

The following conclusions can be drawn from the current study:

1. The main target for conducting this study was to explore the potential of utilizing AIM technique for estimating the pressure drop in pipelines with wide range of angles of inclination.
2. The proposed polynomial GMDH model outperformed the best investigated available models adopted by industry for estimating pressure drop in pipelines for a wide range of angles of inclination with an outstanding average absolute percentage relative error of 19.59%.
3. Statistical analysis revealed that proposed polynomial GMDH model achieved the lowest average absolute percent error, lowest standard deviation, and the lowest minimum error.

4. The superiority of the proposed polynomial GMDH model has been seen when group error analysis has been conducted for different pipe lengths and angle of inclinations with outstanding performance.
5. Accurate results can be obtained if new wide set of data is implemented to generate another AIM model. Hence care must be taken when extrapolating data beyond the original model range.
6. Polynomial GMDH model helps in reducing the curse of dimensionality that lowers the performance of other investigated models.
7. Length of the pipe, angle of inclination, and wellhead pressure were found strongly contributing in estimating pressure drop in pipeline system with the investigated range of data.
8. The common perception that pressure drop relies on the relative proportions of oil, gas, and water flow rates has been proved unrealistic and misleading.
9. No single model had been found reliable for estimating the pressure drop among the investigated old models.

5.2.   Recommendation

The following recommendations may be forwarded for future work:

1. A wide range of data that can be collected from different fields with additional input variables can be used to construct more robust models using AIM technique.
2. A double-verification of the current model results can be assessed through using a smart simulator such as OLGA.
3. GMDH model can be incorporated easily in any commercial production software to serve as an easy programmable tool.

REFERENCES

[1] Abduvayt, P., Manabe, R. & Arihara, N. (2003) Effects of pressure and pipe diameter on gas–liquid two-phase flow behavior in pipelines, *Paper Presented at The SPE Annual Technical Conference and Exhibition*, Denver, CO, USA.
[2] Ayoub, M. A. (2004) Development and testing of an artificial neural network model for predicting bottom-hole pressure in vertical multiphase flow, M.Sc. thesis, King Fahd University of Petroleum and Minerals, Dhahran, Saudi Arabia.

[3] Beggs, H. D. & Brill, J. P. (1973) A study of two-phase flow in inclined pipes, *J. Petroleum Technol.* **25**, 607–617.

[4] Brill, J. (1987) Multiphase flow in wells, *J. Petroleum Technol.* **SPE 16242**, 15–21.

[5] El-Sebakhy, E. A., Sheltami, T., Al-Bokhitan, S. Y., Shaaban, Y., Raharja, P. D., & Khaeruzzaman, Y. (2007, January). Support vector machines framework for predicting the PVT properties of crude oil systems. In *SPE Middle East Oil and Gas Show and Conference*. Society of Petroleum Engineers.

[6] Gomez, L. E., Shoham, O., Schmidt, Z, Chokshi, R. N., Brown, A. & Northug, T. (1999) A unified mechanistic model for steady-state two-phase flow in wellbores and pipelines, *Paper Presented at the SPE Annual Technical Conferences and Exhibition*, Houston, TX.

[7] Ivakhnenko, A. G. & Yurachkovsky, Y. P. (1986) *Modeling of Complex Systems after Experimental Data*, Radio i svyaz, Moscow.

[8] Jekabsons, G., 2010. GMDH-type polynomial neural networks for Matlab. Regression Software and Datasets. http://www.cs.rtu.lv/jekabsons/.

[9] Lockhart, R. & Martinelli, R. (1949) Proposed correlation of data for isothermal two-phase, two-component flow in pipes, *Chem. Eng. Prog.* **45**(1), 39–48.

[10] Madala, H. R. & Ivakhnenko, A. G. (1994) *Inductive Learning Algorithms for Complex System Modeling*, CRC Press, FL.

[11] Osman, E. A., Abdel-Wahhab, O. A., & Al-Marhoun, M. A. (2001, January 1). Prediction of Oil PVT Properties Using Neural Networks. Society of Petroleum Engineers. (SPE Paper#68233) doi:10.2118/68233-MS.

[12] Osman, E. A. a. R. E. A.-A. (2002) Abductive networks: a new modeling tool for the oil and gas industry, *Paper Presented at the SPE Asia Pacific Oil & Gas Conference and Exhibition*, Melbourne, Australia.

[13] Petalas, N. & Aziz, K. (2000) A mechanistic model for multiphase flow in pipes, *J. Canadian Petroleum Technol.* **39**(6).

[14] Sawaragi, Y., Soeda, T., Tamura, H., Yoshimura, T., Ohe, S., Chujo, Y. & Ishihara, H. (1979) Statistical prediction of air pollution levels using nonphysical models. *Automatica (IFAC)*, **15**(4), 441–452.

[15] Tackacs, G. (2001) Considerations on the selection of an optimum vertical multiphase pressure drop prediction model for oil wells, *Paper Presented at the Production and Operations Symposium*, Oklahoma.

[16] Verleysen, M. & François, D. (2005) The curse of dimensionality in data mining and time series prediction, *Comput. Intell. Bioinspired Syst.*, 758–770.

APPENDIX A. RESEARCH DATA

The testing set is being utilized for calculating the pressure drop for all investigated models (Xiao *et al.* and Gomez *et al.*) and correlation (Beggs and Brill).

Training Data Range:

Property	Pressure drop, psia (y-output)	Diameter of pipe, inches (x_1-input)	Wellhead temperature, °F b(x_2-input)	Oil flow-rate, Bbl/d (x_3-input)	Gas flow-rate, MSCF/D (x_4-input)	Length of the pipe, ft (x_5-input)	Water flow-rate, Bbl/d (x_6-input)	Angle of inclination, degrees (x_7-input)	Wellhead pressure, psia (x_8-input)
Minimum	10.00	6.065	63.00	2200.00	1078.0	500.00	0.000	−52.000	160.00
Maximum	240.0	10.02	186.00	24800	19024	26700.0	8335.00	208.000	540.00
Mean	80.620	8.6042	133.756	12852.5	7594.6	11447.4	1523.49	44.952	322.964
Standard Deviation	56.540	1.7412	22.0260	5743.26	3203.1	6247.44	1952.78	59.5522	133.655

Validation Data Range:

Property	Pressure drop, psia (y-output)	Diameter of pipe, inches (x_1-input)	Wellhead temperature, °F b(x_2-input)	Oil flow-rate, Bbl/d (x_3-input)	Gas flow-rate, MSCF/D (x_4-input)	Length of the pipe, ft (x_5-input)	Water flow-rate, Bbl/d (x_6-input)	Angle of inclination, degrees (x_7-input)	Wellhead pressure, psia (x_8-input)
Minimum	10	6.065	82	4400	3346.6	3600	0	−13	160
Maximum	250	10.02	168	25000	19278	26700	8424	208	540
Mean	84.120	9.3729	132.891	13234.4	7384.21	13590.6	2824.01	72.927	265.710
Standard Deviation	46.209	1.14549	19.08965	4877.89	3154.73	7395.66	2377.77	69.03442	92.5294

Testing Data Range:

Property	Pressure drop, psia (y-output)	Diameter of pipe, inches (x_1-input)	Wellhead temperature, °F b(x_2-input)	Oil flow-rate, Bbl/d (x_3-input)	Gas flow-rate, MSCF/D (x_4-input)	Length of the pipe, ft (x_5-input)	Water flow-rate, Bbl/d (x_6-input)	Angle of inclination, degrees (x_7-input)	Wellhead pressure, psia (x_8-input)
Minimum	20	6.065	72	3800	3239	4700	0	−52	170
Maximum	250	10.02	173	22700	19658.2	25000	8010	128	545
Mean	83.75	8.31893	138.5833	12112.8	7583.855	10411.1	1336.9	31.7619	354.96
Standard Deviation	64.4433	1.82076	20.05066	5105.85	2458.774	5196.26	2016.5	46.7587	142.02

APPENDIX B. PRESSURE DROP MODELS IN PIPELINES USING POLYNOMIAL GROUP METHOD OF DATA HANDLING TECHNIQUE

The main program in this code is the *gmdhbuild.m*. The user must have adequate knowledge in GMDH, in general to ease following these steps. The *GMDH_script.m* is only a subroutine to call all the four functions (*gmdhbuild.m, gmdheq.m, gmdhpredict.m, gmdhtest.m*). The concentration will be put on the script file, which is intended to guide the user step by step towards the optimum modeling procedure.

```
clc; % The aim is to clear all input and output from the Command
        Window display, and to give the user a "clean screen."
clf: % it deletes from the current figure all graphics objects.
 clear all;%Clears all variables and other classes of data too.
close all; % It force deletes all figures (hidden and non-hidden
        % strings).
 tic; % To measure the running time ''for comparison purposes''.
```

The first step is to prepare the data in any supported format by MAT-LAB. An example is set here using excel file (Microsoft Excel 2007).

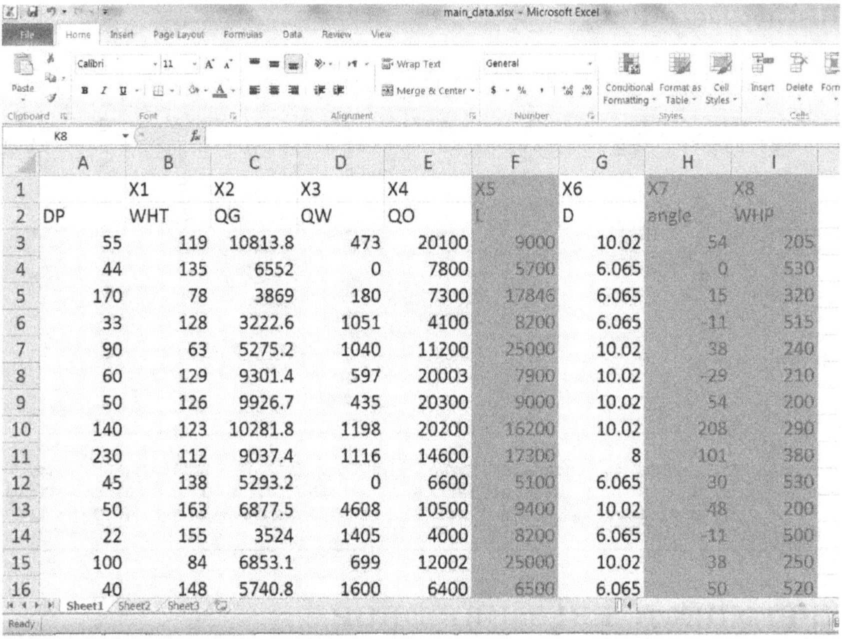

	A	B	C	D	E	F	G	H	I
1		X1	X2	X3	X4	X5	X6	X7	X8
2	DP	WHT	QG	QW	QO	L	D	angle	WHP
3	55	119	10813.8	473	20100	9000	10.02	54	205
4	44	135	6552	0	7800	5700	6.065	0	530
5	170	78	3869	180	7300	17846	6.065	15	320
6	33	128	3222.6	1051	4100	8200	6.065	-11	515
7	90	63	5275.2	1040	11200	25000	10.02	38	240
8	60	129	9301.4	597	20003	7900	10.02	-29	210
9	50	126	9926.7	435	20300	9000	10.02	54	200
10	140	123	10281.8	1198	20200	16200	10.02	208	290
11	230	112	9037.4	1116	14600	17300	8	101	380
12	45	138	5293.2	0	6600	5100	6.065	30	530
13	50	163	6877.5	4608	10500	9400	10.02	48	200
14	22	155	3524	1405	4000	8200	6.065	-11	500
15	100	84	6853.1	699	12002	25000	10.02	38	250
16	40	148	5740.8	1600	6400	6500	6.065	50	520

Fig. B.1. Data configuration.

The input file must contain the input parameters and output target. The target set (DP) is in the first column while the rest of input parameters are located in column 2 to column 9, as represented by Fig. B.1.

The second step is to make the data readable by the code; the MATLAB command is shown below. The main data file called main_data.xlsx and the command is "xlsread".

```
ndata= xlsread('main_data.xlsx');
```

Inside the excel file, the user can partition the data into three components (based on the availability). Those are: training, validation and testing. The partitioning ratio among them can be 2:1:1, 3:1:1, 4:1:1, or 5:3:2 (those are the most commonly used by researchers) or any other portioning ratio. In our case here we used 50% for training, 25% for validation, and 25% for testing (has not been seen during training process).

For-loop has been utilized in this step to read those components (training, validation, and testing). The code reads 168 data sets for training, 83 data sets for validation, and 84 data sets for testing. The code reads:

```
for i=1:168
    atr(i,:)=ndata(i,:);
end
for i=169:251
    aval(i-168,:)=ndata(i,:);
end
%
for i=252:length(ndata)
    atest(i-251,:)=ndata(i,:);
end
```

The data step is not finished yet. It is required that the user must "identify" the training input data and its target. The same goes for validation and testing. This step is crucial and needed by the code since the main program *gmdhbuild.m* utilizes it.

```
Ytr=atr(:,1);
Xtr=atr(:,2:9);
Xtst=atest(:,2:9);
Ytst=atest(:,1);
Yv=aval(:,1);
Xv=aval(:,2:9);
```

The next step is to call the GMDH's main function, which is *gmdhbuild.m*. The input parameters for this function can be obtained directly from the definition part of this function. The output of this function is the model and time.

```
[model, time] = gmdhbuild(Xtr, Ytr, 2, 0, 2, 0, 2, 1,
0.9, Xv, Yv,1);
```

The user can select the level of desired accuracy by setting it in *gmdheq.m* (in this example 3 has been selected).

```
gmdheq(model, 3);
```

Again, calling **gmdhpredict.m** is necessary to check the performance of each data set. Knowing that this step is necessary for training, validation, and testing will produce **Yqtr**, **Yqval**, and **Yqtst** vectors. Those vectors are the predictors by GMDH code, which will be saved and utilized later for performance comparison.

```
[Yqtr] = gmdhpredict(model, Xtr);
[Yqval] = gmdhpredict(model, Xv);
[Yqtst] = gmdhpredict(model, Xtst);
```

Since we know that the testing set is one that we target, the performance basically will be stressed for it. The code can produce a series of statistical properties as seen by the following:

```
[MSE, RMSE, RRMSE, R2] = gmdhtest(model, Xtst, Ytst);
```

Additional statistical parameters can be derived easily, knowing that the target and the actual data vectors are already available. The code can only produce for training set and this is the reason why we need to do it for the rest of data sets. The following shows these statistical derivations.

Cross plot for the training set is shown in Fig. B.2. The coding for this part follows.

```
% Evaluating Relative Error for training set:
%================================================
Et1=(Ytr-Yqtr)./Ytr*100;
[q,z] = size(Et1);
figure
plot(Ytst,Yqtst,'o')
grid off
set(gcf, 'color', 'white')
axis square

title('Predicted Pressure Loss vs. Measured Pressure Loss');
xlabel('Measured Pressure Loss "psig"');
ylabel('Predicted Pressure Loss "psig"')
legend('Training set', 'location', 'Northwest')
% Adding Reference Line with 45 degree slope
```

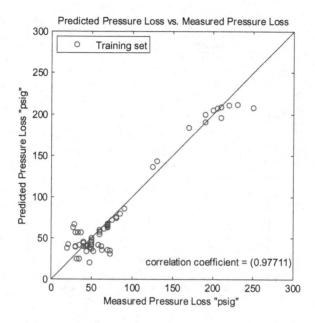

Fig. B.2.   Training set performance (crossplot).

```
line([0 ; 300],[0 ; 300])
%HINT: Select the y-value based on your data limits
Hold

% Evaluating the correlation coefficient for training set:
% ============================================================
Rt1=corrcoef(Yqtr,Ytr);
Rt11=min(Rt1(:,1));
gtext(['correlation coefficient = (' num2str(Rt11) ')']);
hold

% Adding Reference Line with 45 degree slope
%line([0 ; 300],[0 ; 300])
%HINT: Select the y-value based on your data limits
```

Crossplot for the validation set is shown in Fig. B.3. The coding for
this part is as follows.

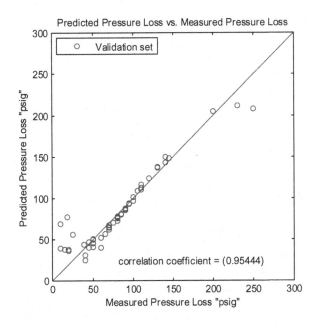

Fig. B.3.   Validation set performance (crossplot).

```
% Evaluating Relative Error for validation set:
%================================================
Ev1=(Yqval-Yv)./Yqval*100;
[m,n] = size(Ev1);
figure

plot(Yv,Yqval,'o')
grid off
set(gcf, 'color', 'white')
axis square
title('Predicted Pressure Loss vs. Measured Pressure Loss');
xlabel('Measured Pressure Loss "psig"');
ylabel('Predicted Pressure Loss "psig"')
legend('Validation set', 'location', 'Northwest')
% Adding Reference Line with 45 degree slope
line([0 ; 300],[0 ; 300])
%HINT: Select the y-value based on your data limits
```

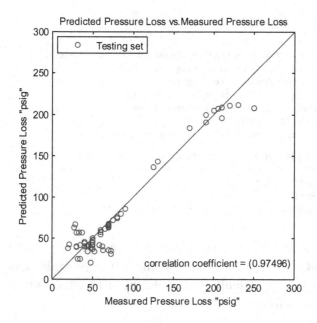

Fig. B.4.   Testing set performance (crossplot).

```
% Evaluating the correlation coefficient for validation set:
% ============================================================
% for the first target Pressure Drop
Rv1=corrcoef(Yqval,Yv);
Rv11=min(Rv1(:,1));
gtext(['correlation coefficient = (' num2str(Rv11) ')']);
hold
```

Crossplot for the testing set is shown in Fig. B.4. The coding for this part is as follows.

```
% Evaluating Relative Error for testing set:
%==========================================
% for the first target Pressure Drop
Ett1=(Ytst-Yqtst)./Ytst*100;
[m,n] = size(Ett1);
figure
%
plot(Ytst,Yqtst,'o')
grid off
```

```
set(gcf, 'color', 'white')
axis square

title('Predicted Pressure Loss vs. Measured Pressure Loss');
xlabel('Measured Pressure Loss "psig"');
ylabel('Predicted Pressure Loss "psig"')
legend('Testing set', 'location', 'Northwest')
% Adding Reference Line with 45 degree slope
line([0 ; 300],[0 ; 300])
%HINT: Select the y-value based on your data limits

% Evaluating the correlation coefficient for testing set:
% =========================================================
Rtt1=corrcoef(Yqtst,Ytst);
Rtt11=min(Rtt1(:,1));
gtext(['correlation coefficient = (' num2str(Rtt11) ')']);
hold
```

Plotting the histogram of the errors distributions can give better view for the data set performance in terms of the possible errors ranges. The histogram for training set is shown in Fig. B.5. The coding for this part is as follows.

```
% plotting the histogram of the errors for training set:
% =========================================================
figure
```

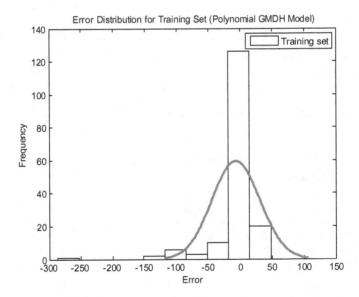

Fig. B.5.   Training set performance (histogram-error distribution).

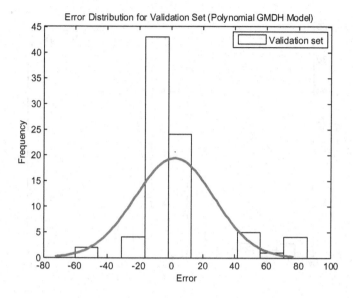

Fig. B.6. Validation set performance (histogram-error distribution).

```
%histfit(Et1,10)
hist(Et1,10)
h = findobj(gca,'Type','patch');
set(h,'FaceColor','w','EdgeColor','k')
title('Error Distribution for Training Set (Polynomial GMDH Model)');
legend('Training set')
xlabel('Error');
ylabel('Frequency')
set(gcf, 'color', 'white')

hold
```

The histogram for validation set is shown in Fig. B.6. The coding for this part is as follows.

```
% plotting the histogram of the errors for validation set:
% ========================================================
figure
%histfit(Ev1,10)
hist(Ev1,10)
h = findobj(gca, 'Type', 'patch');
set(h,'FaceColor','w','EdgeColor','k')
title('Error Distribution for Validation Set (Polynomial GMDH Model)');
legend('Validation set')
xlabel('Error');
ylabel('Frequency')
set(gcf, 'color', 'white')
```

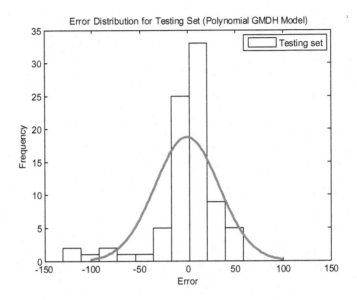

Fig. B.7.   Testing set performance (histogram-error distribution).

```
hold
```

The histogram for testing set is shown in Fig. B.7. The coding for this part is as follows.

```
% plotting the histogram of the errors for testing set:
% =======================================================
figure
histfit(Ett1,10)
%hist(Ett1,10)
h = findobj(gca,'Type','patch');
set(h,'FaceColor','w','EdgeColor','k')
title('Error Distribution for Testing Set (Polynomial GMDH Model)');
legend('Testing set')
xlabel('Error');
ylabel('Frequency')
set(gcf, 'color', 'white')
hold
```

Estimating the residuals for each set offers an invaluable graphical means to check model performance for each individual data set. The residual values will be calculated for training, validation and testing. The residuals for training set is shown in Fig. B.8. The coding for this part is as follows.

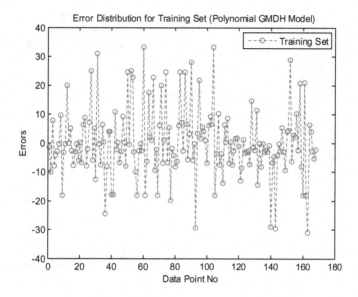

Fig. B.8. Training set performance (residuals-error distribution).

```
% Estimating the residuals for training set:
% =============================================
figure
Errort1 = Yqtr-Ytr;
plot(Errort1,':ro');
grid off
set(gcf, 'color', 'white')
title('Error Distribution for Training Set (Polynomial GMDH Model)')
legend('Training Set')
xlabel('Data Point No')
ylabel('Errors')
hold
```

The residuals for validation set is shown in Fig. B.9. The coding for this part is as follows.

```
% Estimating the residuals for validation set:
% =============================================
figure
Errorv1 = Yqval-Yv;
plot(Errorv1,':ro');
grid off
set(gcf, 'color', 'white')
title('Residual Graph for Validation Set (Polynomial GMDH Model)')
legend('Validation Set')
xlabel('Data Point No')
```

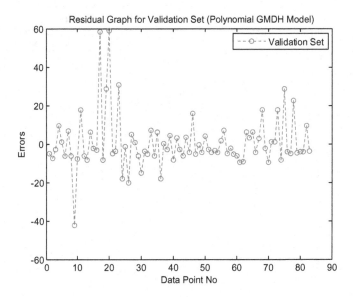

Fig. B.9.   Validation set performance (residuals-error distribution).

```
ylabel('Errors')
hold
```

The residuals for testing set is shown in Fig. B.10. The coding for this part is as follows.

```
% Estimating the residuals for testing set:
% ==========================================
figure
Errortt1 = Yqtst-Ytst;
plot(Errortt1,':ro');
grid off
set(gcf, 'color', 'white')
title('Residual Graph for Testing Set (Polynomial GMDH Model)')
legend('Testing Set')
xlabel('Data Point No')
ylabel('Errors')
```

The remaining statistical analyses can be extracted from their mathematical descriptions as follows:

Minimum Absolute Percent Relative Error:

$$E_{\min} = \min_{i+1}^{n} |E_i|.$$

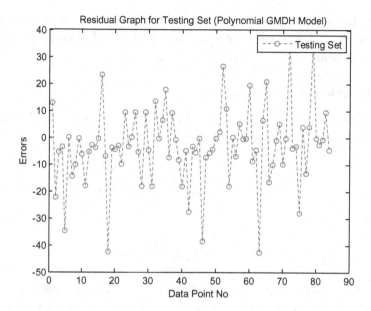

Fig. B.10. Testing set performance (residuals-error distribution).

Maximum Absolute Percent Relative Error:

$$E_{\max} = \max_{i+1}^{n} |E_i|.$$

Root Mean Square Error (RMSE):

Measures the data dispersion around zero deviation, defined by:

$$\text{RMSE} = \left[\frac{1}{n} \sum_{i=1}^{n} E_i^2 \right]^{0.5}.$$

Standard Deviation (STD):

It is a measure of dispersion and is expressed as:

$$\text{STD} = \sqrt{\left[\left(\frac{1}{(m-n-1)} \right) \right] \sum_{i=1}^{m} \left[\left\{ \frac{(\Delta P_{\text{act}} - \Delta P_{\text{est}})}{\Delta P_{\text{act}}} \right\} 100 \right]^2 },$$

where $(m - n - 1)$ represents the degree of freedom in multiple-regression. A lower value of standard deviation indicates a smaller degree of scatter.

The Correlation Coefficient (R):

It represents the degree of success in reducing the standard deviation by regression analysis, defined by:

$$R = \sqrt{1 - \frac{\sum_{I=1}^{n} [(\Delta P)_{\text{act}} - (\Delta P)_{\text{est}}]}{\sum_{I=1}^{n} (\Delta P)_{\text{act}} - \overline{\Delta \Delta P}}},$$

where

$$\overline{\Delta \Delta P} = \frac{1}{n} \sum_{I=1}^{n} [(\Delta \Delta P)_{\text{act}}]_I.$$

three "R" values range between 0 and 1. The closer value to 1 represents perfect correlation whereas 0 indicates no correlation at all among the independent variables.

```
% Training set:
% ============
% Determining the Maximum Absolute Percent Relative Error
MaxErrt1 = max(abs(Et1));

% Evaluating the average error
Etavg1 = 1/z*sum(Et1);

% Evaluating the standard deviation
STDT1 = std(Errort1);

% Determining the Minimum Absolute Percent Relative Error
MinErrt1 = min(abs(Et1));

% Evaluating Average Absolute Percent Relative Error
% =================================================
AAPET1 = sum(abs(Et1))/z;

% Evaluating Average Percent Relative Error
% ========================================
APET1 = 1/z*sum(Et1);
```

```
% Evaluating Root Mean Square
% =============================
RMSET1 = sqrt(sum(abs(Et1).^2)/z);
```

The same can be done for validation and testing set.

The last step is to verify that the GMDH model can predict the true physical behavior, meaning that it is not memorizing the data patterns, rather it learns by training. In order to do that, a trend analysis must be conducted by varying the input parameters between the minimum and maximum values (creating synthetic data) and changing only one parameter and valuing the target output. The model is expected to give the right behavior since it has been trained using the same data sets.

This step can be accomplished through utilizing linspace function:

```
%---------------------------------------------------------------------
---------
% Simulation: Variation of Length of the Pipe while fixing the other
parameters
% ------------Length of the Pipe variation----------------------------
---------
    ps1=[linspace(133,133,10); %WELLHEAD TEMPERATURE [min=63
max=186      mean=134.752]
    linspace(2000,2000,10);%GAS rate [min=1078 max=19024 mean=7622]
    linspace(1527,1527,10);%WATER RATE [min=0.0 max=8335 mean=1527]
    linspace(12920.3,12920.3,10);%OIL FLOWRATE [min=2200 max=24800
mean=12920.3]
    linspace(500,26700,10);%LENGTH OF THE PIPE [min=500 max=26700
mean=11437]
    linspace(7,7,10);%DIAMETER OF THE PIPE [min=6.065 max=10.02 mean=8.6]
    linspace(44.6,44.6,10);%ANGLE OF DEVIATION [min=-52 max=208 mean=44.6]
    linspace(316.8,316.8,10)]';%WELLHEAD PRESSURE [min=160 max=540
mean=321.6]
```

The previous step is needed to generate the synthetic data.

```
% Now simulate
[Yq_length] = gmdhpredict(model, ps1);
% Plot Figures for Length of the Pipe variation
figure
px1=plot(ps1(:,5),Yq_length(:,1),'-rs');
set(gca,'YGrid','off','XGrid','off')
set(gca,'FontSize',12,'LineWidth',2);
```

```
set(px1,'LineStyle','-.','LineWidth',1.5,'Color','k','MarkerSize',6)
xlabel('Length of the Pipe (ft)','FontSize',12)
ylabel('Pressure Drop (psia)', 'fontsize',12)
```

Before concluding that the final model is valid, this step must be repeated until the desired actual behavior is obtained by changing the training parameters in the *gmdhbuild.m*.

PART B
HYBRID GMDH SYSTEMS

Chapter 4

GMDH-BASED POLYNOMIAL NEURAL NETWORK ALGORITHM IN MATLAB

Elaine Inácio Bueno, Iraci Martinez Pereira and Antonio Teixeira e Silva

1. GROUP METHOD OF DATA HANDLING AND NEURAL NETWORKS APPLIED IN TEMPERATURE SENSORS MONITORING OF AN EXPERIMENTAL REACTOR

1.1. Introduction

The studies on Monitoring and Fault Diagnosis have been encouraged because of the increasing demand on quality, reliability, and safety in production processes. This interesting is justified due to complexity of some industrial processes, as chemical industries, power plants, and so on. In these processes, the interruption of the production due to some unexpected change can bring risk to the operator's security besides provoking economic losses, increasing the costs to repair some damaged equipment. Because of these two points, the economic losses and the operator's security, it becomes necessary to implement Monitoring and Diagnosis Systems [11,16,2,3].

There are a great number of variables to be continuously observed in a nuclear power plant; moreover, it is necessary to guarantee performance and safeness. During a fault the operators receive a lot of information through the instruments reading. Owing to this flood of information in a short period of time, the operators are forced to take some decisions in stress conditions, so in some cases the fault diagnosis became difficult. Many techniques using Artificial Intelligence have been used in Monitoring and Fault Diagnosis with the purpose to help the nuclear power plants operators, including the Fuzzy Logic [7], Artificial Neural Networks (ANNs) [14,15], the Group Method of Data Handling (GMDH) [12,15], Genetic Algorithms (AGs) [13,14]. The uses of these techniques are justified because it is possible to model the process without using algebraic equations [18], by using only a database which contains the plant information.

There are many concerns in applications using ANNs due to the appropriate variable input selection to them. There are hundreds of monitored variables in a control room, which indicates the plant status operation. Thus, the correct variables selection is important to choose the lesser possible variable numbers that contain the necessary information to the plant monitoring using ANN. Sometimes, it is necessary to use specialist knowledge to do the appropriate variables input selection, or perform so many tests with different combinations of previously variables until an excellent result will be reached. Because of this, it will be very interesting to have an input automatic selection method which will be used in ANN without using the specialist knowledge. The results obtained will be the use of ANN with a less number of input variables, a faster training time and to discard the use of specialist knowledge to do this work [17].

The GMDH algorithm can be used in automatic input variables selection. The GMDH is a self-organization algorithm of inductive propagation which allows the attainment of a system mathematical model from the database [4].

The purpose of this work is to combine the GMDH and ANN techniques in temperature sensors monitoring of the Ipen experimental reactor. The GMDH will be used to do the automatic variables selection and the Neural Networks to model the system. The monitoring model was implemented through many computational simulations in offline form using a database generated by a theoretical reactor model [6]. Both techniques already mentioned had been used separately [1,5] demonstrating its application viability.

2. GROUP METHOD OF DATA HANDLING — GMDH

The GMDH algorithm proposed by Ivakhnenko is an algebraic method for predicting system states, controller outputs, and actuator functions [4]. He was discouraged by the fact that many types of mathematical models require the knowledge about the system that is generally impossible to find. In fisheries modeling, for example, the modeler may require to know the migration patterns of certain species of fish or the fertility levels of certain age groups. If modelers are forced to make wild guesses at these variables, they can hardly expect to produce a model with great deal of reliability as to prediction. It is necessary to start building purely objective models: in other words, models that characterize the data directly.

In general, the available data are the input and output variables of our system represented by the input variable matrix $X = \{x_{ij}\}$, the output variable vector $Y = \{y_i\}, i = 1, 2, \ldots, n$ and $j = 1, 2, \ldots, m$, where n is the total number of observations and m is the total number of input variables:

$$
X = \begin{bmatrix} x_{11} & x_{12} & \cdots & \cdots & x_{1m} \\ x_{21} & x_{22} & \cdots & \cdots & x_{2m} \\ \cdots & \cdots & \cdots & x_{ij} & \cdots \\ \vdots & \vdots & \vdots & \vdots & \vdots \\ x_{n1} & x_{n2} & \cdots & \cdots & x_{nm} \end{bmatrix}, \qquad Y = \begin{bmatrix} y_1 \\ y_2 \\ \vdots \\ y_i \\ \vdots \\ y_n \end{bmatrix}.
$$

The details of the GMDH algorithm and the systematic procedure for predicting y as a function of $\{x_1, x_2, \ldots, x_m\}$ are given below.

The first step is to take two columns of the X matrix and construct the following regression polynomial. The procedure is repeated for all possible combinations, where p and q are the columns of

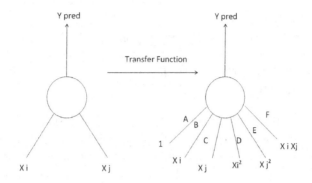

Fig. 2.1.   A node of the GMDH model structure. This node uses a second-order polynomial transfer function.

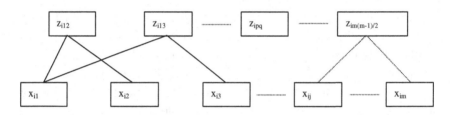

Fig. 2.2.   Computations at a layer of the GMDH algorithm.

matrix X. Figure 2.1 shows a typical computational node, and Fig. 2.2 shows computations at a layer of the GMDH algorithm.

$$y_i = a_{pq} + b_{pq}\, x_{ip} + c_{pq}\, x_{iq} + d_{pq}\, x_{ip}^2 + e_{pq}\, x_{iq}^2 + f_{pq}\, x_{ip}\, x_{iq},$$

$$\begin{cases} p = 1, 2, \ldots, m, \quad p \neq q, \\ q = 1, 2, \ldots, m, \quad q > p, \\ i = 1, 2, \ldots, n. \end{cases} \tag{2.1}$$

For each combination of independent variables (columns of X) we will find a set of coefficients of the regression, resulting in the coefficient matrix C. As we have m input variables, we will have $m(m-1)/2$ different combinations of input variables, resulting in $m(m-1)/2$ lines of the coefficient matrix C:

$$C = \{a_{pq}, b_{pq}, c_{pq}, d_{pq}, e_{pq}, f_{pq}\}, \qquad \begin{cases} p = 1, 2, \ldots, m, \quad p \neq q, \\ q = 1, 2, \ldots, m, \quad p > q. \end{cases}$$

For each set of coefficients C_{pq}, which is a line of the coefficient matrix C, we evaluate the polynomial at every n data points to calculate a new estimate z_{pq}:

$$z_{i,pq} = a_{pq} + b_{pq}\, x_{ip} + c_{pq}\, x_{iq} + d_{pq}\, x_{ip}^2 + e_{pq}\, x_{iq}^2 + f_{pq}\, x_{ip}x_{iq}. \quad (2.2)$$

We repeat this evaluation for all sets of coefficients and for the n data points, generating a new matrix Z (called new generation of variables) where each j corresponds to a pair (p, q)

$$Z = \{z_{ij}\}, \quad \begin{cases} i = 1, 2, \ldots, n, \\ j = 1, 2, \ldots, m(m-1)/2, \end{cases}$$

$$Z = \begin{bmatrix} z_{11} & z_{12} & \cdots & \cdots & z_{1,m(m-1)/2} \\ z_{21} & z_{22} & \cdots & \cdots & \cdots \\ \cdots & \cdots & \cdots & z_{ij} & \cdots \\ \vdots & \vdots & \vdots & \vdots & \vdots \\ z_{n1} & z_{n2} & \cdots & \cdots & z_{n,m(m-1)/2} \end{bmatrix}.$$

One should interpret these new variables as new improved variables that have better predictability properties than those of the original generation (X matrix).

The next step is to compare each column of Z with the dependent variable Y. That is, for each column j of Z we compute the root-mean-squared values r_j:

$$r_j^2 = \frac{\sum_{i=1}^{n} (y_i - z_{ij})^2}{\sum_{i=1}^{n} y_i^2}, \quad j = 1, 2, \ldots, m(m-1)/2. \quad (2.3)$$

We order the columns of Z according to increasing r_j and then pick those columns of Z satisfying some prescribed criterion (for example $r_j < R$, where R is a minimum residual value). One should note that the number of variables saved, say m_1, can be equal, less than, or greater than the original number m.

This new matrix Z will replace the original matrix X. From these new variables we will combine them exactly as we did before. That is, we compute all of the quadratic regression equations of y vs. these new variables (two at a time). This will give us a new set of $m_1(m_1 - 1)/2$

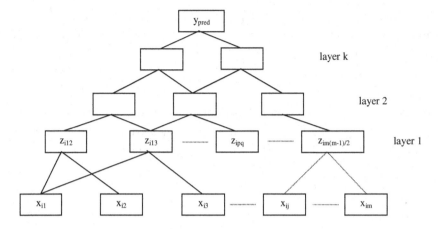

Fig. 2.3.   Self-organizing GMDH model structure with m-inputs and k-layers.

regression equations for predicting y from the new variables. We now select the best of the new estimates, generate new independent variables from the selected equations to replace the old, and combine all pairs of these new variables. We continue this process until the regression equations begin to have a poorer predictability than did the previous ones. This would happen since we test the regression equations against a new independent set of observations. In other words, the model will start to become over-specified. After stopping we pick the best of the quadratic polynomials in that generation.

Figure 2.3 illustrates that the predicted values are propagated successively to higher layers of the algorithm, improving at successive stages. At each stage of the approximation, z_{ipq} is formed from pairs of input signals (to that layer), and new values of the predicted variable are propagated pairwise to the next layer. The iteration is continued until the mean-squared error between the predicted and the measured values of the given output variable is less than a desired value. The stopping criterion for the GMDH algorithm during training is shown in Fig. 2.4.

What we have is an estimate of y as a quadratic function of two variables, which are themselves quadratic of two more variables, and so on. In other words, if we were to make the necessary algebraic substitutions, we would arrive at a very complicated polynomial of

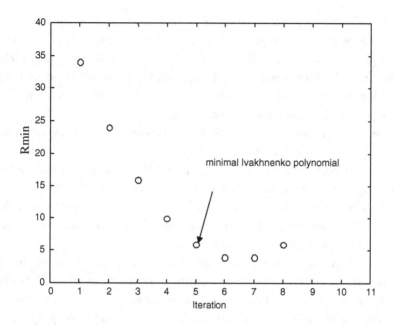

Fig. 2.4.   Stopping criterion for GMDH algorithm during training.

the form:

$$y = a + \sum_{i=1}^{m} b_i x_i + \sum_{i=1}^{m}\sum_{j=1}^{m} c_{ij} x_i x_j + \sum_{i=1}^{m}\sum_{j=1}^{m}\sum_{k=1}^{m} d_{ijk} x_i x_j x_k + \cdots .$$

(2.4)

The polynomial in Eq. (2.4) is known as the Ivakhnenko polynomial [4].

The set of polynomial functions (Eq. (2.1)) is normally sufficient in finding some of the relationships of interest. The choice of the functional forms of the terms depends on the physics of the system. For cases where the relationship is of the form of a rational function approximation, the polynomial regression equation is not adequate. Instead of increasing the order of the polynomial regression, the formulation of Eq. (2.1) can be generalized to include rational and other nonlinear functions of the input variables [6].

An algorithm was developed to select different combinations of the terms of Eq. (2.4). All possible combinations of terms are tested, such as one by one, two by two, three by three in a systematic manner.

The GMDH method consists of an algebraic method to estimate the systems' states, controllers' outputs, and actuators' functions [9,10]. The methodology can be considered as a self-organizing
algorithm of inductive propagation applied at the solution of many
complex practical problems. Moreover, it is possible to get a mathematical model of the process from observation of data samples, which
will be used in identification and pattern recognition or even though
to describe the process itself.

The network constructed using the GMDH algorithm is an adaptive, supervised learning model. The architecture of a polynomial
network is formed during the training process. The node activation
function is based on elementary polynomials of arbitrary order. This
kind of networks is shown in Fig. 2.5.

This method solves the multidimensional problem of model
improvement by the choice procedure and selection of models chosen from a set of candidate models in accordance with a supplied
criterion. The majority GMDH algorithms use reference polynomial
functions. A generic connection between inputs and outputs can be

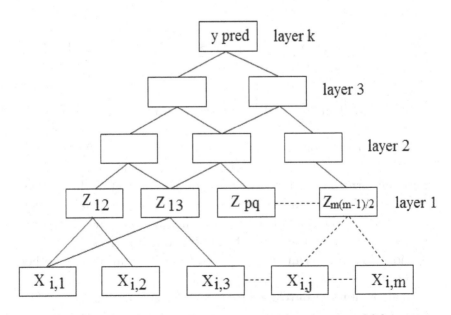

Fig. 2.5.   Self-organizing GMDH structure with m inputs and k layers.

expressed by the series functions of Volterra which is the discrete analogous of the polynomial of Kolmogorov–Gabor, as we can see in Eq. (2.5):

$$y = a + \sum_{i=1}^{m} b_i x_i + \sum_{i=1}^{m}\sum_{j=1}^{m} c_{ij} x_i x_j + \sum_{i=1}^{m}\sum_{j=1}^{m}\sum_{k=1}^{m} d_{ijk} x_i x_j x_k + \cdots,$$

(2.5)

where $\{x_1, x_2, x_3, \ldots\}$ are inputs, $\{a, b, c, \ldots\}$ are polynomials coefficients and y is the node output.

The columns of input matrix can be independent changeable; functional forms or terms of finite differences, moreover, can be used in other nonlinear reference functions. The methods still allow simultaneously finding the model structure and the output system dependence as a function of the most important inputs system values.

2.1. General Description of the GMDH Algorithm

In this section, the basic GMDH algorithm implementation will be described. The following procedure is used for a given set of n observations of the m independent variables $\{x_1, x_2, \ldots, x_m\}$ and their associated matrix of dependent values $\{y_1, y_2, \ldots, y_n\}$ [4].

- Subdivide the data into two subsets: one for training and other for testing.
- Compute the regression polynomial using Eq. (2.6), for each pair of input variables x_i and x_j and the associated output y of the training set which best fits the dependent observations y in the training set. From the observations, $m(m-1)/2$ regression polynomials will be computed from the observations

$$y = A + Bx_i + Cx_j + Dx_i^2 + Ex_j^2 + Fx_i x_j. \qquad (2.6)$$

- Evaluate the polynomial for all n observations for each regression. Store these n new observations into a new matrix Z. The other columns of Z are computed in a similar manner. The Z matrix can be interpreted as new improved variables that have better predictability than those of the original generation $x_1, x_2, \ldots, x_m$.

- Screening out the last effective variables. The algorithm computes the root mean-square value (regularity criterion — r_j) over the test data set for each column of Z matrix. The regularity criterion is given by Eq. (2.7)

$$r_j^2 = \frac{\sum_{i=1}^{nt} (y_i - z_{ij})^2}{\sum_{i=1}^{nt} y_i^2}. \qquad (2.7)$$

- Order the columns of Z according to increasing r_j, and then pick those columns of Z satisfying $r_j < R$ (R is some prescribed value chosen by the user) to replace the original columns of X.
- The above process is repeated and new generations are obtained until the method starts overfitting the data set. One can plot the smallest of the r_j's computed in each generation and compare it with the smallest r_j's of the most recent generation start to have an increasing trend.

3.   ARTIFICIAL NEURAL NETWORKS

An ANN is a massively parallel distributed processor made up of simple processing units, which has a natural propensity for storing experiential knowledge and making it available for use. The knowledge is acquired by the networks from its environment through a learning process which is basically responsible to adapt the synaptic weights to the stimulus received by the environment. The fundamental element of a neural network is a neuron, which has multiple inputs and a single output, as we can see in Fig. 3.1. It is possible to identify three basic elements in a neuron: a set of synapses, where a signal x_j at the input of synapse j connected to the neuron k is multiplied by the synaptic weight w_{kj}; an adder for summing the input signals, weighted by the respective synapses of the neuron; and an activation function for limiting the amplitude of the output of a neuron. The neuron also includes an externally applied *bias*, denoted by b_k, which has the effect of increasing or lowering the net input of the activation function, depending on whether it is positive or negative, respectively [8, 9].

In this work, it was used the Multilayer Perceptron (MLP) neural network architecture. In this kind of architecture, all neural signals

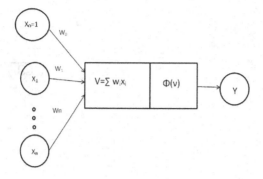

Fig. 3.1. Neuron model.

propagate in the forward direction through each network layer from the input to the output layer. Every neuron in a layer receives its inputs from the neurons in its precedent layer and sends its output to the neurons in its subsequent layer. The training is performed using an error backpropagation algorithm, which involves a set of connecting weights, which are modified on the basis of a Gradient Descent Method to minimize the difference between the desired output values and the output signals produced by the network

$$E = \frac{1}{2} \sum_{m=1}^{m} (y_{dj}(n) - y_j(n))^2, \qquad (3.1)$$

where E is the mean squared error, m the number of neurons in the output layer, y_{dj} the target output, y_j the actual output, and n the number of interactions.

4. IPEN RESEARCH REACTOR IEA-R1

The Ipen nuclear research reactor IEA-R1 is a pool type reactor using water for the cooling and moderation functions and graphite and beryllium as reflector. Its first criticality was in 16th September, 1957. Since then, its nominal operation power was 2 MW. In 1997 a modernization process was performed to increase the power to 5 MW, in a full cycle operation time of 120 hours, in order to improve its radioisotope production capacity. Figure 4.1 shows a flowchart diagram of the Ipen nuclear research reactor IEA-R1.

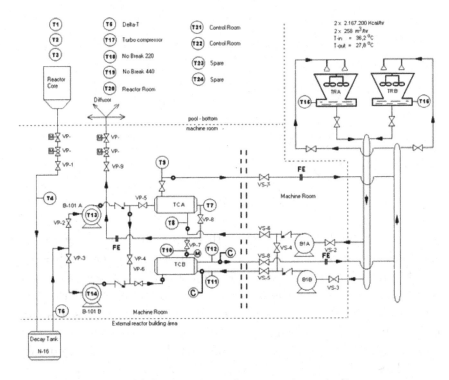

Fig. 4.1.   IEA-R1 experimental reactor schematic diagram.

4.1.   IEA-R1 Data Acquisition System

The Ipen reactor Data Acquisition System (DAS) monitors 58 operational variables, including temperature, flow, level, pressure, nuclear radiation, nuclear power, and rod position (Table 4.1). The DAS performs the storage the temporal history of all process variables monitored and does not interfere with the reactor control.

5.   IEA-R1 THEORETICAL MODEL

The IEA-R1 theoretical model was developed using Matlab toolbox GUIDE (Graphical User Interface Development Environment). The system process equations are based in the IEA-R1 mass and energy inventory balance and the physical and operational aspects, such as length, pipe diameter, flow rate, temperature and pressure drop, are taken into account.

Table 4.1.   IEA-R1 DAS variables.

Z1	Control rod position [0–1000 mm]
Z2–Z4	Safety rod position 1, 2 and 3 [0–999 mm]
N2–N4	% power (safety channel 1, 2 and 3) [%]
N5	Logarithm power (log channel) [%]
N6–N8	% power [%]
mp	Primary loop flowrate [gpm]
ms	Secondary loop flowrate [gpm]
C1–C2	Pool water conductivity [μmho]
L1	Pool water level [%]
R1M3–R14M3	Nuclear dose rate [mR/h]
T1–T3	Pool water temperature [°C]
T4–T6	Decay tank inlet and outlet temperature [°C]
T5	(T4–T3) [°C]
T7	Primary loop outlet temperature (heat exchanger A) [°C]
T8–T9	Secondary loop inlet and outlet temperature (heat exchanger A) [°C]
T10	Primary loop outlet temperature (heat exchanger B) [°C]
T11–T12	Secondary loop inlet and outlet temperature (heat exchanger B) [°C]
T13–T14	Housing pump B101-A and B102-A temperature [°C]
T15–T16	Cooling tower A and B temperature [°C]
T17	Housing turbo compressor temperature [°C]
T18–T19	NO-BREAK temperature −220 V and 440 V [°C]
T20–T24	Room temperature [°C]

The IEA-R1 theoretical model performs the following tasks:

- generation of data in different reactor operation conditions;
- setting the input variable values in an easy and fast way using a graphic interface;
- setting the noise level for the input variables;
- selecting a faulty variable from a list;
- visualization of the results in a dynamical way.

The interface layout was built to look like the reactor process flowchart. Figure 5.1 shows the program interface. The reactor core is represented immersed in the water pool. The temperatures T1, T2 and T3 are the temperatures above the core near the pool surface, at mid high and close to the core, respectively. The nuclear power

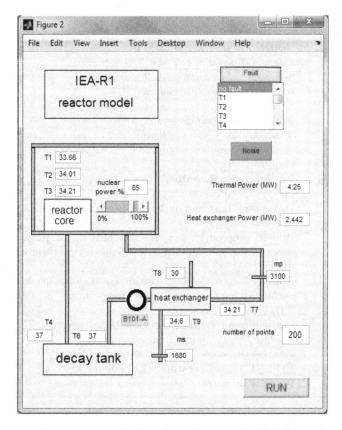

Fig. 5.1.   Program interface developed to compute the IEA-R1 nuclear reactor model variables.

is an input data and a nuclear power of 100% corresponds to the maximum operation power of 5 MW.

The reactor coolant system is represented in the interface. The primary loop water flows through the reactor fuel elements and leaves the pool through a nozzle under the core. Then, the water passes through the decay tank: T4 is the decay tank inlet temperature and T6 is the outlet temperature. B101-A is the primary loop pump. The heat exchanger is also represented. T7 is the heat exchanger outlet temperature (primary loop side). The primary loop flow is measured by mp flowmeter. The primary water loop flows out of the heat exchanger and then returns to the pool. The secondary loop is partially represented by the secondary side of the heat exchanger. The pumps in the secondary side and the cooling towers are not represented. T8 is the inlet temperature of the heat exchanger secondary side, and T9 is its outlet temperature. The secondary loop flow is measured by the ms flowmeter. The units of temperature and flow are the same used in the reactor data acquisition system that is Celsius degrees and gallons per minute.

The interface shows the reactor thermal power (MW) computed from the nuclear power and from the heat exchanger primary side heat balance.

The developed model allows the user to add a fault to a variable by selecting the faulty variable from a list of all the model variables. The first option of the list is "no fault", which means normal operation condition. This option is used to simulate a faulty instrument such as a drifting temperature sensor or a valve actuator, which is faulty.

The input variables noise level can also be set. Choosing this option a new window will be open where one can specify the noise level in % for the variables T3 (core inlet temperature), T8 (heat exchanger inlet temperature — secondary loop), primary and secondary loop flow rates. As the other temperature values are calculated from the input variables, the resulting noise of the others variables are consequences of the input variables noise. This option can be used to simulate malfunction and faults in the instrumentation channel electronics as well as noisy environments.

The user can define the time interval by defining the total number of points and the time step where the variables are to be calculated by the model for a given operational condition. In this case the program calculates for one point, refreshes the values and restarts the computation for the next point.

The user defines the desired variable values for the temperatures, flow rate or nuclear power directly in the interface editable dialog box. After entering the variable values, the noise level, the fault condition and the number of data points, pressing the button *calculate* initiates the program, which calculates the thermal power according to the mass and energy inventory balance equations.

The function *calculate* performs the following tasks:

- read and load the variables values on the screen;
- verify which variable contains fault;
- add noise to the variables T3, T8 and primary and secondary flow rate according to the defined values;
- calculate the thermal power given by the reactor core, using the T3, T4 and primary loop flow rate values;
- calculates the heat exchanger thermal power in the primary and secondary sides;
- refresh the calculated values on the screen;
- places all the values in a data matrix, where the columns are the variable values T1, T2, T3, T4, T6, T7, T8, T9, ms, mp, nuclear power and the lines corresponding to the number of data points;
- creates a plot showing the data generated.

6.   MONITORING AND FAULT DETECTION MODEL

A Temperature Sensors Monitoring System was developed using GMDH and Neural Networks. It was used the first step of the GMDH algorithm, the z *matrix*, to get an estimative of the process from observation of data samples. This z matrix can be obtained in Layer 1 (Fig. 2.3); moreover the z matrix contains a better estimative of data samples, which will be used to train the ANNs. In this way, it was not necessary to use the knowledge specialist because of the z matrix. Figure 6.1 shows the methodology implementation.

The database was obtained from the theoretical model of IEA-R1 research reactor. The data samples were obtained by varying the Nuclear Power variable (Pot) from 5% to 100%, in 5% steps, where 20 patterns were taken for every condition in the power range considered, and totalizing 400 patterns. A 0.4% noise was added to the variable T3 (coolant temperature above the reactor core) and a 1% noise was added to the variables mp (primary loop flow rate). To prevent overfitting, the method of Early Stopping was used, which suggests a database division in three subsets: training (60%), validation

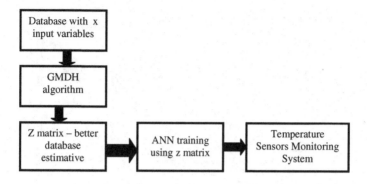

Fig. 6.1.   Methodology implementation.

(20%) and testing (20%). The training set is used to compare different models.

It was used a Multilayer Perceptron Network with three layers: one input layer, one hidden layer, and one output layer. The input layer is composed by 10 neurons and its activation function is linear; the hidden layer is composed by 10 neurons and its activation function is the hyperbolic tangents. The output layer is composed by a neuron that represents the output of the network. Figure 6.2 shows the 3-layers' connections of the Multilayer Perception Network and the neural network training results using Matlab.

It is necessary to create two main folders to develop the Temperature Sensors Monitoring: GMDH + ANNs and ANNs. Copying the files described in above the section to perform the tests described in Sec. 7.

The first step of this work is to use the GMDH algorithm to obtain a better database estimative (the Z matrix). The code (see Sec. 7) shows how it was performed.

The Z matrix is used then as input for the ANN. The number of neurons in the hidden layer is varied from 1 to 10, and the best model is chosen according to the residual value, calculated as shown in Eq. (6.1):

$$\text{residual} = (|y_{dj}(n) - y_j(n)|/y_{dj}(n)). \tag{6.1}$$

Figure 6.3 shows the monitoring results in T3 variable (coolant temperature above the reactor core) and Fig. 6.4, the results in

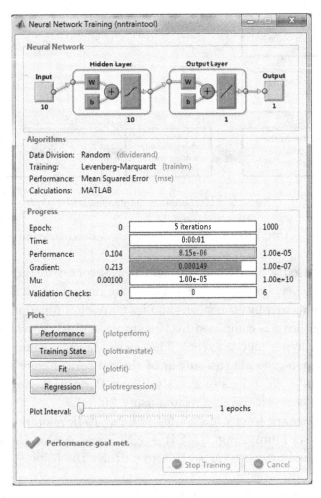

Fig. 6.2.   Connections of the multilayer perception network and the neural network training results.

T8 variable (secondary loop inlet temperature). In both figures the results were shown that obtained using only the ANN with the purpose to study the improvements obtained when the GMDH algorithm was used to obtain a better estimative of input variables, or in other words, performing an input variable selection to the ANNs.

It can be seen that in both cases, T3 and T8 monitoring, results were considerably better using GMDH algorithm as an input

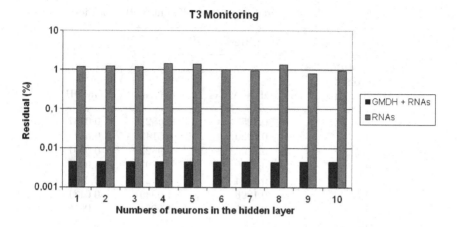

Fig. 6.3.   T3 monitoring using an input selection method.

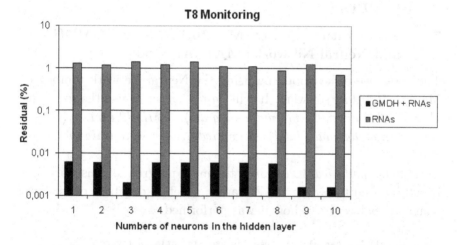

Fig. 6.4.   T8 monitoring using an input selection method.

selection variable than the others obtained using the specialist knowledge to train the ANNs.

Table 6.1 summarizes the results obtained using GMDH + ANNs and only ANNs in temperature sensors monitoring. As we can see, the residuals obtained using the hybrid methodology was better than the others using only ANNs methodology.

Table 6.1.   Mean residual (%) using different methodologies.

Temperature Sensors Monitoring	GMDH + ANNs	ANNs	GMDH
	Mean Residual (%)		
T1	0.2257	0.4821	0.0137
T2	0.1920	0.5142	0.0144
T3	0.2706	0.9822	0.0091
T4	0.2380	0.8297	0.0053
T6	0.2344	0.5924	0.0053
T7	0.1896	1.0946	0.0131
T8	0.1455	1.5001	0.0017
T9	0.2042	0.7424	0.0141

7. RESULTS

7.1. Temperature Sensor Monitoring Using GMDH and Neural Networks MATLAB Code

The codes were developed by using the Neural Network toolbox of Matlab (R2010a) software. It will be necessary to use the following files: *gmdh_iear1_2014.m* (*main program*), *GMDH2iear1.m* (*matlab function*), *dados.mat* (*database*) *and rede1.m* (*used to train the neural network*).

The file *gmdh_iear1_2014.m* is the main program of this work and it will be used to obtain the Z matrix, a better database estimative. The code below shows how it was performed.

```
>> clear all % Clear all the commands used in matlab software
>> close all % Close all the windows used in matlab software
>> load dados % Load de database
>> x = dados;

>> clear dados
```

The database x is a matrix composed by 400 lines and 11 columns. These data were generated from the IEA-R1 theoretical model (see Chapter 5). The data samples were obtained by varying the Nuclear Power variable (potnuc) from 5% to 100%, in 5% steps, where 20 patterns were taken for every condition in the power range considered,

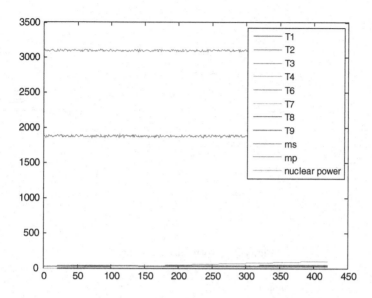

Fig. 7.1. Database used in this work.

and totalizing 400 patterns. A 0.4% noise was added to the temperature variables and a 1% noise was added to the flow rate variables. These values were typical noise reactor operational values. The next step consists to get a plot of the database (Fig. 7.1).

```
>> plot(x);
>> legend('T1','T2', 'T3', 'T4', 'T6', 'T7', 'T8', 'T9', 'ms', 'mp',
nuclear power')
```

Now, it is necessary to normalize the database. In this work, it was used the maximum and minimum values to normalize, and the normalized results are shown in Fig. 7.2.

```
>> MinVal = [20.0 20.0 20.0 20.0 20.0 20.0 10.0 20.0 0 0 0];
>> MaxVal = [45.0 45.0 45.0 45.0 45.0 45.0 40.0 45.0 2500.0 4000.0 100.0];

>> for counter = 1:size(x,1)
>>    xn(counter,:) = (x(counter,:)-MinVal)./(MaxVal-MinVal);
>> end
```

The next step is to use strings to save the results in order to avoid changing when it is necessary:

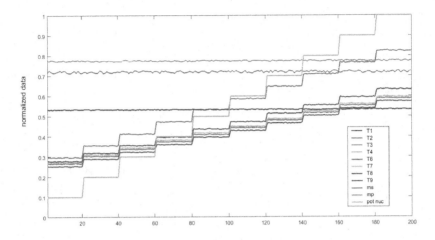

Fig. 7.2.   Normalized database.

```
>> a='save result2_GMDH_';
>> c='coef indc camada_min';
>> todos=['T1 ';...
          'T2        ';...
          'T3        ';...
          'T4        ';...
          'T6        ';...
          'T7        ';...
          'T8        ';...
          'T9        ';...
          'ms        ';...
          'mp        ';...
          'potnuc '];]
```

The commands below shows how to obtain the Z matrix:

```
>> for m = 1
>> b=todos(m,:);
>> d=[a b c];

>> y= xn(:,m); % Output: depends on the m value (see the string called
        %"todos" to know the m value
>> x=[xn(:,1:m-1)  xn(:,m+1:11)];   %input
```

When $m = 1$, the output (y) corresponds to T1 variable, $m = 2$ to T2, and so on. This routine will be performed for all variables of the string called "*todos*" (see previous codes).

Now it will be used as a function to evaluate the GMDH algorithm. This function will return the minimum residual (rmin) in layer n, where $n = 1, 2, \ldots, 10$; a better database estimative (novamatriz_z) which will be used as input to the Neural Networks, the GMDH coefficients (coefs) and the index (see the file *GMDH2iear1.m*)

```
>> for camada=1:10 % refers to layer
>> [rmin,novamatriz_z,coefs,indice]=GMDH2iear1(x,y,camada);
```

The first step is dedicated to divide the database in training and testing. The code below shows how it was performed:

```
% First step: Divide the database in training and testing

>> [np,col]=size(x);
>> ka=1;
>> for i=1:2:np
>>     for j=1:col
>>       xtrain(ka,j)=x(i,j);
>>       xtest(ka,j)=x(i+1,j);
>>     end
>>     ytrain(ka,1)=y(i);
>>     ytest(ka,1)=y(i+1);
>>     ka=ka+1;
>> end
```

After, it will be calculated the coefficients according to Eq. (2.4). It should be done by all the u and v combinations. The codes below show how to perform it:

```
% Coefficients calculation according to equation
% A+Bu+Cv+Du*u...
% It should be done by all the u and v combinations
% These combinations are counted by "cont"

cont=1;
for j=1:col
    for k=j+1:col
        for i=1:200 % Corresponding to the half of the database numbers of
points
            u(i,1)=xtrain(i,j);
            v(i,1)=xtrain(i,k);
            utest(i,1)=xtest(i,j);
            vtest(i,1)=xtest(i,k);
        end
```

```
matrizx=[ones(size(u)) u v u.^2 v.^2 u.*v]; % GMDH equation (see Farlow)
matriztest=[ones(size(utest)) utest vtest utest.^2 vtest.^2 utest.*vtest];

Alpha=0.001;
coeficientes=inv(matrizx'*matrizx+eye(size(matrizx,2),size(matrizx,2))*
Alpha)*matrizx'*ytrain;

coefs(1:6,cont)=coeficientes;
ztrain = [matrizx*coeficientes]; %calculating to training
ztest = [matriztest*coeficientes]; %calculating to testing
% It is the z obtained by the u and v combination. The matrix was written
% in this interval because of the number of matrix columns which is equal
to 10.
% Remember that the matrix size should be the same as the y matrix.

i=1;
z1(:,1)=[ztrain(i:i+9);ztest(i:i+9)];
z2(1:20,1)=z1;
z3(1:20,1)=z1;

for i=11:10:191
    z1(:,1)=[ztrain(i:i+9);ztest(i:i+9)];
    z2(1:20,1)=z1;
    z3=[z3;z2];
end

z(:,cont)=z3;

clear z3;

res=abs((ztrain-ytrain));
restest=abs(ztest-ytest);

% Save the results obtained by the variables combination (only the
% residuals)


residuo_combinacao(cont)=sqrt((sum((y-z(:,cont)).^2))/sum(y.^2));
% This is the root mean square which is called as regularity criterion
cont=cont+1;

end

end


[rmin,contmin]=min(residuo_combinacao);%minimum residual for this layer
zcamada=z(:,contmin);
[residuo_ordenado,indice]=sort(residuo_combinacao);

novamatriz_z=z(:,indice(1:10));
```

Here is the end of the function evaluated by the file *GMDH2 iear1.m*. The main program *gmdh_iear1_2014.m* will continue at this point

```
>> x=novamatriz_z;
>> rminimo(camada)=rmin;

>> coef(:,:,camada)=coefs;
>> indc(:,camada)=(indice)';
>> camada=camada+1;

>> end
```

This routine will continue until layer (*for camada 1:10*) gets the value equal to 10. The next step will save the inputs (matriz_zT1) and outputs (T1) which are better estimative of original database and obtained by the GMDH polynomial equation.

The main program will continue until the m variable gets the value 11 and all the steps previously described will be repeated.

```
>> [residuo_minimo,camada_min]= min(rminimo);
>> save result_GMDH10casoT1 coef indc camada_min
>> T1 = y;
>> save T1 T1
>> matriz_zT1 = novamatriz_z;
>> save matriz_zT1 matriz_zT1

>> end
```

7.2. Neural Networks Training

To perform network training, it is necessary to load the file *rede1.m*. It is necessary to put in the same directory the files: *rede1.m*, *T1.mat* and *matriz_zT1.mat*. The code below shows how it was performed.

```
% Backpropagation algorithm
```

The first step is to load the input and output matrix. The file matriz_zT1 contains the input matrix and T1 the output vector.

```
%%%%%%%%%%%%%%%%%%%%%%%%%%%%%%%%%%%%%%%%%%%%%%%%%%%%%%%%%%%%%%%%%%%
% Load database
%%%%%%%%%%%%%%%%%%%%%%%%%%%%%%%%%%%%%%%%%%%%%%%%%%%%%%%%%%%%%%%%%%%
clc
clear all
load matriz_zT1
```

```
p = matriz_zT1';
clear matriz_zT1
load T1
t = T1';

clear T1
```

After, it is necessary to create the neural network. It was used an MLP (Multilayer Perceptron) architecture, training the backpropagation algorithm. The input layer is composed by 10 neurons and its activation function is linear; the hidden layer is composed by 10 neurons and its activation function is the hyperbolic tangents and the output layer is composed by one neuron.

```
%%%%%%%%%%%%%%%%%%%%%%%%%%%%%%%%%%%%%%%%%%%%%%%%%%%%%%%%%%%%%%%%%%%%%%%%%%
% Number of neurons in the hidden layer
%%%%%%%%%%%%%%%%%%%%%%%%%%%%%%%%%%%%%%%%%%%%%%%%%%%%%%%%%%%%%%%%%%%%%%%%%%
S1 = 10;
%%%%%%%%%%%%%%%%%%%%%%%%%%%%%%%%%%%%%%%%%%%%%%%%%%%%%%%%%%%%%%%%%%%%%%%%%%
% Neural network
%%%%%%%%%%%%%%%%%%%%%%%%%%%%%%%%%%%%%%%%%%%%%%%%%%%%%%%%%%%%%%%%%%%%%%%%%%
net=newfit(p,t,S1);
```

Before training a neural network, it is necessary to initialize the weights and biases. The following command does this:

```
net = init(net);
```

To prevent overfitting, the method of Early Stopping was used: training (60%), validation (20%), and testing (20%).

```
net.divideParam.trainRatio = 60/100; % Adjust as desired
net.divideParam.valRatio = 20/100; % Adjust as desired
net.divideParam.testRatio = 20/100; % Adjust as desired

net.trainParam.goal = 0.00001; % Performance goal
net.trainParam.show = 4; % Epochs between displays
net.trainParam.epochs = 1000; % Maximum number of epochs to train

%%%%%%%%%%%%%%%%%%%%%%%%%%%%%%%%%%%%%%%%%%%%%%%%%%%%%%%%%%%%%%%%%%%%%%%%%%
% Training
%%%%%%%%%%%%%%%%%%%%%%%%%%%%%%%%%%%%%%%%%%%%%%%%%%%%%%%%%%%%%%%%%%%%%%%%%%
tic
[net,tr] = train(net,p,t);

%%%%%%%%%%%%%%%%%%%%%%%%%%%%%%%%%%%%%%%%%%%%%%%%%%%%%%%%%%%%%%%%%%%%%%%%%%
%Testing
%%%%%%%%%%%%%%%%%%%%%%%%%%%%%%%%%%%%%%%%%%%%%%%%%%%%%%%%%%%%%%%%%%%%%%%%%%
```

```
an = sim(net,p);
```

```
toc
```

After training and testing the neural model, it is necessary to calculate the residual value, obtained by the following equation:

```
res = (abs(t-an)./abs(t))*100;
```

This equation will give a residual vector, so it used the mean residual of this vector.

```
y =mean(res);
plot(res)
```

```
legend('residual')
```

Figures 7.3 and 7.4 show the residual obtained from Eq. (6.1), which means the comparison between actual and calculated values.

In this case, the mean residual was 0.1948%.

```
save an an % saving the testing
```

```
save net net % saving the neural network structure
```

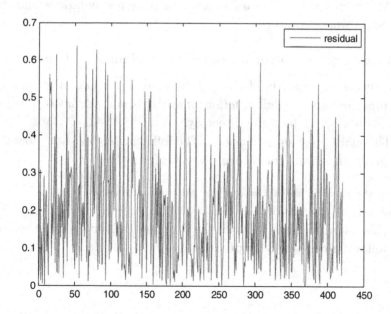

Fig. 7.3.   Residual obtained during the neural network training.

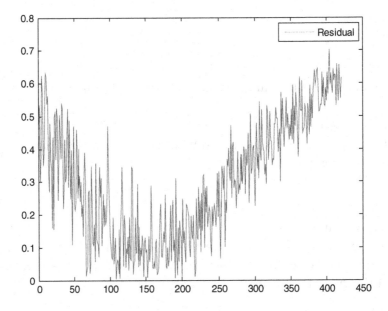

Fig. 7.4.   Residual obtained during the neural network training.

At the end, it is necessary to save the testing simulations and the neural network structure.

7.3.   Sensors Monitoring Using Only Neural Networks

It is necessary for the following files: *rede1.m* (*main program*), *def_input_output* (*matlab function*) *and dados.mat* (*database*). These files should be in the same directory.

The main program is *rede1.m*. The following codes show how the temperature sensors' monitoring was performed:

```
% Call the function which contains the database information
[input,output] = def_input_output;
```

This main program will call the function *def_input_output.m* and the following codes will be performed:

```
Clear all
clc
load dados
dados = dados;
x = dados';
```

```
clear dados
[m,n] = size(x)
```

The first step is to load the database. After, it is necessary to normalize the database in the interval [0,1] by using the maximum and minimum values:

```
%%%%%%%%%%%%%%%%%%%%%%%%%%%%%%%%%%%%%%%%%%%%%%%%%%%%%%%%%%%%%%%%%
% T1
%%%%%%%%%%%%%%%%%%%%%%%%%%%%%%%%%%%%%%%%%%%%%%%%%%%%%%%%%%%%%%%%%
m = 1;
    for n = 1:n
MinVal = [20.0];
MaxVal = [45.0];

for counter = 1:size(x,1)
    xn(counter,: ) = (x(counter,: )-MinVal)./(MaxVal-MinVal);
end

        T1(m,n) = xn(m,n);
end


%%%%%%%%%%%%%%%%%%%%%%%%%%%%%%%%%%%%%%%%%%%%%%%%%%%%%%%%%%%%%%%%%%%
% T2
%%%%%%%%%%%%%%%%%%%%%%%%%%%%%%%%%%%%%%%%%%%%%%%%%%%%%%%%%%%%%%%%%%%
m = 2;
    for n = 1:n
MinVal = [20.0];
MaxVal = [45.0];

for counter = 1:size(x,1)
    xn(counter,: ) = (x(counter,: )-MinVal)./(MaxVal-MinVal);
end
    T2(m,n) = xn(m,n);
    end
T2(1,: )=[];
%%%%%%%%%%%%%%%%%%%%%%%%%%%%%%%%%%%%%%%%%%%%%%%%%%%%%%%%%%%%%%%%%%%
% T3
%%%%%%%%%%%%%%%%%%%%%%%%%%%%%%%%%%%%%%%%%%%%%%%%%%%%%%%%%%%%%%%%%%%
m = 3;
    for n = 1:n
MinVal = [20.0];
MaxVal = [45.0];
for counter = 1:size(x,1)
    xn(counter,: ) = (x(counter,: )-MinVal)./(MaxVal-MinVal);
end
        T3(m,n) = xn(m,n);
    end
T3(1:2,: )=[];
%%%%%%%%%%%%%%%%%%%%%%%%%%%%%%%%%%%%%%%%%%%%%%%%%%%%%%%%%%%%%%%%%%%
```

```
% T4
%%%%%%%%%%%%%%%%%%%%%%%%%%%%%%%%%%%%%%%%%%%%%%%%%%%%%%%%%%%%%%%%%%%%%
m =4;
    for n = 1:n
MinVal = [20.0];
MaxVal = [45.0];

for counter = 1:size(x,1)
    xn(counter,: ) = (x(counter,: )-MinVal)./(MaxVal-MinVal);
end
        T4(m,n) = xn(m,n);
    end
    T4(1:3,: )=[];
%%%%%%%%%%%%%%%%%%%%%%%%%%%%%%%%%%%%%%%%%%%%%%%%%%%%%%%%%%%%%%%%%%%%%
% T6
%%%%%%%%%%%%%%%%%%%%%%%%%%%%%%%%%%%%%%%%%%%%%%%%%%%%%%%%%%%%%%%%%%%%%
m =5;
    for n = 1:n
MinVal = [20.0];
MaxVal = [45.0];
for counter = 1:size(x,1)
    xn(counter,: ) = (x(counter,: )-MinVal)./(MaxVal-MinVal);
end
            T6(m,n) = xn(m,n);
    end
T6(1:4,: )=[];
%%%%%%%%%%%%%%%%%%%%%%%%%%%%%%%%%%%%%%%%%%%%%%%%%%%%%%%%%%%%%%%%%%%%%
% T7
%%%%%%%%%%%%%%%%%%%%%%%%%%%%%%%%%%%%%%%%%%%%%%%%%%%%%%%%%%%%%%%%%%%%%
m =6;
    for n = 1:n
        MinVal = [20.0];
MaxVal = [45.0];

for counter = 1:size(x,1)
    xn(counter,: ) = (x(counter,: )-MinVal)./(MaxVal-MinVal);
end
            T7(m,n) = xn(m,n);
end
T7(1:5,: )=[];
%%%%%%%%%%%%%%%%%%%%%%%%%%%%%%%%%%%%%%%%%%%%%%%%%%%%%%%%%%%%%%%%%%%%%
% T8
%%%%%%%%%%%%%%%%%%%%%%%%%%%%%%%%%%%%%%%%%%%%%%%%%%%%%%%%%%%%%%%%%%%%%
m =7;
    for n = 1:n
MinVal = [20.0];
MaxVal = [45.0];

for counter = 1:size(x,1)
    xn(counter,: ) = (x(counter,: )-MinVal)./(MaxVal-MinVal);
```

```
end
        T8(m,n) = xn(m,n);
    end
T8(1:6,: )=[];
%%%%%%%%%%%%%%%%%%%%%%%%%%%%%%%%%%%%%%%%%%%%%%%%%%%%%%%%%%%%%%%%
% T9
%%%%%%%%%%%%%%%%%%%%%%%%%%%%%%%%%%%%%%%%%%%%%%%%%%%%%%%%%%%%%%%%
m =8;
    for n = 1:n
        MinVal = [20.0];
MaxVal = [45.0];

for counter = 1:size(x,1)
    xn(counter,: ) = (x(counter,: )-MinVal)./(MaxVal-MinVal);
end
        T9(m,n) = xn(m,n);
    end
T9(1:7,: )=[];
%%%%%%%%%%%%%%%%%%%%%%%%%%%%%%%%%%%%%%%%%%%%%%%%%%%%%%%%%%%%%%%%
% ms
%%%%%%%%%%%%%%%%%%%%%%%%%%%%%%%%%%%%%%%%%%%%%%%%%%%%%%%%%%%%%%%%
m = 9;
for n = 1:n
MinVal = [0];
MaxVal = [2500.0];

for counter = 1:size(x,1)
    xn(counter,: ) = (x(counter,: )-MinVal)./(MaxVal-MinVal);
end
        P(m,n) = xn(m,n);
end
ms(1:8,: ) = [];
%%%%%%%%%%%%%%%%%%%%%%%%%%%%%%%%%%%%%%%%%%%%%%%%%%%%%%%%%%%%%%%%
% mp
%%%%%%%%%%%%%%%%%%%%%%%%%%%%%%%%%%%%%%%%%%%%%%%%%%%%%%%%%%%%%%%%
m = 10;
for n = 1:n
    MinVal = [0];
MaxVal = [4000.0];

for counter = 1:size(x,1)
    xn(counter,: ) = (x(counter,: )-MinVal)./(MaxVal-MinVal);
end
        P(m,n) = xn(m,n);
end
P(1:9,: ) = [];
%%%%%%%%%%%%%%%%%%%%%%%%%%%%%%%%%%%%%%%%%%%%%%%%%%%%%%%%%%%%%%%%
% Power
%%%%%%%%%%%%%%%%%%%%%%%%%%%%%%%%%%%%%%%%%%%%%%%%%%%%%%%%%%%%%%%%
m = 11;
```

```
for n = 1:n
MinVal = [0];
MaxVal = [100.0];

for counter = 1:size(x,1)
    xn(counter,:) = (x(counter,: )-MinVal)./(MaxVal-MinVal);
end
    Pot(m,n) = xn(m,n);
end
Pot(1:10,: ) = [];
%%%%%%%%%%%%%%%%%%%%%%%%%%%%%%%%%%%%%%%%%%%%%%%%%%%%%%%%%%%%%%%%%%%%%%%%
clear x m n
```

Now, it is necessary to divide the database into input matrix and output vector.

```
%%%%%%%%%%%%%%%%%%%%%%%%%%%%%%%%%%%%%%%%%%%%%%%%%%%%%%%%%%%%%%%%%%%%%%%%
% Input
%%%%%%%%%%%%%%%%%%%%%%%%%%%%%%%%%%%%%%%%%%%%%%%%%%%%%%%%%%%%%%%%%%%%%%%%
input = [T2;T3;T4;T6;T7;T8;T9;ms;mp;Pot];
clear T2 T3 T4 T6 T7 T8 T9 ms mp Pot
save input input
%%%%%%%%%%%%%%%%%%%%%%%%%%%%%%%%%%%%%%%%%%%%%%%%%%%%%%%%%%%%%%%%%%%%%%%%
% Output
%%%%%%%%%%%%%%%%%%%%%%%%%%%%%%%%%%%%%%%%%%%%%%%%%%%%%%%%%%%%%%%%%%%%%%%%
output = [T1];
clear T1
save output output
```

The main program *rede1.m* will continue from the code below:

```
% Call the function which contains the database information
[input,output] = def_input_output;
%%%%%%%%%%%%%%%%%%%%%%%%%%%%%%%%%%%%%%%%%%%%%%%%%%%%%%%%%%%%%%%%%%%%%%%%
% Input and output definition
%%%%%%%%%%%%%%%%%%%%%%%%%%%%%%%%%%%%%%%%%%%%%%%%%%%%%%%%%%%%%%%%%%%%%%%%
p = input;
clear input
t = output;
clear output
%%%%%%%%%%%%%%%%%%%%%%%%%%%%%%%%%%%%%%%%%%%%%%%%%%%%%%%%%%%%%%%%%%%%%%%%
% Number of neurons in the hidden layer
%%%%%%%%%%%%%%%%%%%%%%%%%%%%%%%%%%%%%%%%%%%%%%%%%%%%%%%%%%%%%%%%%%%%%%%%
S1 = 10;
%%%%%%%%%%%%%%%%%%%%%%%%%%%%%%%%%%%%%%%%%%%%%%%%%%%%%%%%%%%%%%%%%%%%%%%%
% Neural network architecture
%%%%%%%%%%%%%%%%%%%%%%%%%%%%%%%%%%%%%%%%%%%%%%%%%%%%%%%%%%%%%%%%%%%%%%%%
net=newfit(p,t,S1);
net = init(net);
```

```
net.divideParam.trainRatio = 60/100; % Adjust as desired
net.divideParam.valRatio = 20/100; % Adjust as desired
net.divideParam.testRatio = 20/100; % Adjust as desired


net.trainParam.goal = 0.00001; % Performance goal
net.trainParam.show = 4; % Epochs between displays
net.trainParam.epochs = 1000; % Maximum number of epochs to train


%%%%%%%%%%%%%%%%%%%%%%%%%%%%%%%%%%%%%%%%%%%%%%%%%%%%%%%%%%%%%%%%%%%%%%%%
% Training
%%%%%%%%%%%%%%%%%%%%%%%%%%%%%%%%%%%%%%%%%%%%%%%%%%%%%%%%%%%%%%%%%%%%%%%%
tic
[net,tr] = train(net,p,t);
%%%%%%%%%%%%%%%%%%%%%%%%%%%%%%%%%%%%%%%%%%%%%%%%%%%%%%%%%%%%%%%%%%%%%%%%
% Testing
%%%%%%%%%%%%%%%%%%%%%%%%%%%%%%%%%%%%%%%%%%%%%%%%%%%%%%%%%%%%%%%%%%%%%%%%

an = sim(net,p);
toc

res = (abs(t-an)./abs(t))*100;
y = mean(res)

plot(res)
legend('Residual')
```

The mean residual is 0.3045%.

```
save an an
save net net
```

8. CONCLUSION AND FUTURE WORK

It was presented a methodology using the GMDH algorithm and ANN. The methodology was applied to sensor monitoring of the IEAR-1 research reactor. The GMDH algorithm was used during the information preprocessing in two different ways. The GMDH algorithm was used to calculate a better estimative for the original database. This estimative (Z matrix) is then used as input variable for a ANN to calculate the monitoring variable. The result obtained using the GMDH as an input selection method to the ANN was better than that obtained using only ANN and the specialist knowledge.

REFERENCES

[1] Bueno, E. I. (2006) Utilização de Redes Neurais Artificiais na Monitoração e Detecção de Falhas em Sensores do reator IEA-R1, Dissertação (Mestrado), Universidade de São Paulo — IPEN, São Paulo, pp. 98.

[2] Clark, R. N. (1978) Instrument fault detection, *IEEE Trans. Aerospace Electron. Syst.*, **14**, 456–465.

[3] Echendu, J. E. A. & Zhu, H. (1994) Detecting changes in the condition of process instruments, *IEEE Trans. Instrum. Meas.*, **43**, No. 2, 355–358.

[4] Farlow, S. J. (1984) *Self-Organizing Methods in Modeling: GMDH-Type Algorithms*, Marcel Dekker, New York.

[5] Gonçalves, I. M. P. (2006) Monitoração e diagnóstico para detecção de falhas de sensores utilizando a metodologia GMDH, Tese (Doutorado), Universidade de São Paulo — IPEN, São Paulo.

[6] Gonçalves, I. M. P. & Ting, D. K. S. (2005) A theoretical model for the IPEN research reactor IEA-R1, In: *INAC 2005 — Int. Nuclear Atlantic Conf. Proc.* (Cdroom).

[7] Goode, P. V. (1995) Using a neural/fuzzy system to extract heuristic knowledge of incipient faults in induction motors: Part I — methodology, *IEEE Trans. Indust. Electron.*, **42**, No. 2, 131–138.

[8] Haykin, S. (1999) *Neural Networks — A Comprehensive Foundation*, Prentice-Hall, USA.

[9] Ivakhnenko, A. G. (1969) *Self-Teaching Systems of Recognition and Automatic Control*, Tekhnika, Moscow.

[10] Ivakhnenko A. G. (1971) Polynomial theory of complex systems, *IEEE Transactions on Systems, Man, and Cybernetics* **SMC-1**, No. 4, 364–378.

[11] Maki, Y. & Loparo, K. A. (1997) A neural network approach to fault detection and diagnosis in industrial processes, *IEEE Trans. Control Syst. Technol.*, **5**, No. 6, 529–541.

[12] Puig, V. et al. (2007) A GMDH neural network-based approach to passive robust fault detection using a constraint satisfaction backward test, *Eng. Appl. Artif. Intell.*, **20**, 886–897.

[13] Raymer, M. L. et al. (2000) Dimensionality reduction using genetic algorithms, *IEEE Trans. Evolutionary Computation*, **4**, No. 2, 164–171.

[14] Rovithakis, G. A., Maniadakis, M. & Zervakis, M. (2004) A hybrid neural network/genetic algorithm approach to optimizing feature extraction for signal validation, *IEEE Trans. Syst. Man, Cybernet.*, **34**, No. 1, 695–703.

[15] Samanta, B. (2004) Gear fault detection using artificial neural networks and support vector machines with genetic algorithms, *Mech. Syst. Signal Process.*, **18**, No. 3, 625–644.

[16] Sydenham, P. H. & Thorn, R. (1993) Strategies for sensor performance assessment, In: *IEEE Instrumentation and Measurement Technology Conf. Record*, pp. 353–358.

[17] Uhrig, R. E. & Guo, Z. (1992) Using genetic algorithms to select inputs for neural networks, *Int. Workshop on Combinations of Genetic Algorithms and Neural Networks*, pp. 223–234.

[18] Zupan, J., Novic, M. & Ruisanchez, I. (1997) Kohonen and counterpropagation artificial neural networks in analytical chemistry, *Chemometrics Intell. Laboratory Syst.*, **38**, No. 1, 1–23.

Chapter 5

DESIGNING GMDH MODEL USING MODIFIED LEVENBERG MARQUARDT TECHNIQUE IN MATLAB

Maryam Pournasir Roudbaneh

ABSTRACT

System identification techniques are applied in order to model and predict the behaviors of unknown and very complex systems based on given input–output data. A major difficulty in modeling complex systems is the problem of the researcher introducing his or her own prejudices into the model. Ivakhnenko [15] introduced a method, based in part on the Rosenblatt Perceptron [40], that allows the researcher to build models of complex systems without making assumptions about the internal workings.

Group Method of Data Handling (GMDH) algorithm is self-organizing approach that can overcome some practical limitations in Artificial Neural Networks (ANN). Ivakhnenko's GMDH algorithm constructs a self-organizing model (an extremely high-order polynomial in the input variables) that can be used to solve prediction, identification, control synthesis, and other system problems.

GMDH was used to circumvent the difficulty of knowing a priori knowledge of mathematical model of the process being considered. In other words, GMDH can be used to model complex systems without having specific knowledge of the systems. In recent years, the use of such self-organizing network leads to successful application of the GMDH-type algorithm in broad range areas in engineering, science, and management.

The causality relationship between the inputs and the output of a multiple inputs single output self-organizing network can be represented by an infinite Volterra–Kolmogorov–Gabor (VKG) polynomial. The multilayer GMDH network algorithm constructs hierarchical cascades of bivariate activation polynomials in the nodes, and variables in the leaves. Each layer consists of nodes generated to take a specific pair of the combination of inputs as its source. Each node produces a set of coefficients that is estimated using the set of training data. Calculating the coefficients in GMDH can be one of the most difficult and time consuming parts of the algorithm. However, appropriate topology and coefficients have a great impact on their models' performances. GMDH uses a statistical method called the "linear least squares regression" to calculate the values for the coefficients. The standard Levenberg–Marquardt (LM) method or damped least square is a hybrid and self-adaptive approach that is based on Gradient Descent Method (GD) and Gauss–Newton (GN) methods to solve the nonlinear least square curve fitting optimization.

Recently, LM algorithms turned out to be a valuable means for ensuring fast convergence to a solution of the nonlinear system. This algorithm presented here share basic advantages of existing LM methods like fast convergence and the promising practical robustness. The LM iterative algorithm requires initial values to start the fitting procedure. Good parameter initialization results in fast and reliable model/data convergence. This research is developed in the context of a main work which proposes the use of singular value decomposition (SVD) to initialize the parameters in LM method. Approximately 40% computational time is decreased by using the proposed modified LM method.

Evolutionary methods such as genetic algorithms (GA) have been widely used in different aspects of design in neural networks because of their unique capabilities of finding a global optimum in highly multi-modal and/or nondifferentiable search space. This combined application is accomplished by using GA for optimal selection of architecture at the same time as the associated coefficients of each candidate solution in the evolving population are determined using modified LM in an optimal sense. In this work, however, simultaneous design of both architecture and coefficients are performed using GA and modified LM technique, respectively.

In order to illustrate the benefits of GMDH-LM algorithm, it has been applied in an inventory control problem in a Malaysian manufacturing company. The model uses time in the system, work in process, throughput, utilization, stock out, waiting time of the kanbans and predicts the average waiting time of the production ordering. A comparison between basic GMDH algorithm and GMDH-LM algorithm is made and the results show that the accuracy of results modeled by this GMDH-LM is extremely high with a reasonable reduction in processing time.

1. INTRODUCTION

The field of Artificial Neural Network (ANN) and its use in real world's problems experienced an ever-increasing interest over the past few decades. The areas it has been beneficial to include economics, medicine, meteorology, manufacturing, chemistry, financial market, etc. [44]. ANN aims at examining the inputs and outputs provided while training as well as investigating the relationship between the factors. Then, using such information, the neural network is employed to predict the output for a range of almost similar inputs. As they are not restricted to discover the linear relationships, they have gradually been replaced by conventional methods and statistics-oriented approaches [43].

Using ANN for the analysis of data contains several advantages. Firstly, when neural networks are trained, their performances do not considerably decrease when provided with new data that has not been included in the initial learning stage. Secondly, they can manage poor quality data very well. Such problems with data might take place due to measurement errors or other reasons. Thirdly, unlike traditional statistical techniques, the data presented to a neural network do not require strong assumptions. Finally, since the neural network makes decisions on its own, it does not require the user to determine the significance of the variables. Most of the current programs employed to develop artificial neural networks do not need to determine the weights for this purpose. Rather, they train the networks to respond with the ideal output for a particular input, and then record the weights [2].

The "Group Method of Data Handling" (GMDH) adopts a self-organizing attitude by gradually sorting complex models and assessing these models by external criteria on a separate part of the data set. The GMDH was designed for prediction, approximation and identification of multivariate system processes in complex system modeling. It also covers decision support after "what-if" scenarios, diagnostics, and pattern recognition of data samples [15]. More specifically, the GMDH method helps to solve the problem of modeling multi-input data to solo output. General connection between inputs and output variables can be expressed by a complicated discrete form of the Volterra functional series.

Although GMDH offers a systematic procedure of system modeling and prediction, it also suffers from a number of limitations. One hurdle is neurons-weights being calculated by a quadratic polynomial. This helps one to find the exact relationship between neurons in the preceding layer and even hence the most complicated networks will be easily understandable. In addition, the algorithm should create a balance between complexity and accuracy. After the advent of GMDH, it has been developed many different aspects to evaluate coefficients to lessen the problems resulting from the standard GMDH algorithm [9, 10, 31, 37, 39].

Using Levenberg–Marquardt (LM) methods, the researcher requires solving the inverse problem when calculating coefficients for GMDH-LM technique have some restrictions when calculating the change rate for the parameters. Furthermore, an inappropriate selection of the parameters may result in an unfit convergence or a case of divergence. Affective parameters in convergence are variables that might be overlooked by some optimization researchers, while they are usually extremely important for convergence of the models.

In this study, an improved LM method is designed to generate the network rapidly, with least propagation delay, and involving a lot of circuit space, memory, or other hardware resources. Moreover, a hybrid modeling based on LM is introduced with GMDH in comparison with other traditional methods. This algorithm does not necessitate any background knowledge regarding the final network structure.

2. REVIEWED LITERATURE

The initial idea of GMDH belongs to Shankar in 1972. Later on, a number of Japanese and Polish scientists published different variants of GMDH; they concluded that this algorithm is the best method for solving the AI problems for the purpose of "identification", "short-term and long-term forecasting of random processes" and "pattern recognition in complex systems".

2.1. Rationale for Hybrid Systems

In order to elaborate more on justification for "hybridization of intelligent systems", the combined and integrated approaches are essential if the remaining critical issues (imprecision, uncertainty and vagueness, high-dimensionality) in artificial intelligence are to be resolved.

As discussed earlier, the standard GMDH approach has some issues to be resolved. However, in doing so, many research studies attempted to hybridize GMDH with some developing optimization strategies. For instance, in a study by Iba *et al.* [10]; an attempt was made to present the GP-GMDH (Genetic Programming-GMDH) algorithm, it demonstrated that the algorithm functions improved comparing to the conventional GMDH algorithm. Recently, there have been a number of developments in some of the GMDH aspects concerning the area of Genetic Algorithms (GA). Robinson [39] clearly stated that the shortcomings of GMDH are its unchanging arrangement and character which is totally deterministic and looking for the ideal model. However, the mentioned problems and limitations were dealt with by employing multi-objective genetic algorithm (MOGA) to look for the room for potential polynomials to optimize the performance of GMDH. A full fourth order polynomial and a GA are used instead of the Ivakhnenko polynomial to discover the optimal fractional account. In addition, due to the fact that this improvement simply locates the most favorable terms in the fractional accounts and does not modify its arrangement, it has been classified as Term Optimization of GMDH (TOGMDH).

The Structure Optimization of GMDH (SOGMDH) was also recommended by Robinson. The proposed structure optimizes the model's condition and the organization of the ultimate copy together. In that algorithm, a wide stochastic search is done over a large range of possible models by MOGA optimization algorithm. SOGMDH utilizes the form of partial descriptions in TOGMDH but permits the model's development in more than one layer by letting a couple of dissimilar fractional accounts in the next stage to be combined together. Both algorithms have gone thorough examination in both regression and classification tasks where SOGMDH has demonstrated an outstanding increase in accuracy. Nikolaev and Iba [30] improved the GMDH algorithm through least squares fitting during the growing phase; they also optimized the structure of GMDH with neurofuzzy technique. The results show that their version of GMDH (phGMDH) on time series modeling tasks outperforms the "original GMDH", "Neurofuzzy GMDH" and "traditional MLP neural networks". The phGMDH of Nikolaev and Iba has improved the space performance of the "higher order network" through a "backpropagation algorithm" for further gradient descent learning of the weights. A hybrid of genetic algorithm (GA) and GMDH were recommended by Nariman-Zadeh et al. [28] in which it outperforms conventional GMDH approach. It is used for optimal design of generalized GMDH type neural networks models, "combined application of GMDH neural network modeling of numerical input–output data and subsequent non-dominated Pareto optimization process of the obtained models is very promising in discovering useful and interesting design relationships".

Kim and Park [17], to construct a predictive model, a polynomial neural network (PNN) is applied and prediction performance of the PNN was optimized according to the number of input variables and types of polynomials to each node. The performances of predicted model were compared to statistical regression models and the "adaptive network fuzzy inference system" (ANFIS). Results show that, the PNN is efficient and much more accurate from the viewpoint of prediction and approximation strengths. Onwubolu *et al.* [34] presented an enhanced GMDH (e-GMDH) to predict modeling for determining "tool-wear in end milling" operation. They developed predictive model(s) in the form of second-order equations based on the input data and coefficients. Moreover, "particle swarm optimization (PSO) technique" was applied to establish the optimal parameters. The results demonstrated that e-GMDH outperforms polynomial neural network (PNN) and it is more flexible than the basic GMDH, which tends to produce nonlinear predictor even for simple problems.

Another hybrid of differential evolution (DE) and GMDH was proposed by Onwubolu [32] that clearly revealed that this structure outperforms the general GMDH approach. In a more recent study Onwubolu *et al.* [34] offered a hybrid of particle swarm optimization (PSO) and GMDH, they demonstrated that the structure works significantly well compared with the conventional GMDH. A number of methods exist for parametric optimization but they fail to deal with complex situations where singularity arises. The training results show that the "gradient descent algorithm" is generally very slow because it requires small learning rates for stable learning. The conjugate gradient algorithms have fast convergence performances, but function performances are not satisfactory.

2.2. Literature of Levenberg–Marquardt

Levenberg–Marquardt (LM) algorithm is the most appropriate for function approximation problems where the network has up to several hundred weights and the approximation must be precise. Unlike this study, previous researches never suggested improving GMDH through LM technique to modify the GMDH algorithm. The present project research area concerns that type of task.

There are a lot of literatures on improving LM technique by the initial guess factor [36, 41, 45, 46]. Xiang *et al.* [46] developed a direct inversion algorithm for "optimal estimation"; the new algorithm differs from existing one since there is no need for an initial guess for initialization and the estimated parameters are direct solutions from a set of equations. Later on, this group compares the proposed new algorithm with the "standard LM ridge regression algorithm" in terms of adequacy of the models. At last, they managed to find a way to avoid convergence and also to further improve this direct inverse algorithm using gradient algorithm [46].

In 2004, Walker, Varadan and Fushman presented a "novel computer program" named ROTDIF with the aim of "computational efficiency and accuracy"; they instrumented a "six-dimensional optimization search" using an efficient LM algorithm combined with "Monte Carlo generation" of initial guesses. The improvement of this method led to high sensitivity, and robustness, as well as significant time saving advantage compared to all previous approaches in this study area [45].

In addition, Sedighi *et al.* [41] worked on an "inverse problem of optimization" approach based on LM to identify the parameters of two different material constitutive models. He observed that the parameters have relatively low dependency on the initial guess in numerical algorithm. The results indicated the stability of the algorithm while data obtained with Guassian noise. The proposed algorithm was capable of increasing the quality of identification and lowering the cost of calculation by at least 40% with a result error of less than 4% (with input data error of 5%), compared with the original algorithm (using the least squares method).

Finally, Parente *et al.* [36] developed a new Gaussian modeling based on "automatic initial parameter estimation" and examined its performance with the existing technique in modeling of absorption band. In their study, the "nonlinear curve fitting techniques" were investigated by the LM algorithm, and the Total Inversion (TI) algorithm in terms of "accuracy" and "sensitivity analysis of the fitting results with small variations of the initial parameter estimates". Their final results indicated the importance of a "correctly modeled continuum" in the "accuracy and stability" of curve fitting for Gaussian bands to perform on a "low-noise spectra". They stressed that LM is more stable under variations of its parameters, while TI takes into account the uncertainties of the parameters, making it desirable in situations where such uncertainties are known or can be estimated [36].

3. GROUP METHOD OF DATA HANDLING MODEL USING MODIFIED LEVENBERG–MARQUARDT TECHNIQUE FOR INVENTORY SYSTEMS

The proposed algorithm is a combination of the best procedures from these variations on the GMDH method in order to generate the most exact network possible. In addition to having a unique combination of network organization and training techniques, that the new algorithm also supplies a distinctive method of computing coefficients in each layer. The training results show that the some optimization algorithms are not commonly fast because small learning rates and some others algorithms have fast convergence performance, but function performances are not satisfactory. The application of the Levenberg–Marquardt (LM) algorithm is seemingly the quickest possible technique for training of networks. The LM algorithm is best appropriate for function approximation problem where the network has up to several hundred weights and the approximation must be very precise.

Recently, LM algorithm turned out to be a valuable means for ensuring fast convergence to a solution of the nonlinear system if the classical nonsingularity assumption is replaced by a weaker error bound condition so that problems with nonisolated solutions can be treated successfully. This algorithm is a conventional method for solving nonlinear and least squares problems that come from various applications in engineering, physics, and economics. The new algorithms developed are based on the LM algorithm and the algorithms in this area are much less developed than say Gradient's method. The algorithm can be regarded as a regularized LM technique.

This study aims at the design and analysis of new and modified Levenberg–Marquardt type algorithm for solving nonlinear equations in estimation of GMDH algorithm' coefficients. These algorithms share basic advantages of existing LM methods like fast convergence under weak conditions and the promising practical robustness.

The work done for this study is based on the study completed by Kumar titled "Levenberg–Marquardt Algorithms for Nonlinear Equations, Multi-objective Optimization, and Complementarily

Problems" [18] and the research paper by Naveen titled "Modified Levenberg–Marquardt Algorithm for Inverse Problems" [29]. This modified algorithm could be used for a broad range of applications. This research has modified the Levenberg–Marquardt algorithm to use for a specific application in the algorithm of "Group Method of Data Handling". The remaining sections of this chapter will briefly discuss a modified method for use in basic GMDH algorithm.

3.1. The Basic GMDH Algorithm

For many years, in the area of GMDH theory and its applications, numerous papers and books have been published. As it was discussed earlier, the GMDH is referred to as a transmission of the "inductive self-organizing methods" and is applicable for more complex, and practical problems. The main objective of the algorithm is to find a "mathematical model" for the object, specifically the problem identification and pattern recognition; and also, is to "describe the problem of process forecasting". The GMDH solves any "multidimensional model optimization" problem (for example, consequent testing of models, chosen from a set of models-candidates in accordance with the given criterion). This algorithm mostly uses the "polynomial reference functions".

Madala and Ivakhnenko [23] describe the GMDH algorithm as a set of neurons in each layer, connected through a quadratic polynomial that generates new neurons in the next layer. As it is shown in Eq. (3.1), Ivakhnenko employed the "Kolmorovo–Gaborov sentence" to express the input–output relationships. In his theory, Ivakhnenko claims that every function can be outlined by an "infinite Volterra–Kolmogorov–Gabor (VKG) polynomial" of the form. In addition, Volterra functional series express the general connection between input and output variables, and discrete analogue of what is called "Kolmogorov–Gabor polynomial" [6, 27]:

$$
y_n = a_0 + \sum_{i=1}^{M} a_i x_i + \sum_{i=1}^{M}\sum_{j=1}^{M} a_{ij} x_i x_j + \sum_{i=1}^{M}\sum_{j=1}^{M}\sum_{k=1}^{M} a_{ijk} x_i x_j x_k \ldots,
$$
(3.1)

where $X(x_1, x_2, \ldots, x_M)$ is the vector of input variables, $A(a_1, a_2, \ldots, a_M)$ is the vector of coefficients or weights and M is the number of input variables [14]. The input vector X components can be any functional forms, independent variables or finite difference terms. Besides, other nonlinear reference functions (i.e. harmonic, probabilistic, difference, logistic) can be used, as well. The method allows finding simultaneously the structure of the model and the relationship between the output and the values of the most significant inputs of the modeled system. When M increases, given that there are high orders of the resulting polynomial, the equation may lead to harsh calculations. Therefore, Ivakhnenko proposed the solution by the process of breaking down the polynomials, so that, such complex function is transformed to the "VKG series" and consists of several "partial polynomials", with smaller functions of maximum 2 or 3 variables commonly appearing in the form of a nonlinear second-order polynomial function of 2 or maximum 3 inputs [14]. The number of combinations generated before learning each layer is given by Eq. (3.2)).

$$^m C_r = \frac{m!}{r!(m-r)!},\qquad(3.2)$$

where m is the number of input variables and r is the number of points for each node. Equation (3.3) formulates all combinations of two independent variables that are employed in the new algorithm. This is just one of the many possible equations that can be selected for implementing the GMDH algorithm. For even more complex relationships, the equations can be expanded to include more than two inputs in a function

$$G(x_i, x_j) = a_5 + a_0 x_i + a_1 x_j + a_2 x_i x_j + a_3 x_i^2 + a_4 x_j^2. \qquad(3.3)$$

In Eq. (3.3), $G(x_i, x_j)$, x_i and x_j indicate the output of multilayered composition and inputs variables, respectively. By choosing the appropriate layer number of the polynomials, variable coefficients can be determined through GMDH, using training data [11, 13]. Figure 3.1 briefly illustrates schematic diagram of the combinations of two variables and "sq" denotes the square and A_5 is a bias criterion as a noise filtration of variables.

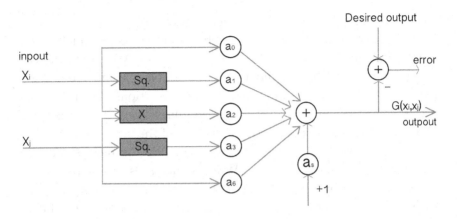

Fig. 3.1.   Combination of two independent variables.

In basic GMDH, the coefficients $(a_1, a_2, a_3, \ldots, a_n)$ are calculated using regression analysis techniques, so that the estimated error for all input variables (x_i, x_j) is minimized. For such parametric optimization, the $(a_1, a_2, a_3, \ldots, a_n)$ coefficients are evaluated using the training data set through one method of optimization [1]. The "Pseudo-Inverse" (PI), "Singular Value Decomposition" (SVD), "Least Square Error" (LSE), "The Gradient Descent" (GD) and "Quasi-Newton" (QN) methods are the five most popular and practiced techniques amongst all techniques of optimization; on the other hand, the "Damped Least Squares" method is a rarely practiced tool for optimization of GMDH-type algorithm. The aim of optimization is to estimate coefficients $(a_1, a_2, a_3, \ldots, a_n)$ using the training data set with one of the mentioned method that results more accurately and prevents from singularity of equations in a timely manner [33]. Employing some of techniques (that was mentioned earlier) to the solution of the coefficients estimation, not only cuts error counts but also it is more likely vulnerable to singularity of these equations. As soon as the system of linear equations is "ill-formed", the case of "singularity" occurs [33]; therefore, in the case of singularity, utilization of alternative methods is needed to produce stable solutions.

3.2. The Damped Least Squares (Levenberg–Marquardt) Method

The Damped Least Squares method is a "iterative technique" that determines the "minimum of a multivariate function" and is represented as "the sum of squares of nonlinear functions in real amounts". So far, this method has been seen as "standard technique for non-linear least-squares problems" and is likely a combination of "Gradient Descent" and the "Gauss–Newton" method while avoiding most problems of the pseudo-inverse's singularity; when the running value is "far from the correct one", the algorithm becomes "a gradient descent method"; it is slow, but guaranteed to converge and also, when the running value is "close to the correct solution", it behaves like a "Gauss–Newton method" [22].

The Damped Least Squares method which is known by Levenberg–Marquardt method is first proposed by Levenberg in [20] and extended by Marquardt in [25]. Levenberg first suggested LM as a "damped GN method" in order to cover the GN weakness; of course, it is applicable when J becomes "rank deficient". Later on Marquardt extended Levenberg concept by adding selections to the method so as to adjust the damping LM algorithm [29].

The objective is to "minimize the sum of the weighted residuals between the real value $y(t_i)$ and the curve-fit function $\hat{y}(t_i; p)$". The value w_i is the measure for the error when $y(t_i)$ is measured. The weighting matrix W is diagonal with $W_{ii} = 1/w_i^2$.

Furthermore, the $\frac{\partial \hat{y}}{\partial p}$ is the "$m \times n$ Jacobian matrix" (noted as J, for the mean of simplicity) that demonstrates the "local sensitivity" of $\hat{y}$ function to the variation of p. The perturbation h goes toward the "direction of steepest descent".

The algorithm suggested by Levenberg updated the diagonal of the Jacobian by the damping parameter as [20]:

$$[J^T W J + \lambda I] h_{lm} = J^T W (y - \hat{y}). \qquad (3.4)$$

And Marquardt [25] updated the Levenberg's relationship by the following equation:

$$[J^T W J + \lambda \operatorname{diag}(J^T W J)] h_{lm} = J^T W (y - \hat{y}), \qquad (3.5)$$

where the small values of the damping parameter λ update the Gauss–Newton and conversely, the large values result in the gradient descent mode. The "GD method" is employed for a stable and convergent progress, as long as values are far from the function minimum. When the solution approaches the minimum value, the "LM method" becomes more likely the "GN method"; the value usually converges quickly to the local minimum [24]. The λ (damping parameter) holds up the incidence of a singular matrix LM is more steady than the GN, since it can work well even if the initial guess is somewhat far from the globally known value [29].

Related to previous sections, LM accuracy is controlled by: the following the initial guess, damping parameter and reduction or amplifications of constant. A proper selection in choosing parameters affects the rapidness and stability of the method, and it is the most critical for effectiveness of the LM algorithm. In addition, estimating these parameters before starting an experiment leads to prevent a great deal of extra time in the modeling process. The proposed algorithm uses for solving these problems and improving of consuming time in basic LM procedures.

3.2.1.   Initial guess

Gradient-based techniques like the LM are highly dependent upon the initial guess, which is commonly unknown to the user. As such, the user needs to go through many trials with various initial guesses in order to reach the global optimum. However, the initial model guess is necessary for success of the heuristic search for an optimal model. LM may lose its effectiveness if the initial guess is not close enough to the actual value. In this case, it will either display slow convergence or a local converge which results in an undesirable match [4,7]. The LM algorithm that works well in practice in case the initial guess is not far from the global minimum. A thorough examination of this front has new ideas in order to guarantee the global convergence of the LM method. Here, algorithm has employed an effective LM algorithm conjuncted SVD technique to create initial guesses. In this work the result of the SVD method in GMDH algorithm as an initial guess for the input of initial guess in LM method is used.

SVD technique is an effective method of dealing with the difficulties, such as matrix inversion, over-determined and under-determined systems of linear models [38]. To avoid getting stuck in a local minimum, the target of function chi square is reduced by generated initial guess by SVD methods, and then choose only those values of the fitting parameters that give the lowest value of the target function. Modified LM algorithm is adjusted for decreasing computational time in classic LM algorithm. In addition, since LM necessitates many function assessments to converge to optimize global values, it may be logical to knock up it when there is marginal betterment in the target function.

Implementations of the modified LM algorithm in GMDH network have the good convergence rate and need less iteration to convergence compared with the classical LM algorithm. Moreover, this technique also yields improved computational efficiency when the Levenberg–Marquardt method is used as the optimization technique for Group Method of Data Handling.

3.2.2. Damping parameter

One of the difficulties of LM method concerns estimating damping parameter, which is used to overcome singularity difficulties of the Jacobian matrix. Stability and convergence rate of the algorithm depend on the suitable selection of the damping parameter. Therefore, selecting a proper damping parameter is the major key in the algorithm. The damping parameter in conventional LM method is selected in a systematic procedure during the iterative process. The damping parameter in the classical LM algorithm is calculated by

$$\text{New damping parameter} = \text{Previous damping parameter}$$
$$\div \text{Reduction constant.} \qquad (3.6)$$

If the OF (objective function) is more than that of the previous iteration,

$$\text{New damping parameter} = \text{Previous damping parameter}$$
$$* \text{Reduction constant.} \qquad (3.7)$$

Moreover, research have been conducted by several authors including Lampton [19] and Evelyn [5] to determine the "amount of the damping parameter based on the prior and the current value of Jacobian". Inappropriate choosing in the damping parameter may lead to pre-convergence. This study modifies LM method using λ as follows:

$$\lambda = \|F\|, \tag{3.8}$$

where $[JTJ + \lambda I]$ is invertible.

Hence, if measurement output is not close to the desirable output function and also errors are large this function converges to a favorite output with large steps. In addition, if the amount of error is small, then the real output converges to a desired output with "soft steps and error oscillation diminish to a great extent".

3.3.   The Modified Levenberg–Marquardt–Fletcher Algorithm

Optimization toolbox of MATLAB represents very mighty apparatus for solution of wide set of optimization problems. Also basic MATLAB provides means for optimization purposes, e.g. backslash operator for solving set of linear equations for nonlinear problems. Let us have a general over determined system of nonlinear algebraic equations:

$$f(x, c) = y \Rightarrow f(x, c) - y = r. \tag{3.9}$$

Its solution, optimal in the least squares sense, is sought by minimizing $\|r\|_2^2 = r^T r$. Necessary conditions for the optimum solution are zero values of partial derivatives of $\|r\|_2^2$ due to unknown coefficients c, i.e.

$$\frac{\partial \|r\|_2^2}{\partial c} = 2 \frac{\partial r^T}{\partial c} r = 2 J^T r = 2\, v. \tag{3.10}$$

Elements of J, which is called Jacobian matrix, are $j_{ij} = \frac{\partial r_i}{\partial c_j}$. Vector v should equal zero vector in the point of optimal solution c^*. It is sought after kth iteration in the form

$$c^{(k+1)} = c^{(k)} + \Delta c^{(k)}. \tag{3.11}$$

Let residual $r(c)$ be smooth functions, and then it holds:

$$r^{(k+1)} = r^{(k)} + \frac{\partial r^{(k)}}{\partial c^{(k)}} \Delta c^{(k)} + \cdots . \tag{3.12}$$

After some manipulations, the equation for the solution increment takes the form

$$A^{(k)} \Delta c^{(k)} - J^{(k)T} r^{(k+1)} = -v^{(k)}. \tag{3.13}$$

The values of λ^{k+1} are varying in dependence on behavior of iteration process. For slow stable convergence of iterations, the new value $\lambda^{(k+1)} = \lambda^{(k)}/v$ is set, which accelerates the process. Should a sign of divergence be observed, the value is changed into $\lambda^{(k+1)} = \lambda^{(k)}v$. The usual value of v is between 2 and 10. Fletcher improved Marquardt strategy of λ adaptation significantly. More to it, he introduced new quotient R which expresses how forecasted sum of squares agrees with the real one in the current iteration step. If R falls between preset limits (R_{lo}, R_{hi}), parameters of iteration do not change, otherwise changes of λ and v follow. The value of λ is halved if $R > R_{hi}$. Provided λ becomes lower than a critical value λ_c, it is cleared which causes the next iteration proceeds like in the Newton method. If $R < R_{lo}$, parameter v is set so that it holds $2 \leq v \leq 10$, and if λ were zero, a modification of λ_c and λ follows. The complete reconstruction of the function named LMF solve appeared in the appendix.

The "LM training process" can be demonstrated in the pseudo-codes:

(1) Initialize the weights and parameters, use the outcome of the SVD method as an initial guess (w) and μ ($\mu = \|F\|$ is appropriate).
(2) Calculate the sum of the squared errors over all inputs $F(w)$.
(3) Solve (2) to create the increase of weights Δw.
(4) Recalculated the sum of squared errors $F(w)$.

Replacing $w + \Delta w$ as the trial w, and judge
IF trial $F(w) < F(w)$ in step 2 THEN

$w = w + \Delta w$

$\lambda = \lambda.\beta \ (\beta = 1)$

Go back to step 2

ELSE

$\lambda = \lambda/\beta$

Go back to step 4

END IF.

4.   EXPERIMENTAL RESULTS AND DISCUSSIONS

Simulation and modeling can give primary vision and approximation of situation for very complex systems. Furthermore, the building and reliability of models are a difficult task. In order to illustrate the benefits of our new algorithm and the resulting network structure that it can develop, the algorithm has been applied to two different applications. The first experiment in this study is an inventory problem in Malaysian industry. The use of simulation and modeling is very common in architect complicated inventory systems, because, generally, a kanban system is a decentralized system in inventory control that harmoniously controls the production of the necessary products in the essential quantities of the required time.

One of the most important conditions that must be met in kanban systems is the aid of accurate prediction in average time in system of products on the final assembly line. The imbalance of time in inventory control influences between processes and the amount of order from subcontractors. In this study, a modified GMDH architecture for prediction average time in kanban systems has proposed; the kanban modeling by GMDH is developed first time in this reaseach.

There are some methods used in the literature to calculate coefficients in GMDH algorithms. To begin with, we have analyzed the performance of different GMDH algorithms, but in later experiments we only look at the performance of our proposed GMDH algorithm, since that is the main focus for this work. Several researchers have successfully demonstrated the use of GMDH based neural network models for prediction in different areas. With the advent of GMDH, there have been variants developed from different angles to evaluate coefficients to lessen the problems resulting from the standard GMDH algorithm [9,10,31,37,39]. Using Levenberg–Marquardt (LM) methods, we managed to solve the inverse problems in the calculating of coefficients in GMDH structure. The LM technique demonstrates some difficulties and constrains related to the calculation of rate of changing of the parameters. Furthermore, an inappropriate selection of these parameters will bring some unfit convergence or divergence. Affective parameters in convergence are variables that sometimes overlooked by optimization researchers, but those are usually far more important in convergence of models.

Recently, with limited resources, even large corporations that realize the savings associated with this type of approach can eliminate all sources of waste and save a significant amount of financial resources. There are conditions and sub-components that must be met, such as total quality control, multi-functioned workers, and inventory control with the aid of kanbans.

Sub-components that seem important in kanban implementation are the number of product kinds that are the level of demand variability of the products that are made on an assembly line; the number of stage on a production line and the number of kanbans that are preserved in different stages. Too many kanban produce excess work — in-progress inventory, while too few lead to production disturbances.

The experimental objective of this chapter is to determine the behavior of kanban controlled JIT production system, which is described in the previous section. This part will achieve to define the relationships between each of the following parameters:

(1) Number of stages on the production line,
(2) Level of processing time variability,
(3) Average throughput,
(4) Average stockout,
(5) Waiting times of the kanban,
(6) Utilization of the production line,
(7) Number of product types assembled on the production line.

One of the most important conditions that must be met in kanban systems is inventory control with the aid of accurate prediction in average time in system of products on the final assembly line. The imbalance of time in inventory control influences between processes and the amount of order from subcontractors. In this study, we have proposed a modified GMDH architecture for prediction average time in kanban systems.

4.1.   Experimental with Kanban System Data

In this section a set of real data sample is used for asses of the validation of our modified algorithm. There are some techniques used in the literature to find all coefficients in GMDH network, such as LSE, SVD and PI methods [21, 42].

All the 68 trials were collected from the industry to do preliminary validation of the proposed method. The outputs and measures were obtained for the 68 trials inputs that are shown in Table 4.1. The input parameters are: number of stages on the feeder line denoted as NSF(a), the level of processing time variability denote as PTV(b), average work in process on the feeder line denoted as WIP(c), average waiting times of the production ordering and withdrawal kanbans on the feeder line denoted as FKTIME(d), throughput at the workstation on the final assembly line during a shift denoted as TPUT(e) and average utilization of all the stages on the feeder line considered for all stage 98% and average time in system of the products being assembled at the workstation on the final assembly line denoted as TYS. This data set constituted five inputs and one output. The targets for average time in kanban system are given in the last columns of Table 4.1. The data have been divided into two sets: training and testing sets. Training set consists of 43 of 68 input–output data pairs and the testing set, which consists of 43 input–output data samples. The outputs of the GMDH-LM learning network reported in this chapter were used to develop the mathematical model of the kanban system in Sec. 4.2.

4.2.   Experiment Results with Kanban System Data

Some of experiments for evaluation of the GMDH-LM parameters were managed in the kanban system model. To performance a valid

Table 4.1. Values for operational factors associated with the kanban.

Trial No.	NSF	PTV	WIP	FKTIME	TPUT	TYS (min)
1	9	20	22	7	1000	7
2	8	15	20	7	950	7.5
3	7	45	23	7	960	7.1
4	8	20	24	5	970	6
5	8	10	21	3	980	9
6	9	40	23	2	970	8
7	10	42	22	3	960	8
8	11	15	24	3	980	7.5
9	12	21	20	2.5	980	7.2
10	13	17	21	2.6	981	7.9
11	9	14	23	2	897	7.8
12	10	41	23	2	898	7.7
13	8	22	24	2	920	7.7
14	8	16	23	1.7	930	9
15	7	22	22	1.9	940	9
16	8	14	21	1.9	950	10
17	9	40	22	2	980	13
18	11	13	22	2	990	7
19	10	42	21	1.7	960	6
20	11	21	21	1.8	890	6
21	11	17	22	1.9	870	12
22	8	18	24	3	980	14
23	12	14	28	4	1200	7
24	14	37	26	4	1300	7
25	13	16	24	4	990	8.1
26	12	31	23	4.2	996	8
27	8	20	18	7	680	9
28	8	32	20	6	1000	11
29	7	21	18	8	980	10
30	6	35	19	8	990	8
31	7	14	21	8	992	9
32	8	71	20	8	982	7
33	10	24	21	9	996	11
34	8	40	22	9	998	12
35	7	45	21	10	1100	10
36	8	42	26	11	1000	14
37	9	45	22	8	1200	8
38	6	13	21	9	1100	9
39	4	21	20	11	990	9
40	7	16	21	14	980	8

(*Continued*)

Table 4.1.   (*Continued*)

Trial No.	NSF	PTV	WIP	FKTIME	TPUT	TYS (min)
41	8	17	22	8	970	11
42	9	32	23	9	960	12
43	7	41	19	11	991	14
44	6	16	20	11	921	14
45	8	18	21	9	978	14
46	9	27	22	8	980	12
47	8	32	20	9	983	13
48	9	51	26	10	989	11
49	10	13	21	2	981	11
50	9	14	22	8	992	11
51	8	16	19	14	994	12
52	9	21	8	10	980	14
53	7	16	9	11	970	12
54	9	37	11	11	920	9
55	12	42	12	11	910	11
56	14	29	15	13	910	9
57	8	31	11	14	920	11
58	9	25	8	11	930	8
59	10	16	11	11	930	9
60	12	37	9	12	960	7.6
61	11	14	12	14	1200	7.6
62	9	31	10	2	910	7.2
63	9	42	10	3	900	7.4
64	9	51	10	2	900	6
65	8	36	12	5	890	6
66	9	26	22	8	920	11
67	9	18	23	8	920	12
68	10	23	22	9	990	14

model, there are some main parameters to choose. Some major factors in the proposed algorithm that used to modify for used together with a crossover probability of cross rate = 0.7 and a mutation probability of mutate rate = 0.07 in a generation number of 150 after which no better progress has been attained for such population size. Table 4.2 shows the GA's factors and the initial information of the GMDH-LM network, which will be optimized to find the best construction for the current query point in the network.

To accomplish to all experimental data, we modeled the prediction efficiency with mean absolute percentage error (MAPE) that refer to

Table 4.2. Design parameters of the proposed method.

Parameters		
GA	Maximum Generation	150
	Population Size	20
	Crossover Rate	0.7
	Mutation Rate	0.07
LM GMDH Network	Number of Layers	2
	Number of Input to be Selected	5
	Polynomial Type	2

training and testing errors, which may be taken for example, from:

$$\text{MAPE} = \frac{1}{N} \sum_{i=1}^{N} \frac{|A_i - F_i|}{A_i} \times 100. \tag{4.1}$$

A number of experts in this field [3] believe that Mean Squared Error (MSE) and Mean Absolute Deviation (MAD) are not much more suitable for accurate forecasting and evaluation because a lot of observations can be preponderated in experiments. Since the MAPE gives the prediction errors from various measurement on real observations, the MAPE is the widely used prediction of accuracy. One general difficulty of the MAPE is when A_i (real observation) to zero. Furthermore, Makridakis discussed that a MAPE criterion is unsymmetrical in that "equal errors above the actual value result in a greater Absolute Percentage Error than those below the actual value". As well as, Armstrong and Collopy clarified that "the MAPE put a heavier penalty on forecasts that exceed the actual than those that are less than the actual."

4.2.1. Comparison result for basic and GMDH-LM networks

The primary focus of this chapter is to develop a flexible algorithm to compare the mean square error with basic GMDH-based algorithm.

Using measured data, the researcher compared the prediction accuracy of basic and proposed GMDH algorithm with the measured values. Table 4.3 shows a comparison between basic GMDH algorithm and GMDH-LM algorithm. The results show that the accuracy of results modeled by this GMDH-LM is considerably high with reasonable reduction in processing time.

4.3. Experimental Result with (SVD, PI and LM) Methods in Kanban System

In this section, the combinations of the coefficients are discussed in different methods by means of singular value description, the pseudo-inverse and modified Levenberg–Maruardt methods and evolutionary Genetic Algorithm methods are evaluated to enhance GMDH-type network systems for experimental input–output data set. The following sections show actual and predicted values for average time on the final assembly line for partial data values with different layers.

4.3.1. Experimental result with two layers in kanban system

Table 4.4 shows actual and predicted values, and Table 4.5 shows comparison values of the error with two layers in different GMDH networks.

4.3.2. Experimental result with three layers in kanban system

In this section, the combinations of the coefficients are evaluated using the training data set by three different methods (SVD, PI and Modified LM) and evolutionary GA methods are applied to design GMDH-type network for the checking set of experimental data set. Table 4.6 shows actual and predicted values for average time on the final assembly line for partial data values with three layers, and Table 4.7 shows comparison values of the error with two layers in different GMDH networks.

Table 4.3. The comparison of the error at two layers.

Trial No.	Basic GMDH	GMDH LM
1	2.322729	0.922617
2	1.685476	0.227774
3	1.404074	0.558004
4	1.42407	0.32585
5	2.50834	0.095952
6	1.417673	0.308776
7	1.429923	0.252215
8	3.298896	0.346476
9	2.425378	0.069549
10	1.649597	0.058035
11	1.560222	0.163698
12	3.672892	0.230914
13	2.209663	0.42018
14	2.230034	0.075986
15	8.374688	0.09283
16	2.637626	0.00177
17	2.229705	0.369168
18	2.799359	0.326032
19	2.167026	0.171276
20	6.107126	0.234681
21	3.522264	0.016007
22	2.991762	0.291886
23	2.202171	0.60623
24	2.062937	0.046677
25	2.445623	0.23801
26	3.721302	0.121525
27	3.15021	0.27996
28	2.18439	0.377955
29	164.1113	0.294162
30	2.880488	0.048123
31	3.372607	0.285012
32	3.542615	1.560397
33	2.316934	0.004835
34	2.51531	0.13726
35	2.416566	0.297963
36	3.872187	0.349053
37	3.083608	1.289199
38	3.552036	0.056
39	24.43898	0.219294
40	7.94728	0.366117

(*Continued*)

Table 4.3.   (*Continued*)

Trial No.	Basic GMDH	GMDH LM
41	3.115869	0.424001
42	2.509889	0.825701
43	4.113579	0.111456
44	3.661861	0.335162
45	2.997564	0.455912
46	2.819119	0.347059
47	2.918142	0.18832
48	3.769493	0.553073
49	3.063366	2.207989
50	2.886467	2.202664
51	3.192149	0.452519
52	2.220497	0.349696
53	2.111972	0.087553
54	2.83089	2.069151
55	2.157615	0.214522
56	7.13792	0.023027
57	2.676013	3.928167
58	3.764977	0.066809
59	2.810014	12.71683
60	3.580773	0.247436
61	2.228115	0.146084
62	2.080842	0.328041
63	2.644759	0.168392
64	6.107126	0.234681
65	2.692093	0.167347
66	3.115869	0.424001
67	2.766532	0.409035
68	2.905396	0.111456
MAPE	**5.7171117**	**0.61667**

4.3.3.   Experimental result with four layers in kanban system

In last section, the combinations of the coefficients are evaluated using the training data set by SVD, PI and modified LM methods and evolutionary GA methods are applied to design GMDH-type network for the checking set of experimental data set with four layers. Table

Table 4.4. Actual and predicted values for partial data values with two layers.

Trial No.	Actual Values TYS (min)	Predicted Values for TYS (min)		
		SVD	PI	LM
1	7	14.17081	15.91137	13.45832
2	7.5	9.498057	8.709776	9.208305
3	7.1	12.11744	8.726021	11.06183
4	6	12.25436	8.151938	7.955097
5	9	10.09144	7.441053	9.863567
6	8	14.73388	10.27385	10.47021
7	8	11.78487	9.324415	10.01772
8	7.5	9.400783	11.71764	10.09857
9	7.2	6.010865	5.600164	7.700754
10	7.9	5.347801	9.353726	8.358477
11	7.8	5.156124	9.069648	6.523158
12	7.7	5.98979	4.873208	5.921963
13	7.7	4.731559	8.263004	4.464611
14	9	5.654272	9.702716	9.683875
15	9	8.313695	4.638746	8.164532
16	10	8.463958	10.9487	10.0177
17	13	8.94692	12.15005	8.200815
18	7	11.24186	10.30593	9.282223
19	6	7.13836	6.167368	4.972347
20	6	5.717444	7.154842	7.408087
21	12	13.46032	9.806214	12.19208
22	14	9.619872	9.74356	9.913602
23	7	10.71582	7.676915	11.24361
24	7	5.424249	7.067658	7.326742
25	8.1	11.69481	9.630034	10.02788
26	8	7.288096	9.211164	7.027798
27	9	7.116901	6.871703	6.480362
28	11	13.37593	10.60942	15.15751
29	10	10.02759	14.4721	12.94162
30	8	6.868317	8.9738	8.384983
31	9	6.874471	6.124995	6.434889
32	7	15.44258	19.8548	17.92278
33	11	7.927429	11.91235	10.94682
34	12	13.55325	11.23066	10.35288
35	10	22.68945	15.03221	12.97963
36	14	10.08809	6.754412	9.113252
37	8	15.13634	15.59027	18.31359
38	9	6.634071	5.375312	8.495996

(Continued)

Table 4.4.   (*Continued*)

Trial No.	Actual Values TYS (min)	Predicted Values for TYS (min)		
		SVD	PI	LM
39	9	9.149807	12.35852	10.97365
40	8	8.554648	4.712446	5.071067
41	11	6.604393	15.81701	15.66401
42	12	3.273505	7.724989	2.091583
43	14	9.861553	5.335834	15.56038
44	14	11.81018	10.40462	9.30773
45	14	7.206193	7.358619	7.617238
46	12	18.8679	6.511733	7.835295
47	13	15.39028	15.14681	15.44816
48	11	13.63549	15.61077	17.0838
49	11	43.15256	44.54688	35.28788
50	11	37.3979	33.87292	35.2293
51	12	5.884573	4.831809	6.569767
52	14	8.865905	15.02937	9.104262
53	12	7.950624	11.62757	10.94937
54	9	33.83094	29.13517	27.62236
55	11	15.90891	10.32446	8.640255
56	9	8.356004	12.29592	8.792757
57	11	59.69966	42.94761	54.20984
58	8	6.340157	5.103612	8.53447
59	9	180.0462	144.1289	123.4515
60	7.6	8.176542	6.700149	5.71949
61	7.6	12.89452	8.701867	8.710242
62	7.2	12.01254	6.907194	9.561894
63	7.4	11.39518	9.896023	8.6461
64	6	5.717444	7.154842	7.408087
65	6	11.1992	9.494348	7.004083
66	11	6.604393	15.81701	15.66401
67	12	6.273505	7.724989	7.091583
68	14	9.861553	10.33583	15.56038

4.8 shows actual and predicted values for average time on the final assembly line for partial data values with four layers, and Table 4.9 shows comparison values of the error with two layers in different GMDH networks.

Table 4.5. The comparison of the error at two layers.

Trial No.	SVD	PI	LM
1	1.024401	1.242729	0.922617
2	0.266408	0.605476	0.227774
3	0.706682	0.324074	0.558004
4	1.042393	0.34407	0.32585
5	0.121271	1.42834	0.095952
6	0.841735	0.337673	0.308776
7	0.473109	0.349923	0.252215
8	0.253438	2.218896	0.346476
9	0.165158	1.345378	0.069549
10	0.323063	0.569597	0.058035
11	0.338958	0.480222	0.163698
12	0.222105	1.652892	0.230914
13	0.385512	0.189663	0.42018
14	0.371748	0.210034	0.075986
15	0.076256	6.354688	0.09283
16	0.153604	0.617626	0.00177
17	0.311775	0.209705	0.369168
18	0.60598	0.779359	0.326032
19	0.189727	0.147026	0.171276
20	0.047093	4.087126	0.234681
21	0.121693	1.502264	0.016007
22	0.312866	0.971762	0.291886
23	0.530832	0.182171	0.60623
24	0.225107	0.042937	0.046677
25	0.443803	0.425623	0.23801
26	0.088988	1.701302	0.121525
27	0.209233	1.13021	0.27996
28	0.215994	0.16439	0.377955
29	0.002759	162.0913	0.294162
30	0.14146	0.860488	0.048123
31	0.23617	1.352607	0.285012
32	1.206083	1.522615	1.560397
33	0.279325	0.296934	0.004835
34	0.129438	0.49531	0.13726
35	1.268945	0.396566	0.297963
36	0.279422	1.852187	0.349053
37	0.892043	1.063608	1.289199
38	0.262881	1.532036	0.056
39	0.016645	22.41898	0.219294
40	0.069331	5.92728	0.366117

(Continued)

Table 4.5.   (*Continued*)

Trial No.	SVD	PI	LM
41	0.399601	1.095869	0.424001
42	0.727208	0.489889	0.825701
43	0.295603	2.093579	0.111456
44	0.156416	1.641861	0.335162
45	0.485272	0.977564	0.455912
46	0.572325	0.799119	0.347059
47	0.183868	0.898142	0.18832
48	0.23959	1.749493	0.553073
49	2.92296	1.043366	2.207989
50	2.399809	0.866467	2.202664
51	0.509619	1.172149	0.452519
52	0.366721	0.200497	0.349696
53	0.337448	0.091972	0.087553
54	2.758993	0.81089	2.069151
55	0.446265	0.137615	0.214522
56	0.071555	5.11792	0.023027
57	4.427242	0.656013	3.928167
58	0.20748	1.744977	0.066809
59	19.00513	0.790014	12.71683
60	0.075861	1.560773	0.247436
61	0.696647	0.208115	0.146084
62	0.668408	0.060842	0.328041
63	0.539889	0.624759	0.168392
64	0.047093	4.087126	0.234681
65	0.866533	0.672093	0.167347
66	0.399601	1.095869	0.424001
67	0.477208	0.746532	0.409035
68	0.295603	0.885396	0.111456
MAPE	**0.815197**	**3.849177**	**0.61667**

4.3.4.   Analysis and description in kanban system

Proposed GMDH-LM model that is shown in the last column of
Tables 4.4–4.10 demonstrates the comparison of the MAPE and estimated time with different methods. The results show that the errors
reduce from layer to layer. Throughout this chapter, TE and EP refer
to the training and testing errors, respectively.

Table 4.6.   Actual and predicted values for partial data values with three layers.

Trial No.	Actual Values TYS (min)	Predicted Values for TYS (min)		
		SVD	PI	LM
1	7	9.39201	8.48307	8.483086
2	7.5	8.390795	8.392236	8.392239
3	7.1	8.411106	8.390515	8.390524
4	6	7.787653	9.030519	8.030513
5	9	8.201901	9.128105	9.128093
6	8	7.841552	9.613829	9.613833
7	8	9.958405	9.544627	9.5446
8	7.5	8.594111	8.404941	8.404946
9	7.2	7.967043	9.576103	9.0761
10	7.9	8.123322	9.816009	9.81601
11	7.8	9.184143	8.529417	8.52942
12	7.7	8.650286	8.939812	8.039801
13	7.7	9.275488	8.706929	8.706927
14	9	9.028739	9.059357	9.059352
15	9	8.719365	9.663608	9.063606
16	10	8.547687	8.774104	8.974096
17	13	11.39311	8.879058	10.87906
18	7	8.263737	8.703692	8.703686
19	6	8.36309	8.674446	7.67445
20	6	5.805579	8.640504	7.640505
21	12	10.49567	11.20084	11.20082
22	14	12.17174	10.39684	11.39682
23	7	8.790371	8.705465	8.705473
24	7	9.083481	8.802269	8.102271
25	8.1	8.554815	8.460486	8.460496
26	8	8.850795	8.724108	7.724104
27	9	8.873058	8.761144	8.761133
28	11	9.921883	8.853306	9.853369
29	10	8.464247	9.59246	9.592481
30	8	9.263189	8.459588	8.459585
31	9	8.684701	9.031328	9.031339
32	7	9.039159	10.4476	9.44759
33	11	9.219502	10.15776	10.15769
34	12	8.826071	8.526414	9.526426
35	10	9.474339	12.21063	11.21058
36	14	8.880067	9.449591	9.449559
37	8	11.57982	10.10912	10.10916
38	9	9.104747	9.288627	9.288603

(*Continued*)

Table 4.6.   (*Continued*)

Trial No.	Actual Values TYS (min)	Predicted Values for TYS (min)		
		SVD	PI	LM
39	9	8.70436	10.42019	9.42013
40	8	11.81082	10.17152	10.17166
41	11	9.159259	10.33528	10.33528
42	12	8.568168	9.630407	9.630379
43	14	12.37334	13.95509	13.95515
44	14	12.76645	9.990143	10.99013
45	14	11.98406	9.739497	9.739486
46	12	13.24542	8.380479	8.380485
47	13	14.61842	10.29298	12.29304
48	11	11.70532	10.68351	10.68355
49	11	24.84925	29.31447	26.3145
50	11	25.11154	30.2589	19.25893
51	12	8.996081	8.810656	9.81066
52	14	8.336765	9.041743	9.041745
53	12	10.16026	8.909459	8.909476
54	9	23.00213	27.21905	17.21913
55	11	8.919277	10.03728	10.03723
56	9	10.71648	8.455046	8.455066
57	11	116.9254	189.5714	109.5678
58	8	11.56341	9.91762	9.917575
59	9	655.1883	534.4172	434.4251
60	7.6	8.214799	8.382241	8.382248
61	7.6	7.768006	8.731639	8.731638
62	7.2	8.392024	9.435654	9.435623
63	7.4	8.680581	9.053177	9.053154
64	6	5.805579	8.640504	7.640505
65	6	8.775645	8.392999	8.393004
66	11	9.159259	10.33528	10.33528
67	12	8.568168	9.630407	9.630379
68	14	12.37334	13.95509	13.95515

Figure 4.1 shows a comparison between basic GMDH algorithm and GMDH-LM algorithm. In Fig. 4.2 the average errors at different layers can be seen. In Figs. 4.3–4.5 represent the performance index on training and testing data set for various layers. It could be showed in Figs. 4.3–4.5 that the error values drop and increase in different layers.

Table 4.7.   The comparison of the error at three layers.

Trial No.	SVD	PI	LM
1	0.341716	0.20682	0.211869
2	0.118773	0.446552	0.118965
3	0.184663	0.257206	0.181764
4	0.297942	0.484545	0.338419
5	0.088678	0.117372	0.014233
6	0.019806	0.239658	0.201729
7	0.244801	0.408106	0.193075
8	0.145881	0.476089	0.120659
9	0.106534	1.998178	0.260569
10	0.028269	0.750729	0.242533
11	0.177454	0.275889	0.093515
12	0.123414	0.724947	0.04413
13	0.204609	0.339211	0.13077
14	0.003193	0.017741	0.006595
15	0.031182	0.966929	0.007067
16	0.145231	0.798088	0.10259
17	0.123607	1.016743	0.163149
18	0.180534	0.401638	0.243384
19	0.393848	2.349385	0.279075
20	0.032404	9.345064	0.273418
21	0.125361	0.54725	0.066598
22	0.13059	0.822615	0.185941
23	0.255767	0.458974	0.243639
24	0.29764	1.143752	0.157467
25	0.05615	0.10028	0.044506
26	0.106349	1.017143	0.034487
27	0.014105	0.126842	0.026541
28	0.098011	0.903517	0.104239
29	0.153575	14.77129	0.040752
30	0.157899	0.40611	0.057448
31	0.035033	0.014739	0.003482
32	0.291308	0.408359	0.349656
33	0.161863	0.274116	0.076574
34	0.264494	2.236334	0.206131
35	0.052566	0.17421	0.121058
36	0.36571	1.163219	0.325032
37	0.447478	0.295546	0.263645
38	0.011639	0.121993	0.032067
39	0.032849	9.480131	0.046681
40	0.476353	3.915132	0.271458

(Continued)

Table 4.7.   (*Continued*)

Trial No.	SVD	PI	LM
41	0.16734	0.151224	0.060429
42	0.285986	0.27154	0.197468
43	0.11619	0.010852	0.003204
44	0.088111	1.831135	0.214991
45	0.143996	0.627116	0.304322
46	0.103785	0.52702	0.301626
47	0.124494	1.132512	0.054382
48	0.06412	0.120088	0.028768
49	1.259023	0.569612	1.392227
50	1.282867	0.729562	0.750812
51	0.250327	0.521524	0.182445
52	0.404517	0.965751	0.354161
53	0.153312	0.763214	0.257544
54	1.555792	0.733724	0.913237
55	0.189157	0.196117	0.087525
56	0.19072	0.846207	0.060548
57	9.629582	3.666789	8.960709
58	0.445426	1.155302	0.239697
59	71.7987	3.071785	47.26946
60	0.080895	1.356781	0.102927
61	0.022106	0.213738	0.1489
62	0.165559	0.464548	0.310503
63	0.173051	0.413793	0.223399
64	0.032404	9.345064	0.273418
65	0.462608	0.460263	0.398834
66	0.16734	0.151224	0.060429
67	0.285986	0.413795	0.197468
68	0.11619	0.010852	0.003204
MAPE	**1.415983**	**1.33417**	**1.018199**

Figure 4.8 represents the graphical schematic of network connections for our proposed GMDH-LM network; this graphical representation is very helpful for realizing how the successful nodes joint from layer to layer until the network find a best solution at the output layer. The accurate behavior of such GMDH-type network in modeling the conjunction with improved Levenberg–Marquardt technique for finding most accurate weights of the polynomials is also displayed in Fig. 4.6. As could be seen, the predicted values closely pursue the

Table 4.8.   Actual and predicted values for partial data values with four layers.

Trial No.	Actual Values TYS (min)	Predicted Values for TYS (min)		
		SVD	PI	LM
1	7	8.385757	8.388655	8.077695
2	7.5	7.526325	10.01482	9.5232
3	7.1	8.475687	9.648308	9.43187
4	6	8.743686	7.838034	7.432652
5	9	8.197017	9.646751	9.603265
6	8	7.896203	8.163063	8.472057
7	8	9.681372	8.895052	7.779383
8	7.5	9.013031	8.028763	8.06548
9	7.2	7.653741	8.348394	8.064278
10	7.9	7.532312	7.50818	7.520411
11	7.8	8.599767	9.342426	9.408336
12	7.7	8.429175	8.83838	8.452098
13	7.7	7.664232	9.71623	7.862252
14	9	9.809427	9.83611	8.953069
15	9	8.630666	9.332181	8.726034
16	10	8.817521	9.285227	10.25593
17	13	10.41251	10.13119	11.51585
18	7	7.501037	4.821087	6.461964
19	6	9.099142	9.035005	7.538478
20	6	7.641761	8.757911	6.066263
21	12	8.556792	9.903318	10.58226
22	14	13.01694	12.17302	13.7145
23	7	8.053197	9.322341	6.465711
24	7	8.224586	8.471864	8.257174
25	8.1	8.864442	8.839417	8.486019
26	8	7.792177	8.883885	9.003305
27	9	10.29003	9.709893	9.590607
28	11	12.06608	10.38453	10.23982
29	10	9.730735	7.810225	8.787593
30	8	8.120702	8.583499	8.832831
31	9	9.015091	8.938809	9.285659
32	7	9.766199	8.736554	8.34043
33	11	7.748487	9.85317	9.388609
34	12	9.748431	10.02501	10.44245
35	10	11.17863	12.37994	10.12274
36	14	10.3811	10.18766	13.37619
37	8	8.710685	10.02188	10.35023
38	9	9.032006	6.967025	8.171915

(Continued)

Table 4.8. *(Continued)*

Trial No.	Actual Values TYS (min)	Predicted Values for TYS (min)		
		SVD	PI	LM
39	9	9.781775	10.19315	8.924657
40	8	12.1713	7.861811	8.421654
41	11	11.32639	11.16147	11.73802
42	12	9.832461	9.281555	9.520726
43	14	13.52455	13.59668	12.53656
44	14	8.924295	14.20394	15.08576
45	14	13.09348	11.17573	11.44973
46	12	10.9797	9.007423	10.85294
47	13	13.00218	11.85906	11.66916
48	11	9.039088	9.96824	10.26221
49	11	68.09621	34.92336	14.00285
50	11	14.56231	23.56214	17.17462
51	12	8.309419	9.01735	9.400295
52	14	7.660391	8.205264	9.028389
53	12	9.48839	10.00885	10.74223
54	9	8.946056	13.41358	12.91555
55	11	12.59188	10.37333	8.874502
56	9	10.9734	8.649952	8.905463
57	11	144.5263	−23.324	30.73042
58	8	9.029521	8.385873	6.691186
59	9	93.00362	22.15699	250.6473
60	7.6	11.46156	10.09521	9.347317
61	7.6	10.2671	9.367011	8.236104
62	7.2	9.370786	9.989403	9.276845
63	7.4	15.97045	10.07663	8.208939
64	6	7.641761	8.757911	8.066263
65	6	11.3324	10.0268	10.71909
66	11	11.32639	11.16147	11.73802
67	12	9.832461	9.281555	9.520726
68	14	13.52455	13.59668	13.53656

actual values, except for experiment numbers 49, 57 and 59 where there is a number of obvious deviations. Figure 4.7 demonstrates the GMDH-LM network's prediction and absolute difference error.

The coefficients in GMDH algorithm are estimated using the singular value decomposition (SVD) method, the pseudo-inverse (PI) method and the Levenberg–Marquardt estimation method. We select

Table 4.9. The comparison of the error at four layers.

Trial No.	SVD	PI	LM
1	0.19325	0.193654	0.150289
2	0.013175	1.258633	1.012584
3	0.274181	0.50789	0.464753
4	0.438684	0.29388	0.229065
5	0.73571	0.592567	0.552724
6	0.015414	0.024215	0.070102
7	0.444235	0.236482	0.058289
8	0.796004	0.278182	0.297498
9	0.381572	0.965739	0.726812
10	0.144067	0.153523	0.14873
11	0.302498	0.583396	0.608325
12	0.426366	0.665638	0.439769
13	0.012049	0.679222	0.054659
14	0.241929	0.249904	0.014027
15	0.538148	0.484014	0.39919
16	0.769822	0.465334	0.166617
17	0.638401	0.70781	0.366179
18	0.118117	0.513669	0.12684
19	2.722462	2.666121	1.351486
20	5.810392	9.760582	0.234513
21	2.357845	1.435769	0.970842
22	0.224436	0.417107	0.065181
23	0.283436	0.624987	0.143788
24	0.777144	0.934071	0.797825
25	0.212652	0.20569	0.107382
26	0.291926	1.241579	1.409326
27	0.685057	0.376981	0.313636
28	0.4487	0.259044	0.319951
29	9.759514	79.36843	43.94371
30	0.106657	0.515603	0.735923
31	0.0071	0.028789	0.134394
32	0.327649	0.20569	0.15877
33	1.058239	0.373248	0.524444
34	1.449586	1.271521	1.002768
35	0.092883	0.187553	0.009673
36	0.925098	0.974547	0.159465
37	0.099587	0.283322	0.329333
38	0.013528	0.859271	0.350004
39	5.218548	7.964581	0.502934
40	7.520626	0.249147	0.760219

(*Continued*)

Table 4.9.   (*Continued*)

Trial No.	SVD	PI	LM
41	0.074254	0.036734	0.167899
42	0.248386	0.311516	0.284109
43	0.114886	0.097457	0.353621
44	2.317864	0.093131	0.495822
45	0.133433	0.415712	0.375382
46	0.148561	0.435734	0.167018
47	0.000912	0.477325	0.556772
48	0.744041	0.391487	0.279944
49	1.77579	0.744058	0.093394
50	0.134947	0.475876	0.233906
51	0.603487	0.487726	0.425106
52	1.234806	1.128677	0.968352
53	0.620246	0.491718	0.310608
54	0.002172	0.177745	0.157688
55	0.324284	0.12766	0.432988
56	3.064305	0.543556	0.146797
57	2.741832	0.70481	0.405145
58	0.620252	0.232476	0.788517
59	0.491117	0.076921	1.41276
60	6.697795	4.327889	3.030685
61	0.503747	0.333743	0.120144
62	0.451069	0.579611	0.431549
63	2.145197	0.669965	0.202479
64	5.810392	9.760582	7.312756
65	1.025619	0.774504	0.907657
66	0.074254	0.036734	0.167899
67	0.378511	0.474714	0.432948
68	0.114886	0.097457	0.111984
MAPE	**1.168731**	**2.111219**	**0.668047**

these methods because they are known and popular methods for parametric optimization. The results show that SVD method is very fast; PI method has great amount of arithmetic computation to prediction error and it is also time consuming than any other methods. It does not have the ability to deal with multifaceted situation where the number of layers and/or neurons increases. On the other hand the LM method has the capability to deal with ill-formed situations where singularity occurs.

Table 4.10. The comparison of errors, MAPE and estimated time in different methods.

	SVD	PI	LM
Training Error	0.378508	5.421033	0.313921
Testing Error	1.517429	1.182044	1.097938
MAPE (Total)	0.815197	3.849177	0.61667
Estimated Time (sec)	130.955249	1005.374115	453.453042

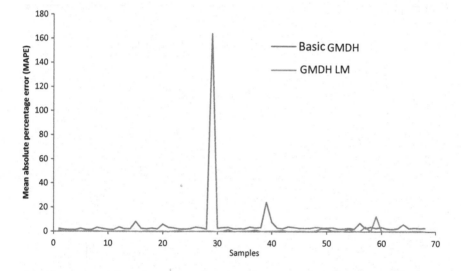

Fig. 4.1. The performance index on training and testing data for two layers.

LM technique for calculation coefficients is better to "direct solving of normal equations particularly" in cases that the number of layers and neurons raises but it is costly in computation. The LM method is the more accurate than SVD method but it is computationally more time consuming than SVD method. PI method does not have the ability to deal with complicated scenario with a lot of neurons and layers. Furthermore, it is most time consuming than other methods. The improved LM method is the optimum method to apply in GMDH algorithm, this architecture focuses on improving the time computing in classic LM method. The GMDH-LM method is a fairly

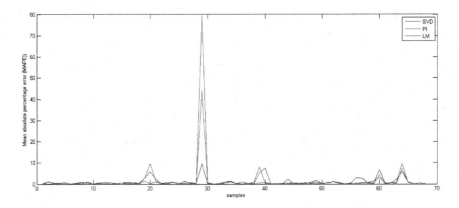

Fig. 4.2.   The average errors at different layers.

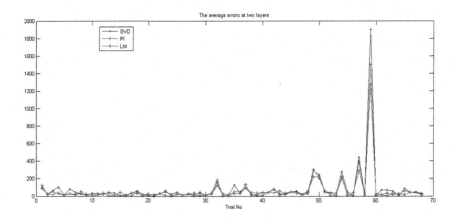

Fig. 4.3.   The performance index on training and testing data for two layers.

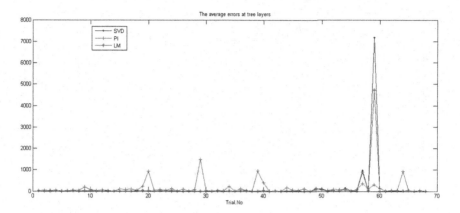

Fig. 4.4.   The performance index on training and testing data for three layers.

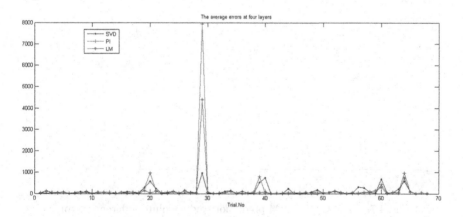

Fig. 4.5.   The performance index on training and testing data for four layers.

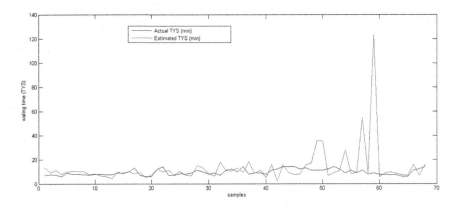

Fig. 4.6.   GMDH-LM actual and predicted plots.

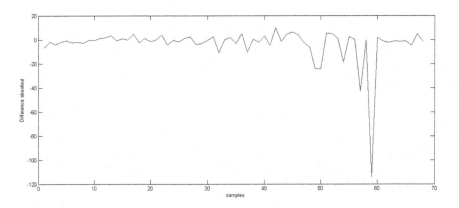

Fig. 4.7.   The GMDH-LM prediction and absolute difference error.

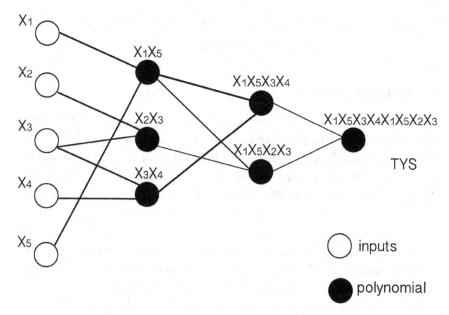

Fig. 4.8. Graphical representation of GMDH-LM network connections structure for kanban system.

agreement between these two tremendous cases and it discovers reasonably good results for real uses. The configuration of such evolved 2-hidden layer GMDH-type network is also illustrated in Fig. 4.8:

$$z_1 = -32.9652 + 0.153768x_1 + 0.076551x_5 - 0.12999x_1^2$$
$$- 4.6E - 05x_5^2 + 0.002662x_1x_5,$$
$$z_2 = 12.43097 + 0.120575x_2 - 0.123869x_3 - 0.0191x_2^2$$
$$- 0.06303x_3^2 + 0.054208x_2x_3,$$
$$z_3 = -0.36839 + 0.511909x_3 - 0.835033x_4 - -0.00839x_3^2$$
$$- 0.0292x_4^2 + 0.000613x_3x_4,$$
$$f_1 = 409.0847 - 43.2289z_1 - 36.9531z_3 + 1.268331z_1^2$$
$$+ 0.908063z_3^2 + 1.789357z_1z_3,$$
$$f_2 = 58.70075 + 1.254165z_1 - 11.8796z_2 - 0.13131z_1^2$$
$$+ 0.518262z_2^2 + 0.166494z_1z_2,$$

$$TYS = 67.4449 - 3.23016 f_1 - 8.29554 f_2 + 0.063436 f_1^2$$
$$+ 0.248207 f_2^2 + 0.220129 f_1 f_2.$$

5.   CONCLUSIONS

We present a new algorithm for the development of architecture that takes the best features of many other methods already available. The new algorithm follows a method similar to the one used in least square methods in order to compute the weights for the neuron functions. Although it is not originally intended for the purpose of calculating weights in a network, it is easily adapted for this modern purpose. least square problems can be solved by general optimization methods, but the researcher offers special methods that are more efficient. Data will usually converge for this method. However, when they do not converge, the method can easily identify this lack of convergence.

In this research an enhanced algorithm for accurate prediction in average time in system of products on the final assembly line was created. Some enhanced GMDH algorithms that can create a model for prediction also compared and evaluated, and demonstrated the effectiveness of the GMDH type algorithm. The classic algorithm that developed by Gilbar, as a part of his Ph.D. thesis, forms the basis for the GMDH algorithm used in this chapter [8]. Finally, it has been modified in order to adjust for the computing time during the experiments.

Currently, many methods exist to form neural networks, but most of these methods will require some prior knowledge of the final network structure. These algorithms can be very time consuming and require tremendous amounts of computational resources.

In most instances, traditional algorithms will not be able to predict whether the network will converge until a significant amount of time and resources have been spent. Therefore, by selecting the best and the most useful principles of traditional methodologies, this new algorithm combines these properties to form an efficient and robust method of creating neural networks.

This algorithm mostly resembles GMDH, which is a method developed by Ivakhnenko [12] — a prominent researcher in the field of cybernetics in 1968. Although, GMDH was not originally created for the development of neural networks, it has evolved significantly to be used for a wide range of applications.

Our new algorithm is adjusted for decrease computational time in LM method that also used for calculate coefficients in GMDH algorithm, its prediction accuracy improves significantly. The testing showed that the lag adjusted GMDH algorithm was very accurate and in some cases almost as exact as the measured time values in kanban system. For instant manufacturing of intricate inventory systems, an executable modeling tool is needed to accomplish effective decision before triggering and reengineering a production line. JIT ideologies are used to the production handling processes and the research proposed a new approach in modeling kanban system by a new GMDH type network modeling.

The main objectives of this research are to develop a new GMDH type network. The ultimate goal of this modification is a prototype artificial intelligent system to a flexible production line for optimization of a material transportation flow and balancing in whole of production lines and making more accurate predictions in order to optimize the arrangement of buffers at stages. A real-balanced material flow system can be attained via balanced material requirement, this optimization can be done by analytical and statistical modeling and evolutionary simulation based approaches.

Case considered in this study, the proposed GMDH-LM based creates an accurate prediction model with better prediction performance in comparison with others method in this search. For the kanban data set, the prediction accuracy of GMDH-LM network is obviously much better than other GMDH combination (SVD-GMDH, PI-GMDH) algorithms. While for this data set, the computational time of SVD-GMDH method is clearly much better than those of the PI-GMDH and LM-GMDH algorithms.

One of the preferences of the proposed method is employing SVD method for using in LM method in estimation of initial guess, the difficulties of the LM method can be overcome by decreasing computational time in LM method. This research employed SVD method within LM method in estimation of initial guess. It decreased the computational time by 40% for the given input parameters. In addition, another advantage of the proposed method is adding GMDH with GA method for optimize structure of GMDH algorithm. Next benefit of predictors is that the training set for each point is much smaller than the global predictors, which involve for all existing training sets, and the space of memory can be saved.

Finally, the major benefit of the proposed GMDH-LM method is its strength to overcome the drawbacks of the primary GMDH algorithm where the structure of the proposed algorithm within the design process is not prespecified and can be self-organized automatically. It comes with a high level of flexibility as each node and connectivity configuration unlike the conventional GMDH algorithm. The new GMDH network is not limited to contiguous layers and becomes fully optimized in structurally and parametrically.

REFERENCES

[1] Amanifard, N., Nariman-Zadeh, N., Borji, M., Khalkhali, A. & Habibdoust, A. (2008) Modelling and Pareto optimization of heat transfer and flow coefficients in microchannels using GMDH type neural networks and genetic algorithms, *Energy Conver. Manage.*, **49**, No. 2, 311–325.

[2] Bishop, C. (1995) *Neural Networks for Pattern Recognition*, Oxford University Press, Oxford.

[3] Chatfield, C. (1988) Apples, oranges and mean square error, *Int. J. Forecasting*, **4**, 515–518.

[4] Dan, H., Yamashita, N. & Fukushima, M. (2002) Convergence properties of the inexact Levenberg–Marquardt method under local error bound conditions, *Optim. Methods Softw.*, **17**, No. 4, 605–626.

[5] Evelyn, A. (2004) A variation of the levenberg marquardt method: an attempt to improve efficiency, MSc thesis, Massachusetts Institute of Technology.

[6] Farlow, S. J. (1984) *Self-organizing Methods in Modeling: GMDH Type Algorithms*, Marcel Dekker Inc, Basel, NY.

[7] Fliege, J., Drummond, L. M. & Svaiter, B. F. (2009) Newton's method for multiobjective optimization, *SIAM J. Optim.*, **20**, 602–626.

[8] Gilbar, T. & Pandya, A. (2002) Software and development and simulation of neural networks using a GMDH type algorithm, In: *Proc. SCI 2002 Conf.*, Orlando, FL, July 14–17.

[9] Hiassat, M., Abbod, M. & Mort, N. (2003) Using genetic programming to improve the GMDH in time series prediction, In: *Statistical Data Mining and Knowledge Discovery*, ed. Bozdogan, H., Chapman & Hall/CRC, pp. 257–268.

[10] Iba, H., De Garis, H. & Sato, T. (1994) Genetic programming using a minimum description length principle. In: *Advances in Genetic Programming*, ed. Kinnear. K. E. Jr., MIT, Cambridge, pp. 265–284.

[11] Iba, H., De Garis, H. & Sato, T. (1995) A numerical approach to genetic programming for system identification. *Evol. Comput.*, **3**, No. 4, 417–452.

[12] Ivakhnenko, A. G. (1968) The group method of data handling-a rival of the method of stochastic approximation, *Soviet Autom. Control*, **13**, No. 3, 43–55.

[13] Ivakhnenko, A. G. (1970) Heuristic self-organization in problems of engineering cybernetics, *Automatica*, **6**, 207–219.

[14] Ivakhnenko, A. G. (1971) Polynomial theory of complex systems, *IEEE Trans. Syst. Man Cybernet.*, **SMC-1**, 364–378.

[15] Ivakhnenko, A. G. (1966), Group method of data handling — a rival of the method of stochastic approximation, *Soviet Automatic Control*, **13**, 43–71.

[16] Ivakhnenko, A. G. & Ivakhnenko, G. A. (1996) A comparison of discrete and continuous recognition systems, *Pattern Recognit. Image Anal.*, **6**, No. 3, 445–447.

[17] Kim, D. & Park, G.-T. (2005) GMDH-type neural network modeling in evolutionary optimization, In: *Innovations in Applied Artificial Intelligence*, Lecture Notes in Computer Science, Vol. 3533, Springer, Berlin, pp. 563–570.

[18] Kumar Shukla, P., "Levenberg–Marquardt algorithms for nonlinear equations, multi-objective optimization, and complementarity problems," Dissertation, Fakultät Mathematik und Naturwissenschaften, Technische Universität Dresden, http://www.qucosa.de/recherche/frontdoor/?tx_slubopus4frontend%5bid%5d=urn:nbn:de:bsz:14-qucosa-27372.

[19] Lampton, M. (1997) Damping undamping stratagies for the levenberg marquardt nonlinear least squares method, *Comput. Phys.*, **11**, No. 1, 110–115.

[20] Levenberg, K. (1944) A method for the solution of certain non-linear problems in least squares, *Quart. Appl. Math.*, **2**, No. 2, 164–168.

[21] Lora, A. T., Riquelme, J. C. & Ramos, J. L. M. (2003) Influence of kNN-based load forecasting errors on optimal energy, production, Lecture Notes on Computer Science, Vol. 2902, Heidelberg, Springer, pp. 189–203.

[22] Lourakis, M. I. (2005) A brief description of the Levenberg–Marquardt algorithm implemened by Levmar, Manuscript, Institute of Computer Science, Vassilika Vouton, Heraklion, Crete, Greece, Foundation for Research and Technology, Hellas (Forth).

[23] Madala, H. R. & Ivakhnenko, A. G. (1994) *Inductive Learning Algorithms for Complex Systems Modeling.* CRC Press, Boca Raton.

[24] Madsen, K., Nielsen, N. B. & Tingleff, O. (2004) Methods for nonlinear least squares problems, Technical Report, Informatics and Mathematical Modeling, Technical University of Denmark.

[25] Marquardt, D. W. (1963) An algorithm for the least-squares estimation of nonlinear parameters, *SIAM J. Appl. Math.*, **11**, No. 2, 431–441.

[26] Monden, Y. (1993) *Toyota Production System*, 2nd Edition, Industrial Engineering and Management Press, pp. 235–260.

[27] Müller, J. A. & Lemke, F. (1999) *Self-Organizing Data Mining: An Intelligent Approach to Extract Knowledge from Data*, Dresden, Berlin.

[28] Nariman-Zadeh, N., Darvizeh, A. & Ahmad-Zadeh, G. R. (2003) Hybrid genetic design of GMDH-type neural networks using singular value decomposition for modeling and predicting of the explosive cutting process, *Proc. Instn. Mech. Engrs.*, **217**, Part B, 779–790.

[29] Naveen, M., Jayaraman, S., Ramanath, V. & Chaudhuri, S. (2010) Modified Levenberg–Marquardt algorithm for inverse problems, In: *Simulated Evolution and Learning*, Lecture Notes in Computer Science, Vol. 6457, Springer, pp. 623–632.

[30] Nikolaev, N. Y. & Iba, H. (2003) Polynomial harmonic GMDH learning networks for time series modelling, *Neural Networks*, **16**, 1527–1540.

[31] Oh, S.-K., Park, B.-J. & Kim, H.-K. (2005) Genetically optimized hybrid fuzzy neural networks based on linear fuzzy inference rules, *Int. J. Control, Autom. Syst.*, **3**, No. 2, 183–194.

[32] Onwubolu, G. C. (2008) Design of hybrid differential evolution and group method in data handling networks for modeling and prediction, *Inform. Sci.*, **178**, 3618–3634.

[33] Onwubolu, G. C. (2009) *Hybrid Differential Evolution and GMDH Systems*, Springer, Berlin.

[34] Onwubolu, G. C., Buryan, P. & Lemke, F. (2008) Modeling tool wear in end-milling using enhanced GMDH learning networks, *Int. J. Adv. Manuf. Technol.*, **39**, 1080–1092.

[35] Onwubolu, G. C., Sharma, S., Dayal, A., Bhartu, D., Shankar, A. & Katafono, K. (2008) Hybrid particle swarm optimization and group method of data handling for inductive modeling, In: *Proc. Int. Conf. Inductive Modeling*, Kyiv, Ukraine, September 15–19.

[36] Parente, M., Makarewicz, H. D. & Bishop, J. L. (2011) Decomposition of mineral absorption bands using nonlinear least squares curve fitting: Application to Martian meteorites and CRISM data, *Planetary Space Sci.*, **59**, No. 5–6, 423–442.

[37] Park, H.-S., Park, B.-J., Kim, H.-K. & Oh, S.-K. (2004) Self-organizing polynomial neural networks based on genetically optimized multi-layer perceptron architecture, *Int. J. Control, Autom. Syst.*, **2**, No. 4, 423–434.

[38] Press, W. H, Flannery, B. P., Teukolsky, S. A. & Vetterling, W. T. (1986) *Numerical Recipes: The Art of Scientific Computing*, 1st Edition, Cambridge University Press, New York.

[39] Robinson, C. (1998) Multi-objective optimization of polynomial models for time series prediction using genetic algorithms and neural networks, Ph.D. Thesis, Department of Automatic Control & Systems Engineering, University of Sheffield, UK.

[40] Rosenblatt, F. (1958) The perceptron: A probabilistic model for information storage and organization in the brain. *Psychological Review* **6**, 386-408.

[41] Sedighi, M., Khandaei, M. & Shokrollahi, H. (2010) An approach in parametric identification of high strain rate constitutive model using Hopkinson pressure bar test results, *Mater. Sci. Eng. A*, **527**, No. 15, 3521–3528.

[42] Sorjamaa, A., Reyhani, N. & Lendasse, A. (2005) Input and structure selection for k-NN approximator, In: *Computational Intelligence and Bioinspired Systems*, Lecture Notes on Computer Science, Vol. 3512, Springer, Heidelberg, pp. 985–992.

[43] Spellman, G. (1999) An application of artificial neural networks to the prediction of surface ozone concentrations in the United Kingdom, *Appl Geography*, **19**, No. 2, 123–136.

[44] Thakkar, J. (2011) A novel NN paradigm for the prediction of hematocrit value during blood transfusion, Masters Thesis, Florida Atlantic University.

[45] Walker, O., Varadan, R. & Fushman, D. (2004) Efficient and accurate determination of the overall rotational diffusion tensor of a molecule from 15N relaxation data using computer program ROTDIF, *J. Magnetic Resonance*, **168**, No. 2, 336–345.

[46] Xiang, J., Cheng, D., Schlindwein, F. S. & Jones, N. B. (2003) On the adequacy of identified Cole–Cole models, *Comput. Geosci.*, **29**, No. 5, 647–654.

APPENDIX

It will be necessary to use the following files: FITTING M-file for Fitting.fig (*main program*),

H = FITTING returns the handle to a new FITTING or the handle to the existing singleton.

FITTING ('CALLBACK', hObject, eventData, handles, . . .) calls the local function named CALLBACK in FITTING.M with the given input arguments.

FITTING ('Property', 'Value'. . .) creates a new FITTING or raises the existing singleton. Starting from the left, property value pairs are applied to the GUI before Fitting Opening Fcn gets called. An unrecognized property name or invalid value makes property application stop. All inputs are passed to Fitting_OpeningFcn via varargin. See GUI Options on GUIDE's Tools menu. Choose "GUI allows only one instance to run (singleton)".

There are several ways to program GUIs to wait for user input. We use one of MATLAB's custom dialog box functions. There is a list of Codes related to dialog box in main program.

The next step is to use global variable to normally store in MAT-LAB. In order to understand function we must first understand that global variables are created using the global command. Variables defined in this function are automatically cleared from memory when the function returns. MATLAB script files store all variables in the calling workspace. If a MATLAB script is called from the command line, the variables are stored in the base workspace. The contents of this workspace can be seen by using the global command. We cannot work directly in the global workspace, but variables in another workspace can be declared global using the GLOBAL command.

str2double converts the string to the MATLAB® double-precision representation. The string can contain digits, a comma (thousands separator), a decimal point, a leading + or − sign, an "e" preceding a power of 10 scale factor, and a complex unit. The commands below show how to use functions.

```
% --- Executes just before Fitting is made visible.
function Fitting_OpeningFcn(hObject, eventdata, handles, varargin)
% This function has no output args, see OutputFcn.
% hObject    handle to figure
% eventdata reserved - to be defined in a future version of MATLAB
% handles    structure with handles and user data (see GUIDATA)
% varargin   command line arguments to Fitting (see VARARGIN)


% Choose default command line output for Fitting
handles.output = hObject;

% Update handles structure
guidata(hObject, handles);

% UIWAIT makes Fitting wait for user response (see UIRESUME)
% uiwait(handles.figure1);

% --- Outputs from this function are returned to the command line.
function varargout = Fitting_OutputFcn(hObject, eventdata, handles)
% varargout cell array for returning output args (see VARARGOUT);
% hObject    handle to figure
% eventdata reserved - to be defined in a future version of MATLAB
% handles    structure with handles and user data (see GUIDATA)


% Get default command line output from handles structure
varargout{1}= handles.output;


function nopop_Callback(hObject, eventdata, handles)
% hObject    handle to nopop (see GCBO)
% eventdata reserved - to be defined in a future version of MATLAB
% handles    structure with handles and user data (see GUIDATA)


% Hints: get(hObject,'String') returns contents of nopop as text
```

```
%         str2double(get(hObject,'String')) returns contents of nopop as a
double
global N_pop
N_pop=str2double(get(hObject,'String'));


% --- Executes during object creation, after setting all properties.
function nopop_CreateFcn(hObject, eventdata, handles)
% hObject    handle to nopop (see GCBO)
% eventdata reserved - to be defined in a future version of MATLAB
% handles    empty - handles not created until after all CreateFcns called


% Hint: edit controls usually have a white background on Windows.
%       See ISPC and COMPUTER.
if ispc && isequal(get(hObject,'BackgroundColor'),
get(0,'defaultUicontrolBackgroundColor'))
    set(hObject,'BackgroundColor','white');
end


function nhl_Callback(hObject, eventdata, handles)
% hObject    handle to nhl (see GCBO)
% eventdata reserved - to be defined in a future version of MATLAB
% handles    structure with handles and user data (see GUIDATA)


% Hints: get(hObject,'String') returns contents of nhl as text
%         str2double(get(hObject,'String')) returns contents of nhl as a
double
global N_HL
N_HL=str2double(get(hObject,'String'));


% --- Executes during object creation, after setting all properties.
function nhl_CreateFcn(hObject, eventdata, handles)
% hObject    handle to nhl (see GCBO)
% eventdata reserved - to be defined in a future version of MATLAB
% handles    empty - handles not created until after all CreateFcns called


% Hint: edit controls usually have a white background on Windows.
%       See ISPC and COMPUTER.
if ispc && isequal(get(hObject,'BackgroundColor'),
get(0,'defaultUicontrolBackgroundColor'))
    set(hObject,'BackgroundColor','white');
end


function crosprob_Callback(hObject, eventdata, handles)
% hObject    handle to crosprob (see GCBO)
% eventdata reserved - to be defined in a future version of MATLAB
% handles    structure with handles and user data (see GUIDATA)


% Hints: get(hObject,'String') returns contents of crosprob as text
%         str2double(get(hObject,'String')) returns contents of crosprob as a
double
```

```
global pc
pc=str2double(get(hObject,'String'));


% --- Executes during object creation, after setting all properties.
function crosprob_CreateFcn(hObject, eventdata, handles)
% hObject    handle to crosprob (see GCBO)
% eventdata reserved - to be defined in a future version of MATLAB
% handles    empty - handles not created until after all CreateFcns called


% Hint: edit controls usually have a white background on Windows.
%       See ISPC and COMPUTER.
if ispc && isequal(get(hObject,'BackgroundColor'),
get(0,'defaultUicontrolBackgroundColor'))
    set(hObject,'BackgroundColor','white');
end


function mutaprob_Callback(hObject, eventdata, handles)
% hObject    handle to mutaprob (see GCBO)
% eventdata reserved - to be defined in a future version of MATLAB
% handles    structure with handles and user data (see GUIDATA)


% Hints: get(hObject,'String') returns contents of mutaprob as text
%        str2double(get(hObject,'String')) returns contents of mutaprob as a
double
global pmm
pmm=str2double(get(hObject,'String'));

% --- Executes during object creation, after setting all properties.
function mutaprob_CreateFcn(hObject, eventdata, handles)
% hObject    handle to mutaprob (see GCBO)
% eventdata reserved - to be defined in a future version of MATLAB
% handles    empty - handles not created until after all CreateFcns called


% Hint: edit controls usually have a white background on Windows.
%       See ISPC and COMPUTER.
if ispc && isequal(get(hObject,'BackgroundColor'),
get(0,'defaultUicontrolBackgroundColor'))
    set(hObject,'BackgroundColor','white');
end


function nene_Callback(hObject, eventdata, handles)
% hObject    handle to nene (see GCBO)
% eventdata reserved - to be defined in a future version of MATLAB
% handles    structure with handles and user data (see GUIDATA)


% Hints: get(hObject,'String') returns contents of nene as text
%        str2double(get(hObject,'String')) returns contents of nene as a
double
global N_Generation
```

```
N_Generation=str2double(get(hObject,'String'));

% --- Executes during object creation, after setting all properties.
function nene_CreateFcn(hObject, eventdata, handles)
% hObject    handle to nene (see GCBO)
% eventdata  reserved - to be defined in a future version of MATLAB
% handles    empty - handles not created until after all CreateFcns called

% Hint: edit controls usually have a white background on Windows.
%       See ISPC and COMPUTER.
if ispc && isequal(get(hObject,'BackgroundColor'),
get(0,'defaultUicontrolBackgroundColor'))
    set(hObject,'BackgroundColor','white');
end

function nted_Callback(hObject, eventdata, handles)
% hObject    handle to nted (see GCBO)
% eventdata  reserved - to be defined in a future version of MATLAB
% handles    structure with handles and user data (see GUIDATA)

% Hints: get(hObject,'String') returns contents of nted as text
%        str2double(get(hObject,'String')) returns contents of nted as a
double
global N_Prediction
N_Prediction=str2double(get(hObject,'String'));

% --- Executes during object creation, after setting all properties.
function nted_CreateFcn(hObject, eventdata, handles)
% hObject    handle to nted (see GCBO)
% eventdata  reserved - to be defined in a future version of MATLAB
% handles    empty - handles not created until after all CreateFcns called

% Hint: edit controls usually have a white background on Windows.
%       See ISPC and COMPUTER.
if ispc && isequal(get(hObject,'BackgroundColor'),
get(0,'defaultUicontrolBackgroundColor'))
    set(hObject,'BackgroundColor','white');
end

function firstseed_Callback(hObject, eventdata, handles)
% hObject    handle to firstseed (see GCBO)
% eventdata  reserved - to be defined in a future version of MATLAB
% handles    structure with handles and user data (see GUIDATA)

% Hints: get(hObject,'String') returns contents of firstseed as text
%        str2double(get(hObject,'String')) returns contents of firstseed as
a double
global first_seed
first_seed=str2double(get(hObject,'String'));
```

```
% --- Executes during object creation, after setting all properties.
function firstseed_CreateFcn(hObject, eventdata, handles)
% hObject    handle to firstseed (see GCBO)
% eventdata reserved - to be defined in a future version of MATLAB
% handles    empty - handles not created until after all CreateFcns called


% Hint: edit controls usually have a white background on Windows.
%       See ISPC and COMPUTER.
if ispc && isequal(get(hObject,'BackgroundColor'),
get(0,'defaultUicontrolBackgroundColor'))
    set(hObject,'BackgroundColor','white');
end
```

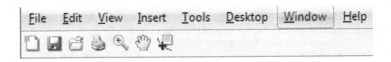

The commands below show how to create menus.

```
function File_Callback(hObject, eventdata, handles)
% hObject handle to File (see GCBO)
% eventdata reserved - to be defined in a future version of MATLAB
% handles structure with handles and user data (see GUIDATA)
% ---------------------------------------------------------------------
function Open_Callback(hObject, eventdata, handles)
% hObject handle to Open (see GCBO)
% eventdata reserved - to be defined in a future version of MATLAB
% handles structure with handles and user data (see GUIDATA)
information = uigetfile('*.m');
if ~ isequal(information, 0)
%open(information);
run information
end
% ---------------------------------------------------------------------
function Exit_Callback(hObject, eventdata, handles)
% hObject handle to Exit (see GCBO)
% eventdata reserved - to be defined in a future version of MATLAB
% handles structure with handles and user data (see GUIDATA)
exit
% ---------------------------------------------------------------------
function Print_Callback(hObject, eventdata, handles)
% hObject handle to Print (see GCBO)
% eventdata reserved - to be defined in a future version of MATLAB
% handles structure with handles and user data (see GUIDATA)
```

In this step we have to choose method for Coefficients Calculation according to the following three below methods.

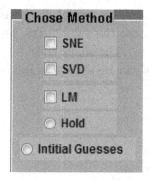

```
function SNE_Callback(hObject, eventdata, handles)
% hObject handle to SNE (see GCBO)
% eventdata reserved - to be defined in a future version of MATLAB
% handles structure with handles and user data (see GUIDATA)
% Hint: get(hObject,'Value') returns toggle state of SNE
global metofcal
if get(hObject,'Value')
metofcal=2;
title('SNE Method','Color','R')
else title('')
end
% --- Executes on button press in SVD.
function SVD_Callback(hObject, eventdata, handles)
% hObject handle to SVD (see GCBO)
% eventdata reserved - to be defined in a future version of MATLAB
% handles structure with handles and user data (see GUIDATA)
% Hint: get(hObject,'Value') returns toggle state of SVD
global metofcal
if get(hObject,'Value')
metofcal=1;
title('SVD Method','Color','R')
else title('')
end
% --- Executes on button press in LM.
function LM_Callback(hObject, eventdata, handles)
% hObject handle to LM (see GCBO)
% eventdata reserved - to be defined in a future version of MATLAB
% handles structure with handles and user data (see GUIDATA)
% Hint: get(hObject,'Value') returns toggle state of LM
global metofcal
if get(hObject,'Value')
metofcal=3;
title('LM Method','Color','R')
else title('')
end
```

The LM algorithm requires an initial guess (IG) for the parameters
to be estimated. We choose the value a=10, b=1, c=35, d=4, e=5 and
f=75 for the initial guess. The main code for the LM algorithm for
refining the parameters can be shown as follows:

```
global IG
global N_Prediction
global informations
IG=[10 1 35 4 5 75]';
run c:\Users\MATLAB\information;
[Rinputs,Cinputs]=size(informations);
for i=1:Cinputs-2
xin(:,i)=informations(:,i+1);
end
y=informations(:,Cinputs);
y=y';
[qwe1,mnb]=size(xin);
Xin_col=mnb;
global N_trn
N_trn=qwe1-N_Prediction
tic
clc
global metofcal
global N_pop
%N_pop=50%input('no pop:');
global N_HL
%N_HL=2%input('Hidden Layer:');
global pc
%pc=.9%input('crossover prob.');
global pmm
%pmm=.1%input('Mutation prob:');
global N_Generation
%N_Generation=150%input('Generation:')
%N_Prediction=5%input('Prediction:');
%metofcal=1
%input('method 1 or 2 or 3:')
global first_seed
%first_seed=-400%input('seed:');
[y,bestfitness,final]=main12
(informations,N_pop,N_HL,pc,pmm,N_Generation,N_Prediction,metofcal,first_seed);
```

The next step is to evaluate the individuals of the population. The
selected individuals are copied unchanged to the next generation (i.e.
to the new population). In order to improve the results, one should
modify the selected individuals, using crossover and mutation. This
function defines a crossover point randomly between two genes in

the chromosomes, and makes two new temporary chromosomes using one-point crossover.

```
Function crosspop=crosso(npop,pc,prob,sortpop,maxlen,xreg,qwe,y,seed)
seed=ran2(-1e6*seed);
crosspop=sortpop;
bcrosspop=sortpop;
nmncross=fix(pc*npop*.5);
jki=1;
beforesele(1)=0.5;
ret=2;
while jki<=nmncross
pl(1)=0;pl(2)=0;
kjk=1;
while (pl(1)==pl(2))|(kjk==1)
seed=ran2(-1e6*seed);
for ha=1:2
seed=ran2(-1e6*seed);
rc(ha)=seed;
end
rc=sort(rc);
fi=1;
ii=1;
while fi<=2
if rc(fi)<prob(ii)
bcrosspop(fi,1:maxlen)=sortpop(ii,1:maxlen);
pl(fi)=ii;
fi=fi+1;
beforesele(jki)=ii;
ii=0;
end
ii=ii+1;
end
[nm,mn]=size(find(beforesele==pl(1)));
[nnm,mnn]=size(find(beforesele==pl(2)));
if (mn>=1)&(mnn>=1)
kjk=1;
else
kjk=2;
beforesele(ret)=pl(1);
beforesele(ret+1)=pl(2);
ret=ret+2;
end
end
[m,n,v]=find(bcrosspop(1,☺));
[mm,nn,vv]=find(bcrosspop(2,☺));
[m,n]=size(v);
[mm,nn]=size(vv);
if n>nn
n=nn;
```

```
end
k=n;
if k==maxlen
k=k-1;
end
seed=ran2(-1e6*seed);
cu=ceil(k*seed);
cu=cu+1;
sav=bcrosspop(1,:);
bcrosspop(1,cu:maxlen)=bcrosspop(2,cu:maxlen);
bcrosspop(2,cu:maxlen)=sav(1,cu:maxlen);
iuy=1;
bB1=find(bcrosspop(iuy,J==bcrosspop(1,1)));
[io,jo,cv]=find(bcrosspop(iuy,:));
[m,n]=size(cv);
[mm,nn]=size(bB1);
bB2=find(bcrosspop(iuy+1,:)==bcrosspop(2,1));
[i,j,cv2]=find(bcrosspop(iuy+1,:));
[m,n2]=size(cv2);
[mm,nn2]=size(bB2);
if (n~ =nn)&(n2~ =nn2)
jki=jki+1;
crosspop(pl(1),:)=bcrosspop(1,:);
crosspop(pl(2),:)=bcrosspop(2,:);
end
end
clear beforesele
```

This function loops through all the genes in a chromosome, and flips the corresponding bit with probability pmut, as specified by the mutation probability variable. In order to implement mutations, enter the following code:

```
function mutpop=muta(pop,len,npop,ninp,pmm,maxlen,sortpop,prob,seed)
seed=ran2(-1e6*seed);
mutpop=sortpop;
nmut=ceil(pmm*npop);
for j=1:nmut
seed=ran2(-1e6*seed);
mupop(j)=ceil(npop*ran2(-1e6*seed));
end
for zx=1:nmut
for ia=1:len(zx)
seed=ran2(-1e6*seed);
poi=ceil(ninp*ran2(-1e6*seed));
mutpop(zx,ia)=poi;
end
end
function [sortpop,prob]=propop(npop,fit,sortfit,pop,maxlen)
```

```
i=1;
while i<=npop
[oo,pp]=find(fit==sortfit(i));
[ii,jj]=size(pp);
for b=1:jj
sortpop(i,1:maxlen)=pop(pp(b),1:maxlen);
i=i+1;
end
end
```

The program just evaluates a single generation and then generates a new population without evaluating it. Almost always, one needs to iterate the processes of evaluation, selection, and reproduction many times. Thus, define a variable number of generations just after the definition of the variable range in the main program. Next, add a for loop that iterates over the number of generations just defined. Finally, add a line that prints the best fitness value, and the corresponding coordinates (x), at the end of each generation;

```
tofit=sum(fit);
prob=sortfit/tofit;
prob=cumsum(prob);
function repop=repro(npop,sortpop,prob,seed)
seed=ran2(-1e6*seed);
for i=1:npop
seed=ran2(-1e6*seed);
rNums(i)=seed;
end
rNums=sort(rNums);
fitIn=1;newIn=1;
while newIn<=npop
if(rNums(newIn)<prob(fitIn))
repop(newIn,:) = sortpop(fitIn,:);
newIn = newIn+1;
else
fitIn = fitIn + 1;
end
end
```

The function The LMFnlsqman serves for finding optimal solution of an overdetermined system of nonlinear equations in the least squares sense. The standard Levenberg–Marquardt algorithm was modified by Fletcher and coded in FORTRAN many years ago. This version of LMFnlsq is its complete MATLAB implementation complemented by setting parameters of iterations as options.

```
function [xf, SS, cnt, res, XY] = LMFnlsqman(varargin)
echo off
if nargin==0 && nargout==0
help LMFnlsqman
return
end % Display help
if nargin==0 ||(nargin==1 && strcmpi('default',varargin(1)))
xf.Display = 0; % no print of iterations
xf.Jacobian = 'finjac'; % finite difference Jacobian approximation
xf.MaxIter = 100; % maximum number of iterations allowed
xf.ScaleD = []; % automatic scaling by D = diag(diag(J'*J))
xf.FunTol = 1e-7; % tolerace for final function value
xf.XTol = 1e-7; % tolerance on difference of x-solutions
xf.Printf = 'printit'; % disply intermediate results
xf.Trace = 0; % don't save intermediate results
xf.Lambda = 0; % start with Newton iteration
return
elseif isstruct(varargin{1}) %
Options=LMFnlsqman(Options,'Name','Value',...)
if ~ isfield(varargin{1},'Jacobian')
error('Options Structure not Correct for LMFnlsqman.')
end
xf=varargin{1}; % Options
for i=2:2:nargin-1
name=varargin{i}; % option to be updated
if ~ ischar(name)
error('Parameter Names Must be Strings.')
end
name=lower(name(isletter(name)));
value=varargin{i+1}; % value of the option
if strncmp(name,'d',1), xf.Display = value;
elseif strncmp(name,'f',1), xf.FunTol = value(1);
elseif strncmp(name,'x',1), xf.XTol = value(1);
elseif strncmp(name,'j',1), xf.Jacobian = value;
elseif strncmp(name,'m',1), xf.MaxIter = value(1);
elseif strncmp(name,'s',1), xf.ScaleD = value;
elseif strncmp(name,'p',1), xf.Printf = value;
elseif strncmp(name,'t',1), xf.Trace = value;
elseif strncmp(name,'l',1), xf.Lambda = value;
else disp(['Unknown Parameter Name -->' name])
end
end
return
elseif ischar(varargin{1}) % check for Options=LMFnlsqman('Name',Value,...)
Pnames=char('display','funtol','xtol','jacobian','maxiter','scaled',...
'printf','trace','lambda');
if strncmpi(varargin{1},Pnames,length(varargin{1}))
xf=LMFnlsqman('default'); % get default values
xf=LMFnlsqman(xf,varargin{:});
return
```

```
end
end
%%%%%%%%%%%%%%%%%%%%%%%%%%%%%%%%%%%%%%%%%%%%%%%
% OPTIONS
% *******
FUN=varargin{1}; % function handle
if ~ (isvarname(FUN) ||isa(FUN,'function_handle'))
error('FUN Must be a Function Handle or M-file Name.')
end
xc=varargin{2}; % Xo
if ~ exist('options','var')
options = LMFnlsqman('default');
end
if nargin>2 % OPTIONS
if isstruct(varargin{3})
options=varargin{3};
else
for i=3:2:size(varargin,2)-1
options=LMFnlsqman(options, varargin{i},varargin{i+1});
end
end
else
if ~ exist('options','var')
options = LMFnlsqman('default');
end
end
% INITIATION OF SOLUTION
% *********************
x = xc(:);
n = length(x);
epsx = options.XTol(:);
le = length(epsx);
if le==1
epsx=epsx*ones(n,1);
else
error(['Dimensions of vector epsx ',num2str(le),'~ =',num2str(lx)]);
end
epsf = options.FunTol(:);
ipr = options.Display;
JAC = options.Jacobian;
maxit = options.MaxIter; % maximum permitted number of iterations
printf= options.Printf;
r = feval(FUN,x);
[A,v] = getAv(FUN,JAC,x,r,epsx);
%~~~~~~~~~~~~~~~~~~~~~~~~~~~~
SS = r'*r;
res= 1;
cnt=0;
trcXY = options.Trace; % iteration tracing
if trcXY
```

```
XY = zeros(n,maxit);
XY(:,1) = x;
else
XY = [];
end
D = options.ScaleD(:); % CONSTANT SCALE CONTROL D
if isempty(D)
D=diag(A); % automatic scaling
else
ld=length(D);
if ld==1
D=abs(D)*ones(n,1); % scalar of unique scaling
elseif ld~=n
error(['wrong number of scales D, lD = ',num2str(ld)])
end
end
D(D<=0)=1;
T = sqrt(D);
Rlo=0.25; Rhi=0.75;
l=options.Lambda; lc=1;
dx = zeros(n,1);
cnt = 0;
% SOLUTION
% ******** MAIN ITERATION CYCLE
while 1 % ********************
feval(printf,ipr,cnt,res,SS,x,dx,l,lc)
cnt = cnt+1;
if trcXY, XY(:,cnt+1)=x; end
d = diag(A);
s = zeros(n,1);
% INTERNAL CYCLE
while 1 % ~~~~~~~
while 1
UA = triu(A,1);
A = UA'+UA+diag(d+l*D);
[U,p] = chol(A); % Choleski decomposition
%~~~~~~~~~~~~~~~~
if p==0, break, end
l = 2*l;
if l==0, l=1; end
end
dx = U\(U'\v);
vw = dx'*v;
fin = -1;
if vw<=0, break, end % The END
for i=1:n
z = d(i)*dx(i);
if i>1, z=A(i,1:i-1)*dx(1:i-1)+z; end
if i<n, z=A(i+1:n,i)'*dx(i+1:n)+z; end
s(i) = 2*v(i)-z;
```

```
end
dq = s'*dx;
s = x-dx;
rd = feval(FUN,s);
% ~~~~~~~~~~
res = res+1;
SSP = rd'*rd;
dS = SS-SSP;
fin = 1;
if all((abs(dx)-epsx)<=0) ||res>=maxit ||abs(dS)<=epsf
break % The END
end
fin=0;
if dS>=Rlo*dq, break, end
A = U;
y = .5;
z = 2*vw-dS;
if z>0, y=vw/z; end
if y>.5, y=.5; end
if y<.1, y=.1; end
if l==0
y = 2*y;
for i = 1:n
A(i,i) = 1/A(i,i);
end
for i = 2:n
ii = i-1;
for j= 1:ii
A(j,i) = -A(j,j:ii)*A(j:ii,i).*A(i,i);
end
end
for i = 1:n
for j= i:n
A(i,j) = abs(A(i,j:n)*A(j,j:n)');
end
end
l = 0;
tr = diag(A)'*D;
for i = 1:n
z = A(1:i,i)'*T(1:i)+z;
if i<n
ii = i+1;
z = A(i,ii:n)*T(ii:n)+z;
end
z = z*T(i);
if z>l, l=z; end
end
if tr<l, l=tr; end
l = 1/l;
lc = l;
```

```
end
l = 1/y;
if dS>0, dS=-1e300; break, end
end % while INTERNAL CYCLE LOOP
% ~~~~~~~~~~~~~~~~~~~~~~~~
if fin, break, end
if dS>Rhi*dq
l=1/2;
if l<lc, l=0; end
end
SS=SSP; x=s; r=rd;
[A,v] = getAv(FUN,JAC,x,r,epsx);
% ~~~~~~~~~~~~~~~~~~~~~~~~
end % while END OF MAIN ITERATION CYCLE
% ************************
if fin>0
if dS>0
SS = SSP;
x = s;
end
end
if ipr~ =0
disp(' ');
feval(printf,sign(ipr),cnt,res,SS,x,dx,l,lc)
end
xf = x;
if trcXY, XY(:,cnt+2)=x; end
XY(:,cnt+3:end) = [];
if res>=maxit, cnt=-maxit; end
return
if nargin==0 && nargout==0
help LMFnlsqman
return
end
```

The main code for the Jacobians' matrices can be shown as follows:

```
function J = finjac(FUN,r,x,epsx)
% FINJAC Numerical approximation to Jacobi matrix
% ~~~~~~~~~~~~~~~~~~~~~~~~~~~~
rc = r(:);
lx = length(x);
J = zeros(length(r),lx);
for k = 1:lx
dx = .25*epsx(k);
xd = x;
xd(k) = xd(k)+dx;
rd = feval(FUN,xd);
% ~~~~~~~~~~~~~~~~~~~~~~~~~~~~
J(:,k)=((rd(:)-rc)/dx);
```

End

This function is used for printing information to the screen.

```
function printit(ipr,cnt,varargin)
echo off
if ipr~ =0 && rem(cnt,ipr)==0
lv = length(varargin); % number of arguments
if lv>4 && ipr<0
lv=lv-2; % no print of l, lc
end
n = min(75-26*(ipr<0),13*lv-3);
hlin = @(n) fprintf(['\n',repmat('*',1,n),'\n']);
if cnt==0 % table header
fulh ={' itr',' nfJ',' sum(r^2)', ' x',...
' dx',' lambda',' lambda_c'...
};
hlin(n);
fprintf('%s',fulh{1:lv+1}); % print header
hlin(n);
end
lx = min(4,lv); % number of printed items - 2
xdx = [varargin{3:lx}];
var = [varargin{1:2},xdx(1,:)]; % 1st row of output
if lv>4 && ipr>0
var = [var varargin{5:6}]; % compl. 1st row by l, lc
end
fprintf(['%4.0f %4.0f ' repmat('%12.4e ',1,lv-1),'\n'], cnt,var); % 1st row
fprintf([blanks(23),repmat('%12.4e ',1,lx-2),'\n'], xdx(2:end,:)'); % others
end
```

.

Chapter 6

GROUP METHOD OF DATA HANDING USING DISCRETE DIFFERENTIAL EVOLUTION IN MATLAB

Donald Davendra, Godfrey Onwubolu and Ivan Zelinka

ABSTRACT

This chapter describes the application of Group Method of Data Handing (GMDH) using Discrete Differential Evolution (DDE). DDE is a discrete variant of the Differential Evolution algorithm, designed to be used in the integer problem space. This makes it an ideal optimizer for the generic GMDH framework. The code is written in the Matlab software and detailed code description is provided with pseudocode representation given in the chapter for all the major functions.

1. GROUP METHOD FOR DATA HANDLING

The framework for modeling chosen for this applied research is based on the Group Method for Data Handling (GMDH) introduced by Ivakhnenko (details are found in [2–4]) as a mean of identifying nonlinear relations between input and output variables. The multi-layered iteration (MIA) network is one of the variants of GMDH.

The MIA relationship between the inputs and the output of a multiple inputs single output self-organizing network can be represented by an infinite Volterra–Kolmogorov–Gabor (VKG) polynomial of the form [2–4]:

$$y_n = a_0 + \sum_{i=1}^{M} a_i x_i + \sum_{i=1}^{M} \sum_{j=1}^{M} a_{ij} x_i x_j + \sum_{i=1}^{M} \sum_{j=1}^{M} \sum_{k=1}^{M} a_{ijk} x_i x_j x_k \cdots,$$

(1.1)

where $X = (x_1, x_2, \ldots, x_M)$ is the vector of input variables and $A = (a_0, a_i, a_{ij}, a_{ijk} \ldots)$ is the vector of coefficients or weights.

When the GMDH network is completed, there is a set of original inputs that filtered through the layers to the optimal output node. This is the computational network that is to be used in computing predictions (in our application, classifications are implied). The best nodes in the input layer (starred nodes in Fig. 1.1) are retained and form the input to the next layer. The inputs for layer 1 are formed by taking all combinations of the surviving output approximations from the input layer nodes. It is seen that at each layer the order of the polynomial approximation is increased by two. The layer 2 best nodes for approximating the system output are retained and form the

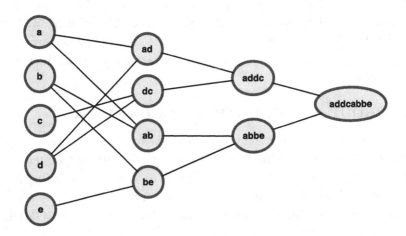

Fig. 1.1.   GMDH Network.

layer 3 inputs. This process is repeated until the current layer's best approximation is inferior to the previous layer's best approximation.

1.1. Advantages of the Basic GMDH Technique

The advantage of using pairs of input is that only six weights (coefficients) have to be computed for each neuron(s). The number of neuron(s) in each layer increases approximately as the square of the number of inputs. During each training cycle, the synaptic weights of each neuron(s) that minimize the error norm between predicted and measured values are computed and those branches that contribute least to the output of the neuron(s) are discarded, the remaining branches being retained and their synaptic weights kept unchanged thereafter. A new layer is subsequently added and the procedure is repeated until the specified termination conditions are met.

There could be summarized that the GMDH-type polynomial networks influence the contemporary artificial neural network algorithms with several other advantages [4]:

(1) they offer adaptive network representations that can be tailored to the given task;
(2) they learn the weights rapidly in a single step by standard ordinary least square (OLS) fitting which eliminates the need to search for their values, and which guarantees finding locally good weights due to the reliability of the fitting technique;
(3) these polynomial networks feature sparse connectivity which means that the best discovered networks can be trained fast.

1.2. Limitations of GMDH Technique

Although standard GMDH provides for a systematic procedure of system modeling and prediction, it has also a number of shortcomings. Anastasakis and Mort [1] have carried out a comprehensive study of the shortcomings of GMDH:

Selection of Input Arguments: One of the main features of GMDH is its ability to objectively select the most appropriate input arguments amongst a set of candidates. However, the identification of these candidate input arguments is not straightforward and may affect its performance.

Inaccuracies in Parameter Estimation: The method of least square estimates is the most popular method to calculate the coefficients of partial descriptions. If the data matrix is well defined its estimates will be accurate however, in the majority of real world systems the data matrix is ill-defined and the least squares biased.

Multicollinearity: Another problem found exclusively in multilayer algorithm, which affects the stability of coefficients, is that of multicollinearity.

Reduction of Complexity: Another shortcoming that found GMDH approach is a tendency to generate quite complex polynomial (since the complexity of the network increases with each training and selection cycle through addition of new layers) for relatively simple systems (data input); also, an inclination to producing overly complex network (model) when dealing with highly nonlinear systems owing to its limited generic structure (quadratic two-variable polynomial).

Formulas of Partial Descriptions: Despite the wide range of partial descriptions majority of researchers follow the argument that Volterra series are capable of identifying any nonlinear system and therefore have adopted polynomial partial descriptions similar to Ivakhnenko polynomial. However, due to the complexity of the model and the requirement of including the theory behind the object, many modifications have been designed in order to adapt to system's properties.

Over-fitting: A consequence of complexity is the over-fitting problem and poor generalization. Partition of Data: The objectiveness of GMDH algorithm is based on the utilization of an external criterion to select the optimum model, which requires the partition of the data.

Low Accuracy in GMDH Method: In many cases and particularly in applications of long range prediction the GMDH has been observed to be inaccurate.

2. DIFFERENTIAL EVOLUTION SCHEMA

The differential evolution (DE) algorithm introduced by Storn and Price [10] is a novel parallel direct search method, which utilizes Np parameter vectors as a population for each generation G. DE is one of the extant evolutionary approaches used to solve complex real-life problems. It was primarily designed for continuous domain space formulation, but was reformulated to solve permutative problems by [5]. DE has a specialized nomenclature that describes the adopted configuration. This takes the form of $DE/x/y/z$, where x represents the solution to be perturbed (such a random or best). The y signifies the number of difference vectors used in the perturbation of x, where a difference vector is the difference between two randomly selected although distinct members of the population. Finally, z signifies the recombination operator performed such as *bin* for binomial and *exp* for exponential. Algorithm 2.1 provides a pseudocode listing of the

---

Algorithm 2.1 Pseudocode for classical Differential Evolution

Precondition:

$Population_{size}, Problem_{size}, Weighting_{factor}(F), Crossover_{rate}(CR).$

1 **function** DE()
2   Population $\leftarrow$ InitializePopulation($Population_{size}, Problem_{size}$)
3   EvaluatePopulation(Population)
4      $\leftarrow S_{best}$ GetBestSolution(Population)
5   **while** $\neg$ StopCondition() **do**
6   NewPopulation $\leftarrow \emptyset$
7   **for** $P_i \in$ Population **do**
8              $S_i \leftarrow$ NewSample($P_{i,population}, Problem_{size}, F, CR$)
9   **if** Cost(S_i) < Cost(P_i)) **then**
10   NewPopulation $\leftarrow S_i$
11   **else**
12   NewPopulation $\leftarrow P_i$
13   Population $\leftarrow$ NewPopulation
14   EvaluatePopulation(Population)
15         $S_{best} \leftarrow$ GetBestSolution(Population)
16   **return** S_{best}

DE algorithm ([6, 7, 9, 10]) for optimizing a cost function, specifically a DE/rand/1/bin configuration.

The overall steps involved in the classical DE are summarized here:

- Step 1: Initialization,
- Step 2: Mutation,
- Step 3: Crossover,
- Step 4: Selection,
- Step 5: Stopping criteria.

3.   DISCRETE DIFFERENTIAL EVOLUTION

The discrete version of differential evolution (DDE) is an integer based approach formulated around the Backward/Forward transformation approach of [6]. The basic outline can be given as follows:

- **Initial Phase**
  - *Population Generation*: a sequence of discrete values is generated within a predefined range, where replication is allowed.

- **Conversion**
  - *Forward transformation*: this conversion schema transforms the discrete individual into the required continuous individual

$$x' = -1 + \frac{x \cdot f \cdot 5}{10^3 - 1}.$$

  - *DE Strategy*: the specified DE strategy is applied to the continuous individual to create the trial individual.
  - *Backward Transformation*: this conversion schema transforms the continuous trial individual back into a discrete individual

$$x = \frac{(1 + x') \cdot (10^3 - 1)}{5 \cdot f}.$$

- **Repairment**: any value which is outside of the given bound is regenerated within the bounds.

The initial phase simply generates a discrete population where each element in the individual is generated within a specified bound.

The difference with the permutative approach of [6] is that this individual is not based on a given permutation, therefore replicated values may exist.

Once the population is generated, it is evaluated for its fitness, and then the forward transformation schema is applied to change each discrete value into a continuous value. The DE schema then operates on the population to generate the trial population. This population, as yet cannot be vetted for its fitness, as it is still in the continuous format. The backward transformation is then applied to the population to regain the discrete population, which is then checked and if required repaired to finally obtain a discrete population. The population is then evaluated for its fitness, and if a trial individual is better than its direct parent, it replaces the parent in the new population. This iterates till a specified termination criteria is met. The outline of DDE can be given as in Fig. 3.1.

4. HYBRID-GMDH NETWORK

Based on the shortcomings of the basic GMDH, hybrids of GMDH were proposed to significantly enhance the performance of GMDH [1]. For ease of reference and clarity to readers, the main design steps for the hybrid group method for data handling-genetic algorithm (GMDH-GA) based approach used for the work reported in this paper which applies to similar hybrid-types are summarized here (interested readers may refer to [8] for details on hybrid-GMDH):

Step 1: Configuration of input variable.

Step 2: Form training and testing data.

Step 3: Decision of initial information for constructing the hybrid GMDH-GA structure: The number of generations, population size, crossover rate, and mutation rate were chosen as 25, 50, 0.9, and 0.1 respectively.

Step 4: Determine polynomial neuron(s) (PN) structure: The vector number of input variables of two, the polynomial order of Type 2 (quadratic), and the input variables were assigned to each node of the corresponding layer.

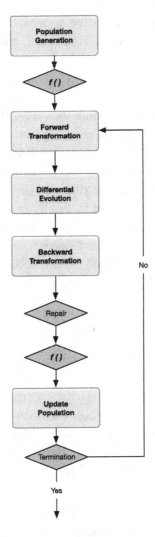

Fig. 3.1.   DDE outline.

Step 5: Parametric optimization: Coefficient estimation of the polynomial corresponding to the selected node (PN): The vector of the coefficients of the partial descriptors (PDs) is determined using a standard mean square error for the training data set subsets.

Step 6: Structural optimization: select nodes (PNs) with the best predictive capability, and construct their corresponding layer: All

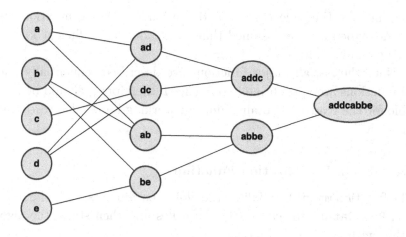

Fig. 4.1.   GMDH-DE network solution.

nodes of the corresponding layer of the hybrid GMDH-DE architecture are constructed by optimization (see Fig. 4.1).

Step 7: Termination criterion: After the iteration process, the final
generation of population consists of highly fit solution population
that provide optimum solutions.

5.   GMDH-DDE IN MATLAB

This section describes the detailed description of the GMDH-DD in
Matlab software. The Matlab software is coded in version R2013a and
backward compatible to R2011a. The generic template of the code is
referenced from Roudbaneh [8]. A number of prerequisites is needed
to make fully understand of the following sections. The reader must
have a working knowledge of Matlab, especially the Mathematics
toolkits and functions. This chapter should be read together with
the supplied codes as there is frequent reference and all nomenclature
follows that of the supplied codes for better correlation. Even though
an effort has been made to make it as generic as possible, many
descriptions requires the understanding of Matlab commands (pinv,
svds, etc.).

Additionally, some basic functions as sorting, pairwise comparison are only generically referenced in the chapter, whereas

printing, plotting, file reading and random number generation are not described as it is assumed that the reader has sufficient knowledge to understand it.

Nevertheless, all major functions are described sequentially and all functions are appropriately referenced, therefore it should be possible for the reader to obtain sufficient working knowledge regarding the code.

5.1.   Main Initialization Function

The function main() initializes the global parameters, calls the function ReadData() to read in the data files and then starts the algorithm with the function main12(...).

There are two components to the global variables. The first is the *problem* variables, and the second is the algorithm *control* variables. The *problem* variables are the problem data files which are stored in the global informations and the global IG is initialized to IG = [1 2 3 4 5 6]'.

The control variables are the global metofcal which is set to 1, global N_pop is the number of individuals in the populations, global N_HL is the number of hidden layers, global pmm is the mutation probability, global N_Generation is the number of generations, global N_Prediction is the prediction ratio, global first_seed is the initial seed, global CR is the crossover constant and global F is the scaling factor in DE. The outline is given in Algorithm 5.2.

5.2.   Data Read Function

The function ReadData() reads in the data from the problem file and assigns them to the appropriate variables. The first procedure is to read in the problem data file. The sample data file named inform.m is given as in Fig. 5.1 where the informations is read into the global informations variable. The first column is the trial number, the next three columns are the tool speed, feed rate and depth-of-cut, whereas the last column is the surface roughness.

The second part is the reading of operating parameters from the data file named mydata.dat, where the variables are the metofcal,

---

Algorithm 5.2 Main

Precondition: None

```
1  function MAIN()
2      global informations    ▷ problem variables from data file
3      global IG                      ▷ IG = [1 2 3 4 5 6]'
4      global metofcal                ▷ problem variables
5      global N_pop                    ▷ Population size
6      global N_HL                       ▷ Hidden Layer
7      global pmm                  ▷ Mutation probability
8      global N_Generation            ▷ Generation number
9      global N_Prediction             ▷ Prediction variable
10     global first_seed                 ▷ Random seed
11     global CR                          ▷ DDE variable
12     global F                           ▷ DDE variable
13     function READDATA()
14     function MAIN12()
```

N_pop, N_HL, pmm, N_Generation, N_Prediction, first_seed, CR and F.

The function description is given in Algorithm 5.3.

5.3. Main Iteration Function

Once the input data has been read into the program, the main iteration function is called as main12(...). This function has the input as all input parameters, and the output of this function is the dimension of the inputs (the number of distinct parameters, 27 in this case as given in Fig. 5.2), the best fitness value, bestfit and the final population, final as given in Algorithm 5.4.

The function is divided into a number of sub-functions which are called iteratively during the generations. The six main sub-functions are the fitn2() (Sec. 5.12), propop() (Sec. 5.4), repop() (Sec. 5.5), DEIteration() (Sec. 5.7), lengha() (Sec. 5.6) and muta() (Sec. 5.11).

```
informations = [
1 27   0.0188 0.5 8
2 27 0.0188 1 2.3
3 27 0.0188 1.5 2.6
4 27 0.059 0.5 1.7
5 27 0.059 1 2.45
6 27 0.059 1.5 2.7
7 27 0.1684 0.5 1.95
8 27 0.1684 1 2.55
9 27 0.1684 1.5 2.85
10 36 0.0188 0.5 2.9
11 36 0.0188 1 3.35
12 36 0.0188 1.5 4.35
13 36 0.059 0.5 3.105
14 36 0.059 1 3.55
15 36 0.059 1.5 4.5
16 36 0.1684 0.5 3.196
17 36 0.1684 1 3.95
18 36 0.1684 1.5 4.65
19 49 0.0188 0.5 4.95
20 49 0.0188 1 5.85
21 49 0.0188 1.5 7.7
22 49 0.059 0.5 5.2
23 49 0.059 1 6.25
24 49 0.059 1.5 10.2
25 49 0.1684 0.5 5.45
26 49 0.1684 1 6.75
27 49 0.1684 1.5 19.52
];
```

Fig. 5.1.   **inform.m** file parameters.

2 5 2 0.07 3 2 5 0.7 0.7

Fig. 5.2.   **mydata.dat** file parameters.

When the DE generation has been completed, the best individual is evaluated for error computations for the training and prediction sets. Three unique identifies are computed as the size of the input (xin_col), N_trn and best_pop which are obtained from the final population.

Algorithm 5.3 Global Data

Precondition: global declarations from `main()` function (Algorithm 5.2)

```
1  function READDATA()
2      global informations ← run inform  ▷ read in the problem data
       file
3      global metofcal ← mydata.txt              ▷ read in the data file
4      global N_pop ← mydata.txt
5      global N_HL ← mydata.txt
6      global pmm ← mydata.txt
7      global N_Generation ← mydata.txt
8      global N_Prediction ← mydata.txt
9      global first_seed ← mydata.txt
10     global CR ← mydata.txt
11     global F ← mydata.txt
12     return globals to main() function (Algorithm 5.2)
```

These variables as passed to the `multip()` function (Sec. 5.13) to obtain the final objective value as `yout` for the given input `y`. Using `yout` the `MRe_Train` can be computed as $MRe\_Train = \frac{\sum_1^{10} Re}{10}$ and the `MRe_Predict` as $MRe\_Predict = \frac{\sum_{11}^{15} Re}{5}$, where `Re` is computed as $Re = \frac{ABS(y-yout)}{y}$ in Algorithm 5.5.

The final output of the software is the plot of the `y` against `yout`^{T} as given in Fig. 5.3 as the fitting of the approximation over the obtained values.

5.4. Propop Function

The `propop()` function takes as input the number of individuals in the population (`npop`), the fitness of the population (`fit`), the sorted population (`sortfit`), population (`pop`) and the maxlength (`maxeln`). Iterating through the sorted fitness, the relative index in the population is obtained. Taking the size of the index, the relative position of the fitness individual is obtained in the population. This indexed individual is then copied to the sorted population (`sortpop`).

The fraction of the fitness to its sum total is computed in the array `prob`. Its cumulative average is then returned to the `main12()`

Algorithm 5.4 Main iteration function (part 1)

Precondition: `global` declarations from `main()` function (Algorithm 5.2)

---

1 **function** MAIN12()

2   maxlen = $2^{(N\_HL+1)}$ ▷ length of the hidden layer

3   qwe = size(y) - N_Prediction   ▷ dimension

4   nlay = $\frac{\log(\max len)}{\log(2)}$ ▷ number of layer

5   ninp = dimension$|y|$ ▷ number of dimension in input

6   **for** $i \leftarrow 1$ to N_{Pop} **do**

7   len (i) $\leftarrow$ maxlen $\times$ rand()   ▷ randomly set the length of
    each individual

8   **for** $j \leftarrow 1$ to N_{Pop} **do**

9   pop(i) = ceil(maxlen $\times$ *rand*())   ▷ population gen

10   **for** $i \leftarrow 1$ to $N_{Generation}$ **do**

11   f(pop(i)) $\leftarrow$ evelute fitness   ▷ Sec. 5.12

12   averfitt $\leftarrow$ average fitness

13   bestfit $\leftarrow$ best fitness value

14   fina $\leftarrow$ best fitness array

15   sortpop, prob $\leftarrow$ propop()   ▷ Sec. 5.4

16   repop $\leftarrow$ repop()   ▷ Sec. 5.5

17   sortpop, prob $\leftarrow$ propop()   ▷ Sec. 5.4

18   pop $\leftarrow$ DEIteration()   ▷ Sec. 5.7

19   len $\leftarrow$ lengha()   ▷ Sec. 5.6

20   f(pop(i)) $\leftarrow$ evelute fitness   ▷ Sec. 5.12

21   sortpop, prob $\leftarrow$ propop()   ▷ Sec. 5.4

22   mutpop $\leftarrow$ muta()   ▷ Sec. 5.11

23   **return** averfit, bestfit, finalpop

---

function alongside the sorted population (`sortpop`). The outline of this function is given in Algorithm 5.7.

5.5. Repop Function

The `repop()` function computes the probability of an individual in the sorted population based on an external randomly generated sequence. The required parameters for this function is the number of individuals in the population (`npop`), the sorted population (`sortpop`), and the probability array (`prob`).

Algorithm 5.5 Main iteration function (part 2)

Precondition: from Algorithm 5.4

---

1 **function** MAIN12()(from Algorithm 5.4)
2   xin_col = size(xin)   ▷ size of the input
3   N_trn = qwe1 - N_Prediction   ▷ dimension
4   best_pop = final_pop   ▷ assign best_pop
5   yout ← multip()   ▷ Sec. 5.13
6   yout ← yout^T ▷ transpose yout
7    $\text{Re} = \frac{\text{ABS}(y-yout)}{y}$ ▷ compute the data set
8    $\text{MRe\_Train} = \frac{\sum_1^{10}\text{Re}}{10}$ ▷ compute training set from 1–10
9    $\text{MRe\_Predict} = \frac{\sum_{11}^{15}\text{Re}}{5}$ ▷ compute prediction set from 11–15
10   **return** End

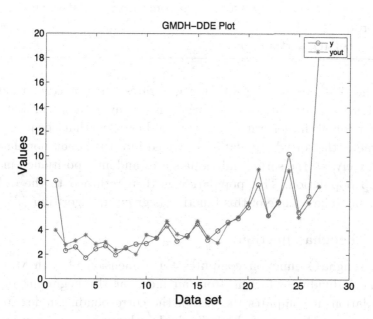

Fig. 5.3. Output plot of y vs $yout^T$.

Algorithm 5.6 propop function

Precondition: number of individuals in the population (`npop`), the fitness of the population (`fit`), the sorted population (`sortfit`), population (`pop`) and the maxlength (`maxlen`)

1 **function** PROPOP()(npop, fit, sortfit, pop, maxlen)
2   **for** $i \leftarrow 1$ to *npop* **do**
3   k = index(sortfit) $\leftarrow$ pop   ▷ index of the sorted population is in the population
4   s = size(k)   ▷ size of the index
5   **for** $j \leftarrow 1$ to *s* **do**
6   sortpop(i) = pop(j)   ▷ create the sorted population
7   tofit $\leftarrow$ sum(fit)   ▷ calculate the total fitness
8   prob $\leftarrow$ sortfit/tofit ▷ divide the sorted fitness by total sum
9   prob $\leftarrow$ cumsum(prob)   ▷ compute cumulative sum of the prob
10   **return** sortpop, prob

The first part of the function generates a sequence of random numbers in `rNums` array. Comparing this array with the probability array `prob`, if the generated random number is less than the probability value, the sorted population is copied into the `repop` population. Iteratively, all the sorted individuals are randomly positioned in the `repop` population. This population is then returned to the calling function. The outline of this function is given in Algorithm 5.7.

5.6.   Lengha Function

The `lengha()` function computes the dimension of each variable in the individual. Starting from an index at the beginning of the population, it computes the size of the corresponding index in the population. The size of the individual (column size) is then stored in the `len` array and returned to the calling function as shown in Algorithm 5.8.

Algorithm 5.7 repop function

Precondition: number of individuals in the population (**npop**), the sorted population (**sortpop**) and the probability (**prob**).

1 **function** REPOP()(npop, sortpop, prob)
2   **for** $i \leftarrow 1$ to *npop* **do**
3   rNums(i) = rand()   ▷ randomly generate a sequence of numbers
4   rNums $\leftarrow$ sort(rNums)   ▷ sort in ascending order
5   g = 1   ▷ index for sortpop
6   **for** $i \leftarrow 1$ to *npop* **do**
7   **if** $rNums(i) < prob(g)$ **then**
8   repop(i) $\leftarrow$ sortpop(g) ▷ copy the sortpop into repop
9   **else**
10   g = g + 1   ▷ increment counter g
11   **return** repop

Algorithm 5.8 lengha function

Precondition: number of individuals in the population (**npop**) and the population (**pop**).

1 **function** LENGHA()(pop, npop)
2   **for** $i \leftarrow 1$ to *npop* **do**
3   len(i) = size(find(pop(i))) ▷ obtain the size of the position of the corresponding index in the population
4   **return** len

5.7. DEIteration Function

The main input of this research is the application of Discrete Differential Evolution (DDE) algorithm as the optimizer for GMDH. Once the population is created and evaluated for its fitness, the population (**pop**), input file data (**xin**), fitness of the population (**fit**), the crossover constant (**CR**) and the scaling factor (**F**) are passed to the DEIteration() function.

The function calculates the size of the population (`npop`) and the best value position in the population (`best`). Iterating through the population, all individuals are converted to *real* numbers in the function `DEForwardTransformation()` described in Sec. 5.8. This is required as the DE algorithm cannot operate on the discrete or integer domain. Once all the individuals are transformed, the main routine for DDE application is called in the `DERoutine()` function as described in Sec. 5.9.

The output of the `DERoutine()` function is the trial population. This population is however in real value form, and needs to be transformed back into integer form using the `DEBackward Transformation()` function given in Sec. 5.10. During this conversion, there may exist some infeasible elements in the individual, which may be outside the bounds given by `xin`. There infeasible values are randomly reset to within the bounds. The final population `DEPopulation` is returned to the calling function. The outline of this function is given in Algorithm 5.9.

5.8.   DEForwardTransformation Function

The `DEForwardTransformation()` function transform the integer values in the population to real values. Each value in the individual is multiplied by 500 and the result is divided by 999. The resultant is then added by -1 as given in Algorithm 5.10.

5.9.   DERoutine Function

Once all the values have been transformed to the real domain, the `DERealPopulation` is passed to the `DERoutine()` function. The parameters needed for the function are the DE population (`DEPop`), population size (`PopSize`), size of the individual (`PopDimension`), best position (`BestPosition`), current iteration (`Iter`), the crossover constant (`CR`) and the scaling factor (`F`).

Two counters are required; the first is the start position (`start`), which is randomly selected in the individual. The second is the `counter` which is used to iterate through the individual. For each index, a random number is generated and if it is less than the value

---

Algorithm 5.9 DEIteration function

Precondition: number of individuals in the population (`npop`), input file data (`xin`), fitness of the population (`fit`), the crossover constant (`CR`) and the scaling factor (`F`).

1 **function** DEITERATION()(xin, pop, fit, CR, F)
2   DERealPopulation ← DEForwardTransformation() ▷ Section 5.8
3   npop ← size(pop)   ▷ size of pop
4   best ← max(fit)   ▷ position of best fitness
5   **for** i ← 1 to *npop* **do**
6   **if** $i = best$ **then**
7   TrialPopulation(i) = DEPop(best)   ▷ copy the best into the trial pop
8   **else**
9   TrialPopulation(i) = DERoutine()   ▷ Sec. 5.9
10   DEPopulation ← DEBackwardTransformation()   ▷ Sec. 5.10
11   DEPopulation ← repair   ▷ check for feasibility
12   **return** DEPopulation

Algorithm 5.10 DEForwardTransformation function

Precondition: DE population (`DEPop`), population size (`PopSize`) and size of the individual (`PopDimension`).

1 **function** DEFORWARDTRANSFORMATION()(DEPop, PopSize, PopDimension)
2   **for** i ← 1 to *PopSize* **do**
3   **for** j ← 1 to *PopDimension* **do**
4   DERealPopulation(i,j) = -1 + ((DEPop(i,j) × 500) / 999)
5   **return** DERealPopulation

Algorithm 5.11 DERoutine function

Precondition: DE population (`DEPop`), population size (`PopSize`), size of the individual (`PopDimension`), best position (`BestPosition`), current iteration (`Iter`), the crossover constant (`CR`) and the scaling factor (`F`).

1 **function** DEROUTINE()(DEPop, PopSize, PopDimension, BestPosition, Iter, CR, F)

2   `VectorIndex[2]` ← 2 pairwise unique indicies

3   start = ceil(PopDimension) × rand()

4   counter = 0

5   **while** $rand() < CR$ and counter < PopDimension **do**

6   `DEIndividual(start) = DEPop(BestPosition, start) + (F ×` `DEPop(VectorIndex(1), start) - DEPop(VectorIndex(2), start))`

7   start = start + 1   ▷ increment start

8   counter = counter + 1   ▷ increment counter

9   **return** DEIndividual

---

of `CR`, then the DE crossover schema is applied to the indexed counter in the individual.

The DE schema used in this research is the DE/best/2/bin, which infers that the best individual in the population is used as the base individual which is added to the difference of two randomly indexed individuals (`VectorIndex`) multiplied by `F`. The resulting trial individual (`DEIndividual`) is returned to the calling function as given in Algorithm 5.11.

5.10. DEBackwardTransformation Function

The `DEBackwardTransformation()` function transforms the real values in the `DEIndividual` to integer values. This is the reserve of the forward transformation, where each value in the individual is multiplied by 999 and the result is divided by 500. The resultant is then added by 1 and rounded to the closest integer as given in Algorithm 5.12.

Algorithm 5.12 DEBackwardTransformation function

Precondition: DE population (`DEPop`), population size (`PopSize`) and size of the individual (`PopDimension`).

1 **function** DEBACKWARDTRANSFORMATION()(DEPop, PopSize, PopDimension)
2   **for** $i \leftarrow 1$ to *PopSize* **do**
3   **for** $j \leftarrow 1$ to *PopDimension* **do**
4   DEDiscretePopulation(i,j) = round(1 + ((DEPop(i,j) × 999) / 500))
5   **return** DEDiscretePopulation

5.11.   Muta Function

The `muta()` function computes a mutation population based on the global `pmm` variable. The required parameters for this function is the number of individuals in the population (`npop`), the sorted population (`sortpop`), the main population (`pop`), the variable array (`len`), the dimension of the data (`ninp`), the global `pmm` variable, the maximum length (`maxlen`), and the probability array (`prob`).

The `mutapop` population is obtained from the sorted population (`sortpop`). The mutation index (`nmut`) is computed as the product of the upper bound of the size of the population (`npop`) and `rand()`. Using `nmut` as the maximum iterator, each variable in the population indexed through the variable array (`len`) is modified by a random number between the dimensions of the problem (`ninp`). This is the mutation function to induce diversity in the population in-between iterations. This mutated population (`mutapop`) is returned to the calling function. The outline of this function is given in Algorithm 5.13.

5.12.   Fitn2 Function

The `fitn2()` function is the objective evaluation function. The required parameters for this function is the input file data (`xin`), the variable array (`len`), the number of individuals in the population (`npop`), the main population (`pop`), the layer (`qwe`), the problem

---

Algorithm 5.13 muta function

Precondition: number of individuals in the population (**npop**), the sorted population (**sortpop**), the main population (**pop**), the variable array (**len**), the dimension of the data (**ninp**), the global **pmm** variable, the maximum length (**maxlen**) and the probability array (**prob**).

1 **function** MUTA()(pop, len, npop, ninp, maxlen, sortpop, prob)
2   mutapop ← sortpop   ▷ copy sortpop to mutapop
3   nmut = ceil(npop × rand())   ▷ compute the nmut index relative to size of population.
4   **for** $i \leftarrow 1$ to $nmut$ **do**
5   **for** $j \leftarrow 1$ to $len(i)$ **do**
6   mutpop(i,j) = ceil(ninp × rand())   ▷ generate a random mutation relative to the ninp
7   **return** mutapop

---

data (**y**), data sample size (**qwe1**), the method (1, 2 or 3 of **metofcal**), and the dimension of the problem (**ninp**).

The first step is to sort the population in ascending order for each pairwise element in each individual. Therefore, elements 1 and 2 are sorted in ascending order, and then elements 3 and 4 are sorted likewise. This process is iterated for all the elements in the individuals over the entire population.

Iterating through the population, the first step is to generate the layers. Taking the **len** as the base for each individual, the neuron(s) (**n**) is calculated. If the value of **n** is 2, then the neuron(s) layer is obtained directly from the indexed population, otherwise the **layer** is computed as $layer = \log(n)/\log(2)$. This computes the number of layers in the network for each neuron(s) layer.

Iterating through the neuron(s) **layer**, each subsequent layer is calculated as neuron(s)$(i + 1, h)$ = neuron(s)(i, j) · $((ninp + 1)^{\wedge}(2^{\wedge}(i - 1)))$ + neuron(s)$(i, j + 1)$, where i is the population iterator, j is the **len** iterator and h is the iterator of the neuron(s) layer. The neuron(s) layer is then pairwise sorted as given in Algorithm 5.14.

Algorithm 5.14 fitn2 function (part 1)

Precondition: input file data (`xin`), the variable array (`len`), the number of individuals in the population (`npop`), the main population (`pop`), the layer (`qwe`), the problem data (`y`), data sample size (`qwe1`), the method (1, 2 or 3) (`metofcal`), and the dimension of the problem (`ninp`).

1 **function** FITN2()(xin, len, npop, pop, qwe, y, qwe1, metofcal, ninp)

2   pop ← **pairwise sort**   ▷ sort each dual individual pairwise in descending order

3   **for** $i \leftarrow 1$ to $npop$ **do**

4   n = len(i)

5   **if** n = 2 **then**

6   neuron(s)(1) = pop(i)   ▷ copy pop into neuron(s)

7   **else**

8   layer = $\frac{\log(n)}{\log(2)}$ ▷ compute layer

9   **if** n = 32 **then**

10   layer = layer - 1; qwe

11             $h = 1$ ▷ set counter

12   **for** $j \leftarrow 1$ to $size(len)$ **do**

13   neuron(s)$(i+1, h)$ = neuron(s)$(i, j) \cdot ((ninp+1)^\wedge(2^\wedge(i-1))) +$ neuron(s)$(i, j+1)$ ▷ compute neuron(s) layer

14   neuron(s) ← **pairwise sort**   ▷ sort each dual neuron(s) pairwise in descending order

15   continued...

Once the **neuron(s)** layer is sorted, we iterate through the number of **neuron(s)** layers. For the initial iteration, we obtain subsequent neuron(s) u and v from the first layer. Each subsequent layer obtains u and v pairwise. If the adjacent neuron(s) are equal, **xnew** is updated from the input data **xin** for the u index. However, if they are unique, then the matrix of coefficients vectors **A** of size **qwe** is generated as $A(w) = \{1, xin(w, u), xin(w, v), xin(w, u)^\wedge 2, xin(w, v)^\wedge 2, xin(w, u) \cdot xin(w, v)\}$. The first column is value 1, the second and third columns are indexed **xin** for u and v, the fourth and fifth columns are the squared values of second and third columns and the final column is the product of the second and third columns.

If the **metofcal** is selected as 1 in the input file, then resultant matrix **a** is computed as the transpose of $a = PINV(A^T \cdot A) \cdot A^T \cdot (y^T)$, where the pseudo-inverse of the product of matrix **A** and its transpose A^T is multiplied by the product of the transpose A^T and input y^T.

If the **metofcal** is selected as 2 in the input file, then the singular values of the coefficients vector **A** is computed as $[U, S, V] = SVDS$ (A), where U and V are orthonormal and S is diagonal matrix. Iterating though the diagonal matrix S, each subsequent entry is checked against a minimum value and adjusted. Thereafter, the resultant matrix **a** can computed as the transpose of $a = V \cdot S \cdot U^T \cdot (y^T)$, which is the product of V, S, U^T and y^T as given in Algorithm 5.15.

Likewise if **metofcal** is 3, then the same procedure for **metofcal** = 1 is used to generate **a**. The external function **run_lm()** and **LMFnlsqman()** is called to generate **a**. Similar approach is also used when **metofcal** is 4, apart from the initial allocation of **a**, instead the transpose of the global **IG** is used. As we have only used **metofcal** of 1 and 2 in our experimentations, the detailed description of the functions **run_lm()** and **LMFnlsqman()** is omitted.

Once the layers have been generated, the coefficients vector is computed as:

$$xnew(w, p) = \begin{pmatrix} a(1,1) + a(1,2) \cdot xin(w,u) + a(1,3) \cdot xin(w,v) \\ + \cdots + a(1,4) \cdot xin(w,u)^\wedge 2 + a(1,5) \\ \cdot xin(w,v)^\wedge 2 + a(1,6) \cdot xin(w,u) \cdot xin(w,v) \end{pmatrix}$$

where w is the iterator for the **qwe1** and u, v are indexes. Subsequently, value in array **len** is then halved and **xin** is updated from **xnew**. The outline of this can be seen in Algorithm 5.16.

If the value of **len** is 32 in any position, a similar procedure to Algorithms 5.15 and 5.16 is applied with the exception being that u = 1 and v = 2.

The **error** is computed as $err(i) = err(i) + (xin(l) - y(l))^2$, where i is the population counter and l is the iterator for **wqe**. The average **error** is given as a factor of $err = err/qwe$ whereas **fitness** is the

---

Algorithm 5.15 fitn2 function (part 2)
Precondition: from Algorithm 5.14.

---

1 **function** FITN2()(continued from Algorithm 5.14)
2   **for** $f \leftarrow 1$ to $size(neuron(s))$ **do**
3   counter $p = 1$ ▷ set counter to 1
4   **for** $g \leftarrow 1$ to $len(i)$ **do**
5   **if** f $= 1$ **then**
6                 $u = $ neuron(s)(f,g)
7                 $v = $ neuron(s)(f,g+1)
8   **else**
9                 $u = $ g
10                 $v = $ g+1
11   **if** neuron(s)(f,g) $=$ neuron(s)(f,g+1) **then**
12   `xnew(p)` $= $ `xin(u)`
13   **else**
14   **for** $w \leftarrow 1$ to qwe **do**
15

$A(w) = \{1, xin(w,u), xin(w,v), xin(w,u)^\wedge 2, xin(w,v)^\wedge 2, xin \quad (w,u) \cdot xin(w,v)\}$ ▷ compute A as a sequence of weighted values of input

16   **if** metofcal $= 1$ **then**
17                     $a = PINV(A^T \cdot A) \cdot A^T \cdot (y^T)$ ▷ compute the pseudo inverse of $A^T \cdot A$ multiplied by $A^T \cdot y^T$
18                     $a = a^T$ ▷ obtain the transpose of a
19   **else** metofcal $= 2$
20                     $[U, S, V] = SVDS(A)$ ▷ compute the singular values of A where U and V are orthonormal and S is diagonal.
21   **for** $r \leftarrow 1$ to $size(S)$ **do**
22   **if** S(r,r) $>$ 1e-3 **then**
23   S(r,r) $= 1 / S$(r,r)
24   **else**
25   S(r,r) $= 0$
26                   $a = V \cdot S \cdot U^T \cdot (y^T)$ ▷ obtain the matrix products
27                 $a = a^T$ ▷ obtain the transpose of a
28   continued...

Algorithm 5.16 fitn2 function (part 3)

Precondition: from Algorithm 5.15.

---

1 **function** FITN2()(continued from Algorithm 5.15)

2   **if** metofcal = 3 **then**

3         $a = PINV(A^T \cdot A) \cdot A^T \cdot (y^T)$ ▷ compute the pseudo inverse of $A^T \cdot A$ multiplied by $A^T \cdot y^T$

4         $a = a^T$ ▷ obtain the transpose of a

5         $[x] = f(xin, qwe, A, u, v, a)$ ▷ call function run_lm() to generate x

6         $a = x$ ▷ assign x to a

7   **else** metofcal = 4

8         $a = [IG]^T$ ▷ obtain the transpose of IG

9         $[x] = f(xin, qwe, A, u, v, a)$ ▷ call function run_lm() to generate x

10        $a = x$ ▷ assign x to a

11   **for** $w \leftarrow 1$ to $qwe1$ **do**

12
$$xnew(w, p) = \begin{pmatrix} a(1,1) + a(1,2) \cdot xin(w,u) + a(1,3) \\ \cdot xin(w,v) + \cdots + a(1,4) \cdot xin(w,u)^\wedge 2 \\ + a(1,5) \cdot xin(w,v)^\wedge 2 + a(1,6) \\ \cdot xin(w,u) \cdot xin(w,v) \end{pmatrix}$$

13 $p = p + 1$

14 len(i) = len(i)/2

15 xin = xnew

16   continued...

---

inverse of the **error** given as $fit = 1/err$. The function returns the polynomial matrices (**yout**), population (**xpop**), fitness (**fit**), sorted fitness (**sortfit**), and average fitness (**averfit**) back to the calling function as given in Algorithm 5.17.

Algorithm 5.17 fitn2 function (part 4)

Precondition: from Algorithm 5.16.

---

1 **function** FITN2()(continued from Algorithm 5.15)
2   **for** $l \leftarrow 1$ to qwe **do**
3         $err(i) = err(i) + (xin(l) - y(l))^2$ ▷ compute error
4   yout $=$ xin   ▷ assign yout from xin
5     $err = {}^{err}\!/_{qwe}$ ▷ cumulative error
6     $fit = {}^{1}\!/_{err}$ ▷ fitness error
7   averfit $\leftarrow$ mean fit ▷ average fitness
8   sortfit $\leftarrow$ sort fit ▷ sorted fitness
9   **return** yout, xpop, fit, sortfit, averfit

5.13. Multip Function

The multip() function is the final objective evaluation function. The required parameters for this function is the input file data (xin), the problem data (y), column size of xin (xin_col), best population best_pop, the data size minus the N_Prediction value (N_trn) and the method (1, 2 or 3 of metofcal).

This function mirrors that of fitn2(), the major difference being the use of the best population in the computations. Once the function is called with the parameters, the neuron(s) counter nn is initialized. The next step involves the pairwise sorting of the best population into ascending order. If the value of the len array n is 2, then the neuron(s) layer is obtained directly from the best population, otherwise the layer is computed as $layer = \log(n)/\log(2)$. If n is 32, then the layer is decremented by 1. The neuron(s) layer counter h is initialized to 1.

The neuron(s) is updated as neuron(s) $(i+1, h) = $ neuron(s)$(i, j) \cdot ((xin_col + 1)^\wedge(2^\wedge(i - 1))) + $ neuron(s)$(i, j + 1)$, with the counter h being incremented after each iteration. The major difference in this calculation is the use of the xin_col and not the problem dimension ninp.

After each iteration of the layer, the population is sorted pairwise as shown in Algorithm 5.18.

Algorithm 5.18 multip function (part 1)

Precondition: input file data (`xin`), the problem data (`y`), column size of `xin` (`xin_col`), best population `best_pop`, the data size minus the `N_Prediction` (`N_trn`) and the method (1, 2 or 3) (`metofcal`).

1 **function** MULTIP()(xin, y, xin_col, best_pop, N_Prediction, N_trn, metofcal)

2     $nn = 1$ ▷ neuron(s) counter

3   best_pop ← **pairwise sort**   ▷ sort each dual individual pairwise in descending order

4   **for** $i \leftarrow 1$ to $size(best\_pop)$ **do**

5   n = len(i)

6   **if** n = 2 **then**

7   neuron(s)(1) = best_pop(i)   ▷ copy pop into neuron(s)

8   **else**

9   layer = $\log(n)/\log(2)$ ▷ compute layer

10   **if** n = 32 **then**

11   layer = layer - 1; qwe

12            $h = 1$ ▷ set counter

13   **for** $j \leftarrow 1$ to $size(len)$ **do**

14   neuron(s)$(i+1, h) =$
neuron(s)$(i, j) \cdot ((\text{xin\_col} + 1)^{\wedge}(2^{\wedge}(i - 1))) + \text{neuron(s)}(i, j + 1)$ ▷ compute neuron(s) layer

15                $h = h + 1$

16   neuron(s) ← **pairwise sort**   ▷ sort each dual neuron(s) pairwise in descending order

17   continued...

Algorithms 5.19 and 5.20 are likewise similar in the application to `fitn2()` function. The major difference is the application of the `multip` matrix which is updated by the coefficients vector **a** after the application of `metofcal` routines. The second difference is the updating of the `yout` by the transpose of `xnew`.

The two error calculations, the error prediction (`err_predict`) and training error (`err_train`) are computed in Algorithm 5.21. The

---

Algorithm 5.19 multip function (part 2)

Precondition: from Algorithm 5.18.

```
1  function MULTIP()(continued from Algorithm 5.18)
2      for f ← 1 to size(neuron(s)) do
3          counter p = 1                                    ▷ set counter to 1
4          for g ← 1 to len(i) do
5              if f = 1 then
6                  u = neuron(s)(f,g)
7                  v = neuron(s)(f,g+1)
8              else
9                  u = g
10                 v = g+1
11             if neuron(s)(f,g) = neuron(s)(f,g+1) then
12                 xnew(p) = xin(u)
13             else
14                 for w ← 1 to qwe do
```

15                  $A(w)$ =
$\{1, xin(w, u), xin(w, v), xin(w, u)^\wedge 2, xin(w, v)^\wedge 2, xin\ (w, u) \cdot xin(w, v)\}$
▷ compute A as a sequence of weighted values of input

16   **if** metofcal = 1 **then**

17                 $a = PINV(A^T \cdot A) \cdot A^T \cdot (y^T)$ ▷ compute the pseudo inverse of $A^T \cdot A$ multiplied by $A^T \cdot y^T$

18                 $a = a^T$ ▷ obtain the transpose of a

19   **else** metofcal = 2

20                 $[U, S, V] = SVDS(A)$ ▷ compute the singular values of A where U and V are orthonormal and S is diagonal.

21   **for** $r ← 1$ to $size(S)$ **do**

22   **if** $S(r,r) > $ 1e-3 **then**

23                      $S(r,r) = 1 / S(r,r)$

24   **else**

25                      $S(r,r) = 0$

26                 $a = V \cdot S \cdot U^T \cdot (y^T)$ ▷ obtain the matrix products

27                 $a = a^T$ ▷ obtain the transpose of a

28   continued...

Algorithm 5.20 multip function (part 3)

Precondition: from Algorithm 5.19.

---

1 **function** MULTIP()(continued from Algorithm 5.19)

2   **if** metofcal = 3 **then**

3        $a = PINV(A^T \cdot A) \cdot A^T \cdot (y^T)$ ▷ compute the pseudo inverse of $A^T \cdot A$ multiplied by $A^T \cdot y^T$

4        $a = a^T$ ▷ obtain the transpose of a

5        $[x] = f(xin, qwe, A, u, v, a)$ ▷ call function run_lm() to generate x

6        $a = x$ ▷ assign x to a

7   **else** metofcal = 4

8        $a = [IG]^T$ ▷ obtain the transpose of IG

9        $[x] = f(xin, qwe, A, u, v, a)$ ▷ call function run_lm() to generate x

10       $a = x$ ▷ assign x to a

11   `multip(nn)` = a   ▷ assign a to multip

12    $nn = nn + 1$ ▷ increment neuron(s) counter

13

14   **for** $w \leftarrow 1$ **to** $qwe1$ **do**

15

$$xnew(w, p) = \begin{pmatrix} a(1,1) + a(1,2) \cdot xin(w,u) + a(1,3) \\ \cdot xin(w,v) + \cdots + a(1,4) \cdot xin(w,u)^{\wedge}2 \\ + a(1,5) \cdot xin(w,v)^{\wedge}2 + a(1,6) \\ \cdot xin(w,u) \cdot xin(w,v) \end{pmatrix}$$

16 $p = p + 1$

17 len(i) = len(i)/2   ▷ decrease len values by half

18 `xin = xnew`   ▷ update xin by xnew

19 `yout = xnew`^{T} ▷ update yout by transpose of xnew

20   continued...

---

error prediction is calculated as $err\_predict = \frac{err\_predict}{qwe1 - qwe}$ and the training error is given as $err\_train = \frac{err}{qwe}$, where `qwe1` is the total sample size and `qwe` is the sample size minus the `N_Prediction`. The function returns **yout** to the calling function.

Algorithm 5.21 multip function (part 4)

Precondition: from Algorithm 5.20.

---

1 **function** MULTIP()(continued from Algorithm 5.20)   err(i) = 0   ▷ initialize error

2   err_predict(i) = 0   ▷ initialize prediction error

3   **for** $l \leftarrow 1$ to qwe **do**

4        $err(i) = err(i) + (xin(l) - y(l))^2$ ▷ compute errors

5   **for** $l \leftarrow qwe + 1$ to $qwe1$ **do**

6        $err\_predict(i) = err\_predict(i) + (xin(l) - y(l))^2$ ▷ compute error prediction

7    $err\_predict = \frac{err\_predict}{qwe1 - qwe}$ ▷ calculate total prediction error

8    $err\_train = \frac{err}{qwe}$ ▷ calculate training error

9   **return** yout

---

6. CONCLUSION

This chapter gives a detailed description of the GMDH-DDE algorithm in Matlab code. The aim is to give a detailed pseudocode representation of the major functions in the GMDH-DDE module, which when used in conjunction with the supplied Matlab codes imparts sufficient information as to enable the reader to discern useful information and modify the code to suit his/her requirements.

The codes are following a modular format, with all functions split into separate files. All the major functions are described in this chapter, each following the same nomenclature as the Matlab codes for easier correlation. All function are described both in terms of application and each is accompanied with a detailed algorithm description in order to describe its hierarchy, functional loops and inputs and output of particular variables. Whenever the function is too complex or large, it is split into smaller modules for better understanding.

ACKNOWLEDGMENT

This work was fully supported by the SGS, Grant Agency of the Czech Republic — GACR and partially supported by Grant of SGS

No. SP2014/42, VŠB — Technical University of Ostrava, Czech Republic, by the Development of human resources in research and development of latest soft computing methods and their application in practice project, reg. no. CZ.1.07/2.3.00/20.0072 funded by Operational Programme Education for Competitiveness.

REFERENCES

[1] Anastasakis, L. & Mort, N. (2001) The development of self-organization techniques in modelling: A review of the group method of data handling (GMDH), Technical Report, The University of Sheffield, UK.

[2] Ivakhnenko, A. G. (1971) Polynomial theory of complex systems, *IEEE Trans. Systems, Man Cybernet.*, **1**, 364–378.

[3] Madala, H. R. & Ivakhnenko, A. G. (1994) *Inductive Learning Algorithms for Complex Systems Modelling*, CRC Press, Boca Raton.

[4] Nikolaev, N. Y. & Iba, H. (2003) Polynomial harmonic gmdh learning networks for time series modeling, *Neural Netw.*, **16**, 1527–1540.

[5] Onwubolu, G. (2009) *Hybrid Self-Organizing Modeling Systems*, Springer, Germany.

[6] Onwubolu, G. & Davendra, D. (2009) *Differential Evolution: A Handbook for Global Permutation-Based Combinatorial Optimization*, Springer, Germany.

[7] Price, K. V. (1999) *An Introduction to Differential Evolution, in New Ideas in Optimization*, McGraw-Hill, UK.

[8] Roudbaneh, M. P. (2013) Group method of data handling model using modified Levenberg–Marquardt technique, Ph.D. thesis, Multimedia University, Malaysia.

[9] Storn, R. & Price, K. V. (1995) Differential evolution: A simple and efficient adaptive scheme for global optimization over continuous space, Technical Report, International Computer Science Institute, Berkeley, CA.

[10] Storn, R. & Price, K. V. (1997) Differential evolution-a simple and efficient heuristic for global optimization over continuous spaces, *J. Global Optim.*, **11**, 341–359.

INDEX

A

abductive networks, 80–81, 84
abductory induction mechanism (AIM), 77
analog complexing (AC), 16
artificial neural networks (ANN), 128, 163, 165
automated data preprocessing, vi

D

data crossover, 22
data mining, 3, 5, 15, 22, 23
DE crossover, 248
DE schema, 235, 248
Discrete Differential Evolution (DDE), 229, 245

E

external criterion, 3, 9, 11, 15, 18, 21, 33, 35, 40, 55, 64, 83, 85, 232

G

gaseous phase, 75
Gauss–Newton (GN), 164, 175–176
Genetic Algorithms (GA), 128, 167
GMDH connections, 30
GMDH layers, 28
GMDH Models, 55
GMDH network, 4–11, 13, 28, 31, 55–57, 64–65, 164, 177, 182, 208, 230

GMDH nodes, 28
GMDH-based PNN algorithm, vii, 127
GMDH-DDE, 237, 259
GMDH-LM network, 184, 196, 198, 207
GMDH-MIA network, 27, 73
Gradient Descent Method (GD), 137, 164
group error analysis, 91, 96, 106
Group Method of Data Handling (GMDH), 3, 27, 77, 93, 128, 163

I

inductive algorithm, 82
Ivakhnenko polynomial, 8, 20, 34, 35, 41, 50–51, 53–54, 56–57, 65, 73, 133, 168, 232

K

Kanban system, 182, 186
knowledge discovery, vi, 3, 23
knowledge mining, vi

L

layer unit, 85
Levenberg–Marquardt (LM) method, 164
liquid hydrocarbon phase, 75

M

MATLAB, vi–vii, 21, 24, 27, 52, 92,
    109–110, 146, 178, 211–218, 221
mean absolute percentage error
    (MAPE), 184
Mean Absolute Deviation (MAD),
    185
mean squared error (MSE), 84, 137
Method of Data Handling (GMDH), v
Modified Levenberg–Marquardt
    Technique, vii
Monitoring and Fault Diagnosis,
    127–128
multilayer algorithm, 20, 232
multilayer network, 87
multilayer network structure, 87
multilayered iteration (MIA), 27, 28,
    73
multiphase flow (MPF), 76–77, 79

N

neural network, 4, 6–7, 16–17, 85,
    136, 143, 146, 152, 154, 165,
    168–169, 180, 231
Neurofuzzy GMDH, 168

P

partial polynomial, 4, 82
polynomial neural network (PNN),
    vii, 168–169
prediction sum of squares (PSS), 7
pressure drop, 76–79, 88, 90, 93,
    95–98, 100, 102, 105–107, 138

Q

quadratic polynomial, 13, 166, 172

R

regression analysis, 5, 7, 9, 34–35,
    80–81, 122, 174
regression coefficients, 83
regularized average error (RAE), 15,
    32, 34
regularized least square (RLS), 32, 51
regularized model selection, 31

S

self-organizing GMDH, 84
self-organizing network, 4, 28, 164,
    230
singular value decomposition (SVD),
    164, 174, 198
solids phase, 75
stock market, vi
Structure Optimization of GMDH
    (SOGMDH), 168

T

Term Optimization of GMDH
    (TOGMDH), 168
time series analysis, vi
time series prediction, vi
training data set, 13, 51, 82, 174, 186,
    188, 236

V

Volterra–Kolmogorov–Gabor (VKG),
    4, 28, 164, 172, 230

W

workflow automation, vi

Printed in the United States
By Bookmasters